BRIGITTE BARDOT

BRIGITTE BARDOT

A Biography

BARNETT SINGER

McFarland & Company, Inc., Publishers
Jefferson, North Carolina, and London

LIBRARY OF CONGRESS CATALOGUING-IN-PUBLICATION DATA

Singer, Barnett.
Brigitte Bardot : a biography / Barnett Singer.
p.   cm.
Includes bibliographical references and index.

ISBN 0-7864-2515-6 (illustrated case binding : 50# alkaline paper)∞

1. Bardot, Brigitte.   2. Motion picture actors and actresses—
France—Biography.   I. Title.
PN2638.B25S56   2006
791.4302'8092—dc22   2006007835

British Library cataloguing data are available

Cover photograph: Brigitte Bardot holding a dog in Une Parisienne
(Les Films Ariane, Cinétel, Filmsonor, Paris, Rizzoli Film, Rome, 1957)

Manufactured in the United States of America

McFarland & Company, Inc., Publishers
Box 611, Jefferson, North Carolina 28640
www.mcfarlandpub.com

Contents

Acknowledgments

I MUST THANK A NUMBER of people (preeminently, Kathy and my daughter Alexandra, but also Serge-Henri Parisot, Pierre Billard, and Eugen Weber), as well as institutions for help in this project. The latter include libraries and/or audio-visual facilities (with videos or DVDs) at the Bibliothèque Nationale and Bibliothèque du Film or BIFI (Paris); and on this side of the Atlantic, at the Library of Congress; the University of Virginia; the University of Washington, Seattle; SUNY, Buffalo; Brown University; the University of Toronto; Niagara University; and Brock University, the latter two institutions especially important for inter-library loans. I also thank conference organizers and journal editors who heard or read earlier swaths of what became this manuscript.

Preface

EVERYONE SHOULD JOIN the Fondation Brigitte Bardot (or Brigitte Bardot Foundation) at www.fondationbrigittebardot.fr/. I wrote that first line only after years of immersing myself in Bardot's chaotic, sad life and many achievements for defenseless creatures—defenseless in a grossly unfair fight against Descartes' "lords and possessors" of the earth. I finally saw animals and an organization that protects and tries to save them as a proper starting point, after viewing Jacques Perrin's documentary movie, *Winged Migration*. That masterly film showed this individual—nothing like a Bardot who has *directly* placed herself amidst animal suffering for several decades—that these are our truest, bloodiest, trapped, ruined heroes, and the ultimate heroes of this book. Its beneficiaries, too, I hope. It's too late for dodo birds and passenger pigeons, but if every journal, newspaper, TV, or radio comment on this book cites that first line, or even paraphrases it (join the foundation now!), I will be happy.

For unique as people like Bardot are as individuals who make a true difference in this realm, they are but conduits, and the animal drama remains central. In *Winged Migration* the exhausting, egalitarian, utterly serious commitment of beautiful birds to their arduous airborne treks slays the viewer. So does the tragedy of hunters' guns, and traps here, traps there, oil or factory sludge, not to mention killing heat over deserts, or windswept cold of the Arctic or Atlantic. To reiterate, Perrin's film provided the direct hit necessary to place animals at the very top of this treatment.

What follows as an extended rationale for a new biography of Bardot takes off from that starting point. Only then comes the human—and what a *human*, fascinating person we deal with in these pages. On Brigitte Bardot, the first and most obvious thing to say is that for the growing majority who don't know much about her former stardom, she was easily Europe's equivalent of Marilyn Monroe, and her life, as the reader will see, has contained much hurt, upset, and tragedy, including a number of serious suicide

1

attempts. As I have elsewhere noted: "He (or she) who has had a lot of lovers has had a lot of loneliness." To which one could also add a lot of heartbreak. Bardot has had all three—quite a number of loves, much solitude (which on the plus side helped give her the depth I detail), and heartbreak so awful it didn't take war or mugging, but on a number of occasions her own hand to nearly snuff out a fine and necessary existence. Saul Bellow's literary characters have nothing on Brigitte: the confusions of a Herzog seem small potatoes compared to the vicissitudes of such a life. But had she been only the female equivalent of a Herzog, or another Monroe, I wouldn't have written this biography. Bardot also became a rare star who made a considerable difference, especially to suffering animals, but also to many humans.

And speaking of Herzog and his (or Bellow's) brainy side, Bardot's intelligence truly shines through in her own, extraordinarily detailed memoirs. Significant people, I've always felt, invariably write or co-write significant autobiographies. Brigitte didn't publish her first volume of recollections until the late '90s, and while the many previous biographies of her were generally interesting, they then became, in varying degrees, inaccurate and outmoded.

I noted that significant people in their fields—people who are intelligent and who have demanded a lot of themselves, and who have honesty and courage—generally write fine memoirs. I think, too, that their pasts usually contain some suffering—no suffering, no wisdom or depth; and Bardot is certainly of that tribe.

Who are such great autobiographers? In terms of work I have admired, I could cite memoirs by distinguished sufferers like Solzhenitsyn—*One Day in the Life of Ivan Denisovich*, a novel-memoir perhaps; and Elie Wiesel (*Night*). In the field of popular music one could mention Brian Wilson's *Wouldn't It Be Nice*—he was of course the main force behind the Beach Boys, and fortunate to be alive. In sports I could cite Lance Armstrong's *It's Not About the Bike*, which can't be put down, and Maury Wills' *On the Run*, also a favorite for someone like myself who grew up in baseball's golden era, and a book that shows how hard it was for a black man to make the majors then, let alone star for the Dodgers, as he did.

As for Bardot, the first thick volume of her autobiography, covering childhood, the cinematic years, and yes, her loves to the early '70s, came out as *Initiales B.B.* in 1996. And my mouth was open pretty well all the way. In her work she reveals much sensitivity, vivacity, and taste, and a historian's sense of the concrete and chronological. And she offers many acute vignettes. Her recollections will surprise those who know her only as a beautiful face and body of now old movies. And again, because she is so comprehensive, no biography that appeared before these memoirs can any longer be considered even remotely definitive, and there have been none since.

When Bardot added a second, even thicker volume on her "animalian" years from 1973 to 1999—a touch less fascinating than the first, but still compulsively interesting and important—that lack of definitiveness in earlier secondary treatments became even more glaring. And one really has to pay attention to her autobiography, for Bardot has already been betrayed more than enough in an ultra-thronged life.

Her obvious intelligence again may come as a shock to many who know her only by hearsay. For openers one really needs to stress her written French: elegant, rhythmic, sonorous, lovely; punchy, pungent, poetic, potent; jazzy, neologistic, realistic, classic, delicate, forceful! Bardot's high school dropout literacy fairly glitters by comparison to today's undergraduates turned out by the millions in the United States, and in a France that has imitated American hyper-democracy. She may not have had a ton of time to read when she was young; but after leaving the cinematic high wire, she made up for it during the '70s and '80s, when remote-controlled television—especially in ten-years-behind France—hadn't yet eroded book cultures. Bardot's reading in both contemporary and classic literature has been omnivorous, and her vocabulary would put many of today's putatively educated to shame.

What she also had behind her is a Catholic background that has now evaporated in France and in formerly hard-shell parishes of American cities like Chicago or Detroit. And I believe we need to see more than is usual in those standards of primary and secondary education that still obtained in her period, and in Catholic "éducation" taken in the wider French sense. In this biography I emphasize the effect of this rigid Catholicism on someone who certainly revolted famously against it, as she did against the upper-bourgeoisie of her parents; but who also retained positive aspects from that upbringing.

Perhaps that is why Bardot thankfully fails to edit out of herself the emotions, the animal in her that helped turn her into the great protectress of supposedly lower creatures. And of course she has combined high intelligence with a healthy sense of the erotic. In fact, we shouldn't artificially split the physical from the mental in someone like Bardot. As if physical and mental reside in different countries separated by vast oceans! In other words we can—and should—drop from the empyrean into the earthy and back with an easy rapidity? Well, Brigitte certainly has, and that's one reason she is so special, and if one wishes to call that hypocritical, so be it.

Why, however, do we need a new biographical treatment of Bardot? How can I improve on her exhaustive account of her own life? The answer is: It would be vain and crass to think that I can. However, to read her two volumes of memoirs, one has to give oneself the time to read nearly 1,300 pages, and not many have that kind of time or inclination anymore. So I wanted to offer a much crisper treatment here. A second reason is that Bardot's memoirs are in French—as noted, rich, slangy, savorously untranslatable French, and a challenge even for American francophiles who feel they are fluent in that language. Just as she has asked a lot of herself in what she has given to men, the cinema, and especially animals, so Bardot gave herself a high ceiling indeed to lodge these memories. And the results leave no peers in the field. No Hepburn, Peck, or Loren. What I'm saying is that an English translation will never get Brigitte Bardot right—not even close. Bardot uses snatches of Latin, Spanish, English, even Arabic (French slang includes quite a bit of the latter, a remnant of their colonial years); as noted, she uses the high and literary, and the lowest of the low.

To which one may retort: didn't artists like Leonard Tancock translate Penguin classics by writers such as Zola into fine Cockney and get away with it? And I agree—it *can* be done at one level, but really, it can only be done approximately.

Are there other reasons for offering a new biography of Bardot in this new century? Well, we have a load of troubles, and among that ton of troubles is the possible extirpation of an entire planet! Yes, its creatures, along with its air, its water, etc. If Bardot has decided to make *that* her life's work since the early '70s, and if with much difficulty she launched and fought to strengthen a foundation that helps save seals, whales, elephants, and any and every kind of animal, right down to dogs and cats stuck in cages, why not give such efforts exposure in the English-speaking world? If she helps us see the tortured and suffering, and remove ourselves at least intermittently from an insulated world of cars, computers, and TV screens, then we ought perhaps to help her back.

What a reason to write a biography! one may again retort. How moralistic. And it does indeed sound so. But don't we all at some level want to make a difference? And if this effort makes a bit of difference itself, then there will be some justification for it. Bardot's evolution since her movie days—not least, with a personal menagerie of dozens of cats, dogs, and other animals, constantly evolving—may show the way to us all. Here is a woman who has had the financial wherewithal simply to prance around on the Riviera and in Paris, living much the same life as many current Hollywood stars or retired ones live. Instead she has gone out and contacted reality—the reality of heart-tearing, omnipresent suffering. I hope this book may inspire others in such worthy directions.

I believe I am also a kind of revisionist here of clichés about Bardot. One mentioned is that she was just a fetching body and face, a dumb beauty who traded her pulchritude for what she could get in life. A second is that she is a shameless right-winger, and mean-spirited. Again, false. A third is that she does everything for publicity, which is also untrue. To sum up, my ultimate revision is in writing a biography of Bardot that respects the terms and sentiments of her own work, and that respects the person herself, as much as she herself respects animals.

This book, then, is a kind of positive reassessment of Bardot, and that includes her career as an actress. Brigitte, in fact, greatly underplayed her own cinematic contributions; but the more I viewed her films, the more a certain revisionism was thrust upon me in this domain, too. To be brief, Bardot was a much better actress than many know.[1]

Even something she truly did on the side in her heyday, singing, can use some attention as well. When I was first in France for research years back, and sat in mournful Breton cafes sipping and listening to a jukebox, the one Bardot hit one would hear was more like sex than a song—Serge Gainsbourg's "Je t'aime, moi non plus." And in fact the song featured Jane Birkin, for reasons detailed below. But listening more carefully to Bardot's recordings from the '60s and early '70s, I again found a natural, despite evident range limits. The one song I'd want to listen to a number of times was a kind of signature song, "La Madrague," named for her famous spread on the Gulf of Saint-Tropez. Her sweetness shines out in this simple but fine, well-arranged ditty of a more innocent era than ours.

Onward, then, to that "more innocent era," and the travails as well as joys of Bardot's early life and formative influences.

1

A Parisian Childhood

THE FRANCE THAT BRIGITTE BARDOT was born into on September 28, 1934—how should one describe it? If countries' fortunes are rather like those of sports teams, or lives themselves, France had passed its heyday, but was still unique. Its apogee had undoubtedly come earlier during the *Belle Epoque*—roughly from 1880 to the outbreak of World War I in 1914. Politically, that heyday coincided with the Third Republic, a surprisingly long-lived regime still going when Bardot was born, though things were beginning to shake internally, and not only due to the impact of the war, then the Depression. There was also the shattering of a united spirit that had carried the country through the dark days of 1914–1918. France of the mid–'30s was anything but unified; it was badly split between a Right tending more and more toward Fascism, and a socialistic, pacifistic Left. And of course by the year of Bardot's birth Hitler had already in short order become German chancellor across the Rhine, then one-party dictator, openly flouting the Versailles Treaty's restrictions and arming his country to the teeth. In response the French poured billions into a defensive Maginot Line, hunkering down and hoping for the best.

Meanwhile, enjoyment reigned, especially in a Paris that was still the loveliest, most romantic city on earth. If you wanted to live well and had a little money, this was the place for it. And if you wanted a break from the rigors of a still-regnant British or American puritanism, here was—since the demise of Weimar Berlin—the capital of decadent pleasure. What astonished visitors was the wide variety of ladies of the evening one could behold in different *quartiers*. The city also had an ample array of government-permitted brothels, the *maisons de tolérance*—houses of prostitution that unlike individuals working the streets, received a free pass from legislators.

But Brigitte was born into a Paris family that gave short shrift to these racier sides of the great city. Her family was part of the rock-solid, conservative, Catholic upper-bourgeoisie of that era. Brigitte was born and had her earliest memories on the Avénue de la Bourdonnais of the classy seventh *arrondissement* (or district), not far from the Invalides and a stone's throw from the Eiffel Tower. Her mother, Anne-Marie Bardot, nicknamed Toty, and father, Louis Bardot, or Pilou, were strict, money-respecting, by-the-book types, against whom their oldest daughter would eventually, and perhaps predictably, rebel.

Louis had graduated from an engineering school and gone into the family business, Charles Bardot and Company, which manufactured liquid air and acetylene. Sixteen years older than his wife, he was 38 when the girl they would dub Bricheton or Bri-Bri was born. Father Pilou had two distinct sides—one lighthearted, the other strict, repressive, and touchy. He enjoyed sailing, making wine, and telling jokes that he jotted in a notebook he carried everywhere. But at work he was very punctual and responsible, usually arriving at his office by six a.m. (the firm had offices both in Paris and at a factory in the suburbs).

Each parent retained all the then unmitigated traits of their class; but they somewhat eluded the caricature as well, because both had some *artiste* in them, obviously influencing the next generation to come. Brigitte's mother Toty was very dramatic and had studied theater and dance in Milan as a young lady; Pilou wrote poetry in his notebook and would eventually publish a few volumes of it. Yet he also participated in currents of his time—in those days one couldn't arbitrarily withdraw from the mainstream—and that had included being wounded in World War I, where he had earned a *croix de guerre*. But at least a part of him liked the finer things. Did that father unconsciously instill the acting bug in his daughter by acquiring a then rare movie camera to film the baby's moves?[1] Or did a succession of nannies play as much of a role there?

These included Brigitte's lifelong favorite, Dada, from Italy, who became a kind of second mother to the intelligent child, one sorely required, as Churchill needed his "Woom." Given Toty's difficulty having Brigitte, her wish for a boy, and her own rather standoffish elegance, this nanny more than filled the slack, telling "Brizzi" bedtime stories in mixed Italian-French and teaching the little girl to roll her R's in a warm southern manner. The family also had cats that pleased a future animal lover. But though it was a simpler era than ours for children—few media distractions near at hand—it would not be a simple childhood for Brigitte. Increasingly, the child perceived her beautiful mother as a somewhat strange, unpredictable, often rejecting creature, and as a hypochondriac. Papa Bardot, too, seemed frequently nervous, and was sometimes morbidly silent, until his inner geyser exploded.

With her mother pregnant again just before the war, Brigitte remembers her own stomach pains, then being put out in a suffocating feeling she never forgot, especially when it came to animal suffering (she had had her appendix removed). On the bright side her maternal grandmother and grandfather returned after that operation from Italy, where they had been living and had first engaged Dada. Brigitte came to adore "Mamie" Mucel and especially her "bon-papa," known from then on as "Boum papa," or simply "Boum," whom she calls the one man who truly counted in her life. Most every other adult around her seemed to indulge in prevarication, and nothing and nobody could be firmly relied upon. Even her beloved Dada was replaced at the time of her mother's pregnancy, going over to her grandparents' new apartment, and of course Brigitte ardently loathed the new recruit.

With her mother set to deliver, Brigitte remembers a lovely dinner at Mamie's and Boum's, then sleeping the night beside a reassuring Dada, while her grandparents went off to the hospital. Toty and Pilou definitely wanted a boy as their number two—the normal upward limit for bourgeois families of the time—but in the scary year of Munich (1938), with Europe on the brink of another war, a second girl was born, Marie-Jeanne, henceforth nicknamed Mijanjou.

Not only did Brigitte have to get used to a new nurse, Pierrette, she also needed to habituate herself to this crying, pink thing she at least got to hold. Having been the only child and only girl for four years, she was jealous of the competition, especially since her mother parceled out attention and affection so haphazardly. But there were sun-in-fog interventions of happiness, as when Brigitte went out on the town alone with her dad to watch a stirring military parade, feeling exalted; or for a walk under the trees of the Champ de Mars, where French revolutionaries had once gathered to plot strategy; or by the Seine with its bookstalls and strolling lovers. She also got to push Mijanjou's carriage in the Bois de Boulogne that Emperor Napoleon III had upgraded at one end of Paris almost a century earlier. With all its goods and bads, Bardot's Parisian childhood certainly *was* a childhood, compared to that of later latchkey children.

There were also periodic visits to her other grandparents, equally fascinating, but not so open-hearted. Brigitte remembers Grandpa Bardot bending for hours over his roses, sniffing, then unable to right himself. And she realized early on that there were more limits with Grandma Bardot, or "Mémie," than with her maternal grandmother, Mamie Mucel. Grandma Bardot would have extended family dinners at a long table full of tinkling glassware, where the bright girl helped prepare but was then relegated to the kids' table for the meal, wanting furiously to be adult. To the child these family functions meant lots of people talking loudly, pinching her, pulling her hair, and planting saliva-laden kisses on her cheeks (though her beautiful, fastidious mother kissed more cleanly).

There were also visits to a widowed aunt Tapompon, who had lost her husband to wounds from the Great War. Bardot remembers the odors of wax and dry gâteau and moldiness there, but also marvelous hot chocolate and cookies at teatime. Childhoods were more physical then, and she recalls rushing into the arms of Tapompon's handsome son Jean, whom she loved, and who would later suffer tragically from what the French call a *déception sentimentale*. She remembers Jean holding her hand, accompanying her back to the subway, and how she was scared by the clank of the automatic green gates shutting down there, as they still do in Paris subway stations.

From early on Bardot had a full and giving heart. Her nightly prayers might include the following: "Petit Zézus, protézez tous ceux que z'aime, sauf Pierrette et la couturière!" ("Little Jesus, protect all those I wuv, 'cept Pierrette and the seamstress.")[2] As a small child Bardot already showed the extreme sensitivity that remained constant throughout her life.

In 1939 all the big people seemed inexplicably worried, and the girl could feel something unnameable but palpably tense invading the air. When her mother started stocking cupboards with piles of off-limits candy bars and other items, the child wondered even more what could be afoot. Of course even when explained, the word "war" can never really be grasped by small children, for it is hard for them to believe the pervasive cruelty, envy, and aggression of adults that have caused such conflagrations to break out throughout history. Indeed, when Brigitte kept hearing this word "guerre," she found it hard to fathom. Her mother finally explained that it was like a girlfriend taking your toys, then you fighting to get them back.

The actual, adult cause of a Second World War in the offing was of course British and French reluctance to stand up to the growing territorial appetites of Herr Hitler. Defeatism gnawed at the French soul and few wanted another bloodletting à la World War I. After the Munich capitulation, the French and British had bought themselves (it turned out) a year's time before the outbreak of another war. The English used the year profitably, hugely augmenting their air force and developing radar, while the French continued to squabble politically and enjoy themselves on the equivalent of a volcano.

If you weren't dancing or listening to the songs of a Charles Trenet or Maurice Chevalier at a Paris music hall, you could go to the cinema to watch romantic French fare, featuring actors like Jean Gabin, later to star with a youthful Bardot, or American imports. Or you could sip at outdoor cafés, watching passers-by for hours on end. Or take a vacation! One of the important and lasting reforms of Léon Blum's Popular Front administration brought in the then revolutionary innovation of annual vacations with pay; so for the first time workers swelled the summer exodus to coastal beaches of the Bordelais or Normandy, irritating many belonging to the Bardots' class.

Whichever ideological side you were on, and whatever your class, the piper had to be paid by the end of summer 1939. Hitler had started screaming over the airwaves that he wanted the Polish Corridor, an area filled with Germans but given to Poland by the 1919 peacemakers, and also "internationalized" Danzig. This time Neville Chamberlain and French Prime Minister Daladier stood firm. But emboldened by a stunning non-aggression agreement signed with his arch-enemy Stalin in late August 1939, Hitler decided a week later to invade Poland anyway (September 1). On September 3 Britain and France reluctantly declared war, and in Paris the Gare de l'Est would soon be thronged with soldiers leaving weepy wives, mothers, and girlfriends to join their garrisons.

After Poland was carved up between Hitler and Stalin, there ensued eight months or so of "phony war," or what the French labeled the "drôle de guerre." That is to say, nothing really happened in the West between September 1939 and the lovely spring of 1940. Of course Bardot's own memories, slipping so readily into the child's optic, cannot distinguish between that era and the sudden fall of France in May-June 1940 at the hands of the blitzkriegers, crossing the Meuse, then winging tanks over the great plain of northern France, and pincering French and British troops against the Channel coast.

What she does remember—undoubtedly from the period just before France's fall—is that the family decided to make a disruptive move out of Paris, with the old family Renault, nicknamed "the veal," stuffed with valises, and Brigitte and her father importantly alone in it, while her mother and Mijanjou followed in another car bearing Mamie and Pierrette, the nursemaid. The roads were thick with people on foot, bikes, and horseback, as well as in cars. Reaching Dinard on the Channel coast, and with Brigitte content that Pierrette had decamped en route somewhere in Normandy, they procured a two-room place in the resort town, and her father volunteered for his old 155th regiment of Alpine infantry.

Still no more than five at the time, Brigitte was about to enjoy some enforced close-ness with an elusive mother. Toty, having little else to do, now spent a good deal of time trying to teach her daughter how to read from a Babar book, but it was difficult for the sensitive child and brought tears. Mijanjou also got on Anne-Marie's well-bred, fastidi-ous nerves, and then the family abruptly returned to Paris, for Papa was needed by the French more for his factory than for his martial skills.

Back at the Avénue de la Bourdonnais, with its two rooms heated by a lone electric radiator, Bardot remembers constantly being cold and sleeping in her clothes between her mother and dad, also in their clothes. When German planes began bombing the city in June 1940, Brigitte remembers the family descending into the cellar with a can-dle, which she hated. She recalls how traumatic the shrieking sirens were and remained to her. She remembers starting school, but more fondly, spending forty days in bed with measles and having her mother read to her from *Les Petites Filles modèles* by the Countess of Ségur, using pleasingly different voices for the different characters. Toty would inter-mittently fail, but kept getting nudged to continue by her curious, intelligent child.

For most everyone, wartime in Europe would bring food problems, and as the Nazis spread their occupational veil across the continent, shortages developed and caloric intakes spiraled downward in cities like Paris. One now had to get what one could. Unbeknownst to the little girl, her Dada was sometimes out as early as three a.m., spelled in line a couple hours later by Mamie, queuing up for luxuries like the lamb's brains Brigitte's mother fed her one day, a delicacy hard to procure, but intended to help the girl stay healthy. All white and sticky on the noontime plate, the dish repelled the child, and she refused to touch it. In those days the bourgeoisie still had inflexible limits, and Brigitte sat until dinnertime in front of the untouched dish, until finally her exasperated mother, impulsively pinching her nose, pushed the now icy, gluey stuff into her daugh-ter's mouth, making her vomit all night and avoid lambs' brains the rest of her life! A great antipathy to unfairness would emerge from this bourgeois rearing, but so would the tenacity that later came to characterize a mature Bardot.

One of the child's sole distractions in Nazi-occupied Paris, where one went out less than in the prewar era, was dancing at home to Pilou's phonograph, making her mother see the possibility of ballet here. Brigitte was duly pushed in that direction, but more discipline went with the territory. She remembers, for example, having to walk around the apartment with a pot of water on her head. One false move and the water fell all over her, and she would receive a slap on her cheek into the bargain. This training had a lot to do with the regal posture and walk that would so often get Bardot recognized in adult life, even when disguised to elude fans or paparazzi. Enrolled in a once-a-week dance course, she remembers the sweaty, dusty odors of a typical French ballet school of the time, but at least found that she preferred entrechats and pliés to arithmetic.

Still in wartime Anne-Marie decided on a move to a different Paris residence, and proudly, Brigitte got to comb the city on a bike, with her father accompanying her on another, looking for signs indicating apartments to rent. They located a huge one of nine rooms on the fifth floor of 1, Rue de la Pompe, in the tony 16th district where she would also live in adulthood. For vacations and on some weekends they traveled to the family place in Louveciennes, about 25 kilometers from Paris, but still the country then, with old trees (good for wood in winter), no running water, and many rabbits, some of whose babies Brigitte tried to feed with a bottle. Others were penned in by her father, and at first she didn't notice when the family kept consuming rabbit for dinner. Brigitte had a special fondness for one named Noiraud, and then one day he was gone—to the forest, said her mother. That night they dined on *civet de lapin*, but Brigitte wouldn't eat, crying her eyes out, sure her mother had lied and that this was Noiraud on her plate. Neither mama nor papa ended up eating, either, and much later Anne-Marie confessed that they had indeed killed Noiraud, due to the exigencies of wartime. Needless to say, Bardot has not eaten rabbit since.

Her best friend, Chantal, often accompanied her to Louveciennes, but Brigitte felt inferior to her in that her father had died during the Nazi invasion of 1940, where Pilou had only been wounded, not killed, in the previous war. Toty, however, told Brigitte that she was privileged just to *have* a father, so from then on the sensitive girl offered Chantal half her papa.

Did that father's factory help the occupying Germans? Bardot is vague on this, as she probably ought to be, given that she was but a child at the time. She does say that he would plead that the machines weren't working and also notes that he could speak some German, owing to his Lorraine background, which probably helped with Occupation authorities. Getting the payroll each month was, however, stressful for an already uptight man—noises in the apartment supposedly led to bookkeeping errors, then Louis would erupt, Anne-Marie would follow suit, and the two china-doll girls, terrified and mute, picked up the bad vibes, becoming nervous wrecks themselves. In those days no parents of that class psychologized themselves; instead they were more than allowed to take out the horrors of their own repressions in child-directed sadism. One result was Brigitte's harassed body pleading for help, in the form of regular eczema outbreaks.

But again, what of forms of collusion with the Nazis in occupied Paris? The subject is a thorny, complex one, and has raised much debate. It was an era that from the beginning demanded a return to moral order, personified by the aged Marshal Pétain— to family, roots, soil, and the Church. At first de Gaulle, speaking for the Resistance from England, was little heard. But by 1942 with roundups and shortages increasing, more and more young French people enrolled in the *maquis*, and many were deported, tortured, or murdered for their efforts. On the far Right were out-and-out Collaborationists, and a "Milice" (Militia), helping the Nazis hunt Resistants or Jews.

What of well-known stars like Trenet or Chevalier? Did they sing for the Nazis? In fact Trenet always tried to avoid such engagements, and some of his songs, considered to contain hints of resistance, were banned. Still, Parisians flocked to music halls to see him or Chevalier, if partially to get warm. In September 1943 Trenet and Edith Piaf were finally forced to sing for French prisoners in Germany (there were well over a million there), but Trenet says he did his worst, so as not to be reinvited. The case of his male rival in song, Chevalier, was murkier, and near the end of the war he barely eluded a French lynch mob.

But the young Bardot was quite removed from these adult currents during wartime. The change of residence had taken her at age seven to a fancy new private school, the Cours Hattemer, where at first she needed only to attend three days a week, making up the rest with home schooling. She was thus free to consecrate three days per week to what she loved far more than school—dancing. These lessons, at first conducted at home by a man from the Opéra Ballet, now took place at Madame Bourget's dance studio in the Rue Spontini. A succession of housemaids who lived in a cramped, stiflingly hot or freezing spot under the roof of the Bardots' apartment accompanied her to school, as they did to catechism, while Grandma Mamie took her to dance classes and often home afterward to her apartment. There, Brigitte gladly ate whatever Dada could concoct in wartime, such as fricasseed rutabagas, or a cake made from ersatz chocolate.

In this period of her childhood Chantal was Brigitte's only real friend, since Toty and Pilou always asked the occupations of kids' fathers, generally finding them unsuitable. The dance courses had too many concierges' offspring, averred Madame Bardot with bourgeois certitude. For Anne-Marie the making of a respectable daughter seemed to be her key aim. Talk about the memoirs of a *jeune fille rangée*—the book of that title (in English, *Memoirs of a Dutiful Daughter*) by another bourgeois product, Simone de Beauvoir, seems near beer compared to what Bardot endured. In sum, Toty rejected most friend possibilities her daughter had, and since Brigitte was a quiet girl, her childhood was a rather lonely one. This partially explains why in adulthood she would have such deep and long-lasting friendships with members of both sexes.

Her mother was also fussy about her dress, making the girl obsessive about pulling up her underclothes sufficiently in order to ward off germs. Toty also kept windows shut in the apartment to save on heating costs, and in summer, fearing a break-in, would do so from 6:30 p.m., making the place on hot evenings a shuttered furnace. (Since then Bardot has always liked things open.)

Besides repressing herself and her children, Anne-Marie also kept everything she could under lock and key—liquor in the liquor cabinet, valuables in commodes, etc.— and would often lose the keys, joining the kids in hysterical hunts for them, which sometimes ended in a locksmith's visit to pick and change locks. Brigitte also had to show maniacally correct standards making her bed, with Papa generally judging the final result. If his mood was beneficent that day, she might pass, but if not, parental unfairness, a great teacher, reared its ugly head, and the child would have to do her bed over and over again, in grim, angry silence.

When the body goes through such repressive situations it can't abide, it pays back its owner with ulcers, respiratory ailments, or in Brigitte's case, allergic rashes. Thankfully she had grandparents who were a little looser, particularly Mamie and Boum. She loved visiting these people at their flat, or at the Bardot grandparents' Norwegian chalet at Louveciennes. Here Brigitte felt less stifled. She loved getting away from a regimented Parisian life of rigid discipline and routines. Getting away was to become one of the hallmarks of a peripatetic adult life, as would her contrasting love of secure nests.

Bardot remembers one especially traumatic incident in that wartime childhood, occurring when she was about seven and a half and Mijanjou four. The two were playing at cowboys and Indians, with the *bonne* as the enemy, and while hiding under the table and using the tablecloth as a tent, the Bardot sisters somehow managed to knock over a fine oriental vase, one of their mother's favorites. Unfortunately it smashed into smithereens. On discovering the damage, an irate Toty gave each girl two hard slaps, then their father, in a teeth-gritted rage, whipped their behinds twenty times each. Mama thundered that this was *her* home, not theirs, and that she had the power to throw such disobedient children into the street at any time. She said her daughters would henceforth be treated as strangers, and from that time on ordered the children to use the formal "vous" with each parent, not "tu." It was a splash of cold water indeed, and for Brigitte a turning point in her young life; in some sense she felt she had already lost her parents, facilitating her later precocious revolt into a new lifestyle. But there was also a fear of abandonment that never quite left her, waves of intermittent terror that in childhood provoked those attacks of eczema and even suicidal feelings. Only after her father died in 1975 did her now needy mother beg for a return to the less formal "tu"; but the celebrated actress couldn't oblige.

From the era of the vase incident, Brigitte was in constant conflict with Anne-Marie, envying Chantal, whose mom loved *her* to death, spoiling her with the choicest of toys. So passed this *jeune fille rangée*'s childhood, one where Brigitte's parents worried inordinately about what the Joneses—or Dubois—might think. Even her First Communion of May 1943 was no mere celebration, but a kind of imposed threat—*now* you will turn into a good girl seemed to be the message.

Another traumatic incident followed in November of that year. Brigitte had just danced, the one place where she felt moderately safe and natural, and on arriving home, her father motioned her into the dining room, locking the door to announce something of ominous importance. His announcement to the sweaty girl? That there was really no Santa Claus, and that in fact her parents had been buying her Christmas presents all along. The stunned girl sobbed uncontrollably, another of her illusions gone.

Christmas was nonetheless the best day of the year for her—with *crèche*, tree, and many guests, including down-at-heels family acquaintances, bachelors from the factory, and numerous gifts. By contrast New Year's Day was a bore, where Brigitte saw once-a-year cousins, but where she and her sister feared soiling their good clothes. Brigitte also disliked her September 28 birthday, for French schools then started up at the beginning of October, so she generally received notebooks, briefcases, and other scholastic fare as presents. Was her hatred of things academic inherent, or environmental? Her mother certainly approved of Brigitte's proclivity and aptitude for dance, while Mijanjou, as the "boy," was more encouraged in school. Pound for pound Mijanjou was probably the favorite, and Bardot sees it as a phenomenon that increased during her childhood, especially with her mother, who would frequently cite her little sister as the model child. That sister continued to shine at school, especially in mathematics, while Brigitte, ensconced at the bottom of her class, simply didn't care for school, and was the one punished at home for poor marks.

Wartime even for the better-off classes exacerbated such adolescent insecurities and traumas, and often Bardot found herself waking in a sweat, thinking Paris had been or would be bombed into rubble. Plus she would look in the mirror with adolescent uncertainty, thinking she was ugly and wanting to look like her sister, wondering even at times whether she had been adopted.

Another school change also disrupted her—from Hattemer to L'Institution de la Tour, where she was suddenly surrounded by mystifying nuns. Constant genuflexion, rosaries kept in pockets, girls encouraged to spy on each other—this was another difficult atmosphere for Brigitte. Chantal attended the school, and Bardot knew that even her friend would have sold her out for a good grade. But pneumonia got Brigitte out of this institution, and when she began recovering, she was happily sent back to Hattemer.

Her psychological problems, however, never seemed close to abating. Near the end of the war, a vacation at Chantal's mother's farm in Normandy showed her again a child showered with maternal affection, while Brigitte, who needed love herself, cried in bed at night. These examples of childhood suffering clearly contributed to the making of Bardot's adult character, not least as a future animal protectress.

Of course larger things *were* happening, including imminent Allied landings in France—Operation Overlord unfolding for the night of June 5–6, 1944, on the Channel beaches. From that exciting era Bardot remembers Papa Louis coming to get her up at Chantal's mother's farm in Normandy, and without a car, carrying her twenty kilometers on his shoulders to reach the train back to Paris. Then from the Gare St. Lazare at two in the morning, she remembers being borne again through Paris' streets, full of love for her brave father in wartime.

Final bombardments leading to the French capital's long-awaited liberation were, however, scary, and her parents pushed mattresses against the windows to avoid being hit by flying shards of glass. Food tickets were becoming useless by this time, but in August 1944 the Americans, with plenty of goods to distribute, hit the streets, though they had considerately allowed General Leclerc's French division into the city first. De Gaulle himself entered Paris from suburban Rambouillet on August 25, and the next day was at the Arc de Triomphe, wildly acclaimed by the crowds. With his generals and Resistance leaders behind him, le grand Charles marched down the Champs-Elysées to the Place de la Concorde, amidst a sea of vigorously applauding Parisians.

But Bardot recalls the American soldiers best, greeting little girls carrying paper French flags with presents of chewing gum, chocolate—and kisses. Brigitte didn't even know how to chew gum, but when school started up again she would trade what she had for copied homework at Hattemer, until her teacher found out and punished her for it.

In this liberated Paris de Gaulle became a new enlightened despot, replacing Pétain and doing a fine, if dictatorial job of keeping the prosecution of collaborators and other such business somewhat orderly. But the young Brigitte—like most young people—remained ensconced in her insular family world. Toward the end of the war the arrival of a new governess, Madame Legrand, who spoke some English and became Brigitte's "la Big," was a significant event for her. It turned out that she would love this "Big" until her death. But the family atmosphere remained very tense. Bardot remembers her mother blowing up at "Big," the governess screaming at the nursemaid, and the *bonne* then taking it out on the kids, provoking an outburst of tears. In retrospect Brigitte thinks the separate bedrooms of her parents somewhat contributed to the problem; their repressed sexuality, partly a matter of birth control, providing tinder for these frequent family conflagrations. She says those scenes between her parents traumatized her and still in recollection, make her feel panicky today. She remembers ultra-quiet meals, then her parents suddenly leaving the table, flaring into loud arguments behind closed doors, her mother sobbing, and the two children sitting alone like bereft parrots at the table. At night she would hear her father slam doors and cry out, and a frightened Mijanjou often jumped into Brigitte's bed for protection.

One day Pilou packed his bag to leave for good, and Toty on her knees was crying hysterically in front of the kids and "Big." Impulsively, Louis then decided to climb over

The Bardot family, clockwise from lower left: Sister Marie-Jeanne, father Louis, mother Anne-Marie, Brigitte and grandfather "Boum."

the balcony and jump, threatening to splatter his brains on the pavement below. The mother grabbing for dear life at her husband's leg over the balcony, and the subsequent yelping cries of these two wounded-animal parents still come back clearly to Bardot.

Would life in the postwar era become a little easier for such an uptight bourgeois family? In fact it would (that is, before Brigitte discovered boys). After the war the Bardots resumed their habit of giving dinner parties that had been difficult to convene during the Occupation, with card games crackling on as many as ten bridge tables, good food, and lots of laughter in the air, and Brigitte sneaking out to inhale this parade of adult elegance, taking a kind of mental newsreel, and dreaming herself of rapidly becoming a grown-up. Mémé Bardot was up from Cannes where she had spent the war, and Pilou found her an apartment in their building, which she shared with Brigitte's Uncle René, a widower, and his four daughters, four cousins for Brigitte to play hide-and-seek with in the corridors, a joy. These girls had lost their mother to tuberculosis and Brigitte felt sorry for them. It was also enjoyable to attend the wedding of Jean Marchal, Tapompon's son, in La Rochelle, and to meet his new brother-in-law, a handsome blond athlete of 17, Brigitte's first crush.

The eldest Bardot daughter now had to prepare for her confirmation, an important family event. The nuns on her Paris street belonging to the Sisters of Providence order put her through daily prayers from eight a.m. till six in the evening, trying to rid her of impure thoughts, including for this 17-year-old Bernard, by whom she was plainly stricken. Brigitte couldn't wait to wear the white organza dress that her mother and Mamie had once worn at their confirmations. Confirmation of course meant receiving the Holy Spirit and in fact, entering spiritual adulthood. But what Bardot remembers best is the elegant dinner served by sleek *maîtres d'hôtel* and a plethora of gifts—mainly religious articles intended to help produce a lady. These included about a dozen rosaries, five or six missals, and a crucifix in ivory and ebony. But taking off her beautiful communion outfit made Brigitte feel horrible; how badly she longed to become an adult—the sooner, the better!

Weekends at Louveciennes continued at the Norwegian chalet, and for Bardot some of her best early memories still come from these trips to the "country," though her mother didn't much like it there. Brigitte's first kisses also occurred here at age 12, when she and Chantal took turns with an unprepossessing older boy named Guy.

At age 13 back in Paris, Bardot came tenth (some sources say eighth) out of 150 in a tough ballet competition, making it into the prestigious Conservatoire Nationale de Danse, where "La Big" would watch her sweat out moves, then take her afterward for a lemonade. In school the teenager continued to languish, though a self-taught Boum Papa did her Latin homework for her, until she was nabbed for it. Meanwhile, her sternest critic remained her mother, not only in scholastic matters, but also in the field of dance.

However, to reward Brigitte for winning a ballet competition, an ever unpredictable Toty gave with one hand by awarding the children a vacation to Megève in the Alps, near the beginning of summer; then took away with the other. For Brigitte, trusting such a mother was always a losing proposition. They stayed in a nice hotel, and on discovering a pool, Brigitte and her friend Chantal, who had come along, lit up with happiness. Plus there was a handsome blond lifeguard here who made Brigitte's heart go pitter-patter. Surveying the cool teens around her, she felt ugly and different, but could at least look forward to a month of learning to swim, and of checking out the mores of a young society very different from what she had ever encountered before.

That night in bed, she and Chantal, excited by their day out of the Paris cocoon, were laughing together, and behind a curtain, where Anne-Marie Bardot was lodged, those laughs were easy to hear. Suddenly Toty came storming in to ask whether they were laughing at *her*, deciding impulsively to rip up Brigitte's one-month swim pass as punishment. A depressed Brigitte cried all night, and even in the '90s remained thunderstruck by the awful memory. Somehow we think that people with privileges, fame, and money just forget a mother's injustice, yet there it is—Bardot's greatest education was visited on her by this random sadism, bourgeois sadism, to be sure, not the Nazi or Khmer Rouge variety.

For the next few days Chantal and Mijanjou enjoyed the pool, while her mother's special target (and maybe object of jealousy) stared from the hotel balcony at Mont Blanc, seething inside with the kind of trapped anger she would later observe in incarcerated animals. But a week later Mijanjou came down with typhoid fever, life-threatening and requiring a quarantine. So Brigitte had to remain outside and was now tacitly allowed to return to the pool with Chantal, finally learning how to swim adeptly. Nietzsche's old

Brigitte Bardot, the young ballet dancer whose posture remained unmistakeable later in life.

saw—that which doesn't kill you makes you stronger—had become a theme of her life, and remained so.

More jolts were in store. Though Mémie Bardot wasn't her favorite grandma, her death in her eighties was a blow to Brigitte, and her first look at a dead body laid out at the wake induced a horror of death that stayed with her. One repercussion came at Louveciennes; with the place Brigitte loved reverting by inheritance to Pilou, his wife, a Madame Bovary of redecoration, decided rapidly to modernize it, discarding priceless old items and changing the atmosphere quite dramatically.

On one of those Louveciennes weekends Louis Bardot chased a terrified mouse with a broom, leaving it for dead in the wine cellar. Soft-hearted Brigitte stealthily descended, picked up the stunned creature and put it gently up her sleeve, where it crawled back and forth during dinner, gradually reviving itself. Finally after dinner the future animal activist released the dazed rodent into the wilds, silently cheering her private victory.

By this time Brigitte had quit the Conservatory, henceforth taking dance courses with a Russian taskmaster named Boris Kniaseff. One of his other dancing protégées was Leslie Caron, who would of course attain worldwide fame in the film world. Well before the term "abuse" became a catchall for every form of discipline, Kniaseff never hesitated to goad his girls forward to new balletic heights with smacks of his stick. One result, as noted, was that Bardot would always walk with a dancer's grace, seen most readily in her movies.

Toty would certainly not have minded had her daughter ended up doing something cultural that was legitimate, i.e., like ballet. But as an adult Brigitte would to a degree punish that repressive, holier-than-thou mother by *not* going legit, *not* becoming classical. Instead, with her coming cinematic sexiness and unstable love life, Bardot would grow into the respectable mother's intermittent nightmare, repeatedly confirming a bad girl image she felt stuck with, and never fitting a pattern of which her parents could really approve. But as one writer says, women seldom sin alone; and to aid her in becoming one of the world's sauciest film stars of the '50s and early '60s, Bardot would soon meet her Svengali: Roger Vadim.

2

The Vadim Years

WHEN BRIGITTE HAD BEEN ABOUT at confirmation age, Charles de Gaulle, growingly disgusted by political wrangles in the country he loved, resigned his post as France's provisional president in the fall of 1946. Postwar France was plagued with shortages—the economy as gray as late November—and the Black Market thrived. Nationalization of key industries and the beginnings of a welfare state did less to revive French fortunes than American largesse bestowed by the Marshall Plan of 1947, plus the country's own zest for renewal, reflected in a baby boom, and an explosion of new cultural trends.

The form of government which repelled le grand Charles was that of the Fourth Republic, barely accepted at the end of 1946, and soon a succession of cabinets falling and new ones taking their place, topped by a figurehead presidency. Abroad, France tried to atone for its supposed decadence revealed in the 1940 defeat, sending some of its best and brightest young to die in droves during a nine-year attempt to regain a French Vietnam, followed by a difficult war in Algeria.

France also had to adjust to the reign of two new superpowers, Russia and the U.S., locked in a Cold War that seemed to relegate other European countries to pawn-like status. The recent past under the Nazis beclouded this *après-guerre* France as well, with everyone trying to disavow former affiliations with Pétain or the farther Right.

And yet, it was time for the French to try different pathways, and even a conservative Anne-Marie Bardot was not immune to that post-bellum "nouveaumania." During the war she had already started sewing hats to make extra money, and then began designing them and contracting out the work. In 1948, perhaps inspired by Christian Dior's "new look" of the previous year, she decided to start up her own hat boutique at home in the Rue de la Pompe.

To show one man's collection Toty conceived the idea of her daughter Brigitte dancing a classical theme to each group of apparel presented. The result was that the

17

thin teenager got noticed not only by clients who came around, but by the editor of the magazine *Jardin des modes*, for whom she did a spread. (Family connections were part of that too, for one of Louis Bardot's cousins worked on the magazine, supervising the "Junior Miss" section.) From there, in the concentrated world of Paris journalism, word spread to *Elle*, France's top women's magazine of the era, which now sought Brigitte for an appearance on its pages. To accept such a gig the girl had to argue strenuously with a mother who found this venue potentially scandalous; but finally Brigitte got to do it by virtue of a compromise—a cover profile in *Elle*, but with no name used other than initials that would later become world-famous, BB.

Elle's cover photo of Brigitte that appeared on May 2, 1949, reached a lot of people, then a second, where she looked prim and schoolgirlish, led her to the man who would have as much influence on her life and career as anyone: the dashing young Roger Vadim. Vadim was the offspring of a Russian father from Kiev, Igor Plemiannikov, and was born in Paris in 1928. The boy's first name would have been Vadim, but French law of the time required a French first name; so Igor put a "Roger" in front of Vadim, and when older, the boy simply abandoned his cumbrous last name.

Like many Russians the father had immigrated to France at the time of the Bolshevik Revolution, which he vigorously opposed. Becoming a diplomat in France, Igor died suddenly of a heart attack at 34, leaving the boy of eight to start making his own way in life. His mother, Marie-Antoinette, was French, and though she went on to a brief second marriage, Vadim was one of those Parisian kids who basically had to grow up on his own and quickly, which he did. At a precocious age he would become a journalist and screenwriter, and his deepest ambition was to be an accomplished film director.

When he started earning a living, Vadim moved about incessantly—crashing in this or that apartment of friends he made easily. In heady Saint-Germain-des-Prés of the postwar era, *the* place to be in that period, he rubbed shoulders with artists, philosophers, writers, and musicians.

Where Montmartre had been Paris' cultural center in the '20s, and Montparnasse in the '30s, after the Liberation the action shifted back to the Left Bank—to the Latin Quarter and especially, Saint-Germain. By war's end the intellectual vogue of existentialism was firmly anchored there, and at night the area became a paradise for those who loved to hear singers or jazz at cool haunts like the Tabou Club, especially American bebop players. Despite hostility toward the U.S., French intellectuals of the era received these black jazz artists from the States as nothing short of royalty. Sartre himself might stud his conversation with references to Nietzsche or Baudelaire, but he also greatly admired the sounds of a Charlie Parker.

Vadim met many luminaries here, even if like others, he couldn't quite grasp all the intricacies of existentialism. Its bottom line held what no longer seems so original— that *you* had to make yourself each day; and a young, impetuous, and talented Vadim took that part at face value. He didn't need to know the ins and outs of Sartre's and de Beauvoir's sexual experimentation to realize that the postwar world would change dramatically in that regard as well. All the ambitious young man needed was a vehicle, and he was soon to locate her.

When Vadim came upon the fateful *Elle* and its cover face, he was living at the Paris flat of the actress Danièle Delorme and her actor husband Daniel Gélin, for whom he also babysat. One day their three-year-old son wanted Roger to make him a paper airplane, so the sitter thought he would take the most recent issue of *Elle* and rip out a page. While doing so, he encountered Brigitte's photo and began staring raptly at it— the little boy waiting impatiently for his airplane. Vadim was then an assistant to the tasteful French film director Marc Allégret, who was about to film one of his scripts, and excitedly, he showed Allégret the photo. Impressed, Allégret agreed to a screen test for this young face, with Vadim somehow obtaining her home address and sending her a letter to that effect. Allégret was a great locator of talent, including such unknowns of the time as Jean-Paul Belmondo.[1] But predictably, both Toty and Pilou put their bourgeois feet down—no daughter of *theirs* was going to enter this cinematic demi-monde! So the screen test was definitely out.

Thankfully, Grandma Mamie and Grandpa "Boum" vouchsafed their contradictory two cents, supporting the girl's desperate pleas for a shot at the big time. Brigitte would remember Boum Papa finally dominating the discussion by smashing his fist on the table, declaring heatedly that whether the girl turned out to be a whore or didn't *wouldn't* be changed by a possible career in films! And somehow they carried the day.

Still at an age when today teens are scarcely allowed to consort with adults outside of school, and when puerility is prolonged, Brigitte went to Allégret's apartment, meeting his dark, handsome, worldly assistant there. Compared to a father who would plot each kilometer of a trip and practice his jokes, Vadim seemed pleasantly relaxed and informal. A gawky Brigitte, breaking out in familiar eczema tension spots under the hot lights of her screen test, did not receive Allégret's part; but she did get Vadim's attention. He had written a youthful novel entitled *The Wise Sophie*, and somehow Brigitte seemed the closest human embodiment of this Sophie that he had met.

For a few months he tried giving her a wide berth, knowing what a parental fortress he would have to assault for any kind of intimacy; but then one day, having nothing else to do, he impulsively went to a café, dialing Brigitte from there with his last bit of change. Her parents were blessedly away on vacation, and Vadim found unexpectedly easy entry to the inner sanctum on the Rue de la Pompe, where Mamie was chaperon. It was, as they say in the American song, the start of something big, and as early as age 15 Bardot would even be considering marriage!

Maman, however, wanted her daughter to concentrate on preparation for her baccalaureate degree; but once she fell quickly and desperately in love, the girl found Vadim the only education she wanted. And indeed, he would soon give her a first taste of Tout Paris, including a dinner at the restaurant of restaurants, Maxim's, where older, more practiced women made her feel decidedly out of place. It was all, however, bracing to a girl who had grown up inside such rigid boundaries.

Brigitte's parents predictably found Vadim rather unkempt, though he was a minor league bohemian compared to future hippies. The first time they had him over Toty checked the silver when he left. The young couple met where and when they could, including at a friend's apartment. Louis Bardot was the typical surveillance-heavy, interventionist kind of father we have to a great degree lost. When Bardot kept skipping school to rendezvous with Vadim, and her father finally found out, he flew into a rage, planning to ship her to a boarding school in England, which seemed the end of the earth to her. Her tearful entreaties somehow averted the paternal decree, but she was no longer allowed to see Roger until she was of age.

From then on Brigitte was fully in the resistance, finding opportunities to meet her man *en cachette* and to make love, for she had lost her virginity quite early on. Louis and Anne-Marie, the good bourgeois, kept trying to woo their daughter away from a dangerous presence they still scented in the air, fixing her up with the equivalent of country club offspring in the U.S.—French *fils à papa*. On one of those boring dates Bardot returned ten minutes after her midnight curfew, and an irate Pilou, pulling down the teenager's dress, vigorously spanked her bottom. It was doubly shameful for Brigitte that her shocked date witnessed this punishment, and that it was her first night clad in adult stockings and garter. The punishment wasn't, however, severe enough to make her respectable, and she remained even more dedicatedly at war with her parents, while Vadim stayed her secret love.

The truth is of course easy to feel, and to get her away from this persistent menace, her parents next put Brigitte on a two-week cruise to dance ballet for passengers, along with another French woman who would become famous, Capucine. It turned out to be hard work, but Brigitte found Capucine a warm, lovely role model, and the ship's beau monde interesting.

Once back in Paris, however, she continued her worldly education at the hands of Vadim, who even took her to meet the celebrated author Colette, the latter enthusiastically pronouncing Brigitte a Gigi incarnate. She also met the popular "existential" singer Juliette Greco; the sexually scandalous playwright Jean Genet, recently pardoned from a life sentence in prison; Cocteau; and other cultural figures of the day. She even bumped into an unkempt young Marlon Brando when he stayed for a time in Vadim's apartment building; but Brando was still abed in the early afternoon and merely grumbled at Brigitte's intrusion.[2]

Since Vadim wanted to get his protégée into the film world, a probably jealous Pilou allowed an old friend of his to scoop the young screenwriter by procuring Brigitte her first part in a movie called *Le Trou normand* (released in 1952). For her this debut was both an enjoyable and hellish experience, especially when makeup artists sadistically worked her over, telling her essentially that good treatment only arrived when one became a star.

But no personal downside comes through in the finished product, still an enjoyable Bardot film. With Paul Misraki providing a fine score, as in later Bardot efforts, this black and white picture is pure *Clochemerle*, a portrait of rural France at its best and worst. The French comic actor Bourvil plays the major role here as the village idiot whose conspiratorial aunt and Bardot's Javotte try to swindle him out of his inheritance—a Normandy *auberge* and estate that would enrich him.[3]

On the whole a pertly youthful Bardot seems happy and effervescent in the movie; but real life was quite another thing. Near the end of the shoot came the ultimate bourgeois horror of the day, something she had been fearing: an unwanted first pregnancy. Stuck in Normandy she started feeling nauseous, and as she finished working on "Trou," found herself vomiting continually. One result was that she couldn't eat, a case of nerves undoubtedly a part of it.

Learning of her daughter's illness, Mama hauled her off to an important specialist,

Brigitte as the scheming Javotte Lemoine, playing opposite Bourvil as the village idiot Hippolyte, in her first movie, *Le Trou normand* (*Crazy for Love*). (Cité-Films, 1952)

who in a typically French way confidently labeled the problem viral jaundice, prescribing a regime of total rest. Brigitte asked if she might take part of that rest at the place where she had learned to swim in a pool, Megève, up in the French Alps. Getting an affirmative answer, she met Vadim there, and they went directly to nearby Switzerland for an abortion. This gritty experience had a great effect on Bardot, both in the immediate aftermath of feeling half dead from it, and in a longer-term fear of maternity.

Back in Paris her parents, unaware of the abortion, still tried half-heartedly to keep Brigitte away from her *éminence grise* and their probable future son-in-law. One night, however, Brigitte got a "pass" to attend a movie with Vadim, and the usual twelve midnight curfew was prescribed for their return. Arriving home at 1:30 a.m., the couple blithely rationalized their lateness by announcing that they had walked slowly, and an overprotective Pilou blew a fuse, doubtless aware that the couple's relaxed look had a sexual origin. Taking a revolver out of the cupboard, Papa Bardot pointed it at Vadim, threatening that if he got too cozy with his daughter, i.e., took her virginity, he would shoot him! Pilou's face was livid with rage and the threat seemed plausible. In her bathrobe Toty emerged from the bedroom, managing to pry the gun away from her out-of-control husband, which she then pointed again at Vadim; and with all the drama of a perhaps frustrated actress, and frustrated woman generally, she announced that if Louis hadn't the courage to pull the trigger, she most certainly would! So—no untoward behavior before marriage...

All this repression emboldened Brigitte, but also got her down, and her first of a series of suicide attempts came during the difficult courtship, with Vadim away working in the South of France. Depressed by his absence, and perhaps worried about his fidelity, Brigitte refused a night on the town in the family car to see Parisian monuments reilluminated after the wartime blackout. In the nick of time she was found on their fortuitous early return home, her head stuck in an oven, and the gas on. A shocked Louis and Anne-Marie Bardot now decided to allow their daughter freer access to Vadim, and even to permit a marriage, but only when she turned 18. Pilou also pushed Vadim into taking regular work at the offices of *Paris-Match*, and impelled his religious change from Orthodox to Catholic, involving twice-a-week catechism lessons.

What they could not control was Vadim's mental hold on his protégée, whom he continued promoting like mad. Showing her photos around, helping her obtain more modeling gigs, and getting her face into magazines, he also put her into acting school, which only lasted a few months for the stubbornly autodidactic Bardot. His money needs remained acute—Vadim wasn't one to hold onto it—so his wife-to-be took a second movie role for a film to be made mostly in the Midi, *Manina, la fille sans voiles*, with Vadim accompanying her to Nice for the shoot. "Le Trou" would rake in a few million dollars, and Bardot was en route to becoming a somewhat more well-known commodity, especially when she revealed a good deal of herself in *Manina*.[4] It was the first swallow of a long, liberating western summer, though when released, the bikini shots would anger her father.

Her 18th birthday had special meaning for Bardot—and one good thing about the Catholic bourgeoisie: it mostly kept promises on matters as important as marriage. That landmark birthday was September 28, 1952, and several months later Roger and Brigitte were married—on December 21. The ceremony took place at the Eglise de Notre-Dame-de-Grâce of Passy in the 16th *arrondissement*. At the wedding Daniel Gélin and Danièle Delorme were witnesses, then the newlyweds left to honeymoon in the French Alps, where Brigitte enjoyed the tonic winter air.[5]

They returned to marital reality in a small flat purchased by Brigitte's parents in of course Paris' 16th, or at least on the edge of it—Rue Chardon-Lagache. Trying to be domestic, Brigitte taught herself to cook sturdy, simple fare, and like other housewives of the period worried about the effect of chocolates on her weight and complexion. She got a cocker spaniel she named "Clown" and a house lady named Aïda, a 70-year-old Russian princess. Frequently she trekked across the city to save money on household goods. She also wanted what seemed to Vadim a lot of love and feedback. This husband who was as much her brother or mentor wished to divert his wife's enthusiasm to other, more marketable things, and within a year the marriage became a tempestuous one. Vadim too was a bon vivant living a full life in the big city. Bardot says that he would plead the need for all-night work sessions at the *Match* editorial offices and meanwhile, she would have to stay home, cuddling the dog.

Their extreme differences in handling money became one of their recurring marital problems. At one point the couple bought a lemon of a car from a friend of Vadim's and it promptly died in the Bois de Boulogne. After spending a good deal of money for towing and repairs, they finally got rid of it six months later. Vadim was certainly a good-time Charlie, careless with cash, whereas Bardot was better at financial planning, and unfairly, would later incur a reputation in France of being rather tight with a franc.

She especially wanted her love to be beautiful and the central thing in life, and for Vadim, it obviously wasn't. However, the resultant Bardot pout eventually became a patented screen trademark and also an attraction to other men, provoking in some the natural response of wanting to help.

Despite the money she earned, Bardot's first two films, along with a brief appearance in *Les Dents longues* with Delorme and Gélin, received largely indifferent reviews, leading her to write a hesitant letter to an agent, Olga Horstig, in order to procure better material and roles. That letter yielded unexpected results. Originally from Yugoslavia,

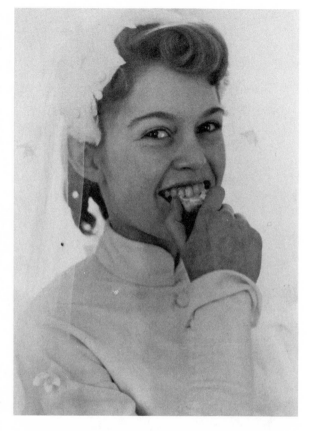

A happy Brigitte in wedding garb, December 1952.

Horstig soon became and would remain Bardot's agent right down to the end of her film career, growing into a kind of second mother for Brigitte. Immediately "Mama Olga" found her another film project, *Le Portrait de son père*, which didn't do much better than the earlier ones.[6] In the same era (1953) Anatole Litvak decided to test the young French actress in an American film, *Act of Love*, set at the time of France's liberation in World War II; and despite her halting English, Bardot received a part, playing a servant, Mimi, anything but the major role.[7]

A turning point portending the decidedly two-edged sword of fame that would make Bardot a ubiquitous target of paparazzi occurred at her visit to the Cannes Film Festival in April 1953, coinciding with the release of *Act of Love*. Vadim was on hand to interview Leslie Caron for *Match*, a star now, and one who made the young Bardot feel like nothing. It was a moment when the Riviera was still almost as young and undiscovered as Bardot, who would help make it famous internationally. A U.S. Navy aircraft carrier, the *Midway*, filled with U.S. sailors, was moored at Cannes, and Bardot was invited to a party on board with the likes of Gary Cooper and Lana Turner. Vadim dressed her in a raincoat, which then came off, revealing a gorgeous teen in a tight dress, and suddenly flashbulbs began popping, and the Yank sailors went crazy for Brigitte. Bardot wasn't yet a household name, but certainly she had gotten launched.[8]

The young Brigitte, appearing in *Manina, la fille sans voiles* (*The Girl in the Bikini*)—in too skimpy a bikini for her father. (Sport Films, 1952)

She then took a role in a Jean Anouilh play, though theater would not be an enduring outlet for her; and next received a small part as the one-night-stand mistress of King Louis XV in the film *Si Versaille m'était conté*. Production people and cast included a famed artist besmirched by the Occupation, Sacha Guitry, as well as Jean Marais and Orson Welles. Some of Bardot's roles seemed hardly worth the trouble, such as in her next French film, *Le Fils de Caroline chérie* (*Caroline and the Rebels*), another poor one, in her estimation. However, a contemporary viewing shows this to be quite a good historical film of its era, even if Brigitte is used intermittently and sparingly in it. Set in Spain during the Napoleonic occupation, parallels to France's own recent experience of occupation and resistance keep being drawn.

Meanwhile, Bardot and Vadim had become an attractive couple hobnobbing with some heavy hitters, though such society types weren't really to her taste. At one point she accompanied her husband to the Countess of Luynes' chateau on the Loire, where he was to interview the noble lady for an article in *Match*. A big hunt was scheduled, and Bardot heard the horn and dogs barking enthusiastically, and instantly identified with the hunted deer. Later at the chateau she beheld its bloody body sprawled out in the courtyard, and profoundly sickened, conceived an instant and lifelong antipathy toward

Bardot and first husband Roger Vadim at the Negresco Hotel in Nice, 1954. (SIPA/NewsCom)

hunters. When it came time to clink champagne glasses with these people, she slipped outside in a silent huff, determined to walk if need be all the way back to Paris. After she had done a few kilometers, Vadim approached in his car stuffed with suitcases, ready to give in and drive her home.

To raise cash Bardot went off to work in *Tradita* with a small Italian company in that country; but exhaustion and hemorrhaging on the set led to a hospital stint. The last part of the shooting up in the Dolomites (where *Cliffhanger* would be shot) was the coup de grâce for her. After convalescing, Bardot went right home to the soothing arms of Mamie, Boum, and Papa, and they loved having her. Her worried parents, however, urged her to get out of movies and have a child.

But she was back in Rome in the spring of 1954 for a part in the American-made extravaganza *Helen of Troy*, leaving her husband at home with Clown, and rooming with another future star, Ursula Andress. She also received positive reinforcement from the paparazzi, not yet the great irritant of her life, as well as from Italian locals. Vadim later arrived on the scene, and found himself bunked in with two great beauties, though a ménage-à-trois never eventuated. Instead, he thrilled Bardot and Andress with bedtime tales of vampires, succubae, incubi, etc., eventually writing a book of stories on the subject, translated into English as *The Vampire* (1963). If Vadim was indeed working in part for the Devil, Bardot didn't seem to mind.

But this is again anything but a siren Brigitte in *Helen...*, cast as a slave to the Spartan queen (played by a blond Rossana Podesta). The film is opulently American, directed by Robert Wise (*West Side Story, Sound of Music*), and with sumptuous music by Max Steiner. Bardot's Andrasty helps spirit Paris and the smitten queen to the water, where they hide, waiting for a Phoenician ship to sail and galley paddle them back to Troy. In return she obtains her freedom and disappears from the film! On the whole the movie is still rather enjoyable to watch, as is the young, as yet unfamed Bardot in her restricted role.[9]

Making money remained a necessity in her marriage, and Bardot honored a commitment to act in Marc Allégret's *Futures Vedettes*, playing a student in love with her music teacher in Vienna (Jean Marais). Bardot was anything but the shrewd business person some have painted her to be, but her husband was a free spender and his gullibility kept getting him swindled out of big sums, even at the hands of a con artist housemaid. Bardot also had a continuing case of nerves from counting days of the month, in a period when the pill wasn't available and when she and Vadim weren't very adept at "Catholic" birth control. The result was a second unwanted pregnancy and illegal abortion, again, in a time when one risked prison and possible death from such a procedure. Death in fact nearly intervened, but for cardiac massage in a dingy Paris apartment, rousing Brigitte out of her torpor.

Recovering, the shaken young actress continued on her film-making merry-go-round, pushed both by Vadim and by Mama Olga. Though refusing to appear in the States, partly due to the recent execution of the Rosenbergs there, she consented to make one of the British doctor films of that era, opposite Dirk Bogarde for swaths of the film. Beginning her shoot in February of 1955, and up at five each day to work on puritanical schedules, it took time to get used to the country of Shakespeare. But she certainly fascinated the Brits, and crowds of admirers were thicker here than in France. For the English, Bardot was becoming the sex kitten from that frivolous country across the Channel—her face and body now starting to displace established French actresses like Martine Carol. If older women came to fear Bardot as the scourge of married men, younger ones in Britain and elsewhere would soon model themselves in droves on her look. It was the perfect moment to be an erotic pioneer—for in Britain puritanism still had vestigial power, and in America staid figures like Dwight Eisenhower or Ed Sullivan reigned as well. In both countries puritanism would obviously be lost in spades during the next decade, but for the moment, Europe was more liberal in that regard. And of course a feline Vadim hardly minded Brigitte being identified as the new "Mam'selle Striptease"—in fact, he encouraged it.

Doctor at Sea, however, remains pretty tame stuff. In a movie where the clipped English may be semi-comprehensible even to Americans, the young Bardot does well by her role—perfectly natural as French singer Hélène Colbert, ending up on the S.S. *Lotus* and becoming Dr. Simon Sparrow's love interest. To fit so well here, and with such apparent ease is a tribute to Brigitte, given her age.

Bogarde plays the British doctor fleeing a woman by running to sea, and is supported by a fine cast, including an overweight, red-bearded captain incarnate (James

Brigitte as an entertainer, Hélène Colbert, on board ship in *Doctor at Sea*. (Group Film Production, 1955)

Robertson Justice); and a middle-aged English blond on board, driving this Captain Hogg to drink and eventual craziness by prodding him toward marriage. Holding her own, a wasp-waisted Bardot with reddish hair in a bun, clad in strapless gowns, nurse's garb, or dresses, is fresh as a salt breeze blowing from Technicolor skies off the freighter's bow. There is plenty of slapstick, but never enough to bowl over her good-humored, spirited dignity in the film.[10]

In her next picture, *Les Grandes Manoeuvres* (*Summer Maneuvers* in the English title), directed by René Clair and begun at Paris' Boulogne studios in April 1955, Bardot plays a girl getting the attention of a soldier on the eve of World War I. In reality she was anything but self-assured, appearing alongside two legendary French actors, Gérard Philipe and Michèle Morgan. On the set Bardot found herself reddening uncontrollably and hating herself for it. She does not have much of a part—Philipe and Morgan are the stars with by far the most lines, and the central romantic interest in this movie.

Clair truly agonized about the ending, consulting intellectual friends like Aragon and Jean Cocteau, shooting two versions, and finally choosing the sadder one. As for Brigitte, though clearly in a subordinate role, she outshines other young people in the film by her out-of-the-bourgeois-cage élan. It's the palpable glitter of someone who is happy to be dramatic, yet still stable in her life with Vadim, and not man-ravaged or experienced enough to be anything like a sex symbol. Though she stands out, her short hair and general look make her cute at most here.[11]

However, Vadim kept pushing her to be sexy and so did a new friend and producer, Christine Gouze-Rénal, whom Bardot met working on her next film of 1955, *La Lumière d'en face*. Outwardly, Brigitte began to project a racier image, but inside, had quite a divided soul—brutally put, between her rebellious, unfettered side, and her bourgeois, "square," thrifty upbringing, some of which remained intact.

That soul division would later be seen when she tried guiltily to juggle two men, and indeed, Vadim knew already that he couldn't do what Brigitte perhaps wanted him to do—prevent her from falling in love elsewhere. There was always a voyeuristic quality about this screenwriter-director, and he undoubtedly sensed the coming female vogue of much enhanced personal liberty. The theme of being torn between two lovers would become a mainstay of Bardot's life ... but not yet.

The Light Across the Street (in its English title) is quite a good black-and-white film of its period, but as with *Manoeuvres*, one sees why it wouldn't make it in the English-speaking world.[12] Nothing here to rival *High Society* et al. Bardot wasn't yet a complete femme fatale, not least due to rather prim reddish hair that comes off as brown on screen. She is still not a blond bombshell à la Monroe. However, the film was banned in several parts of France for supposedly suggestive content, involving a sick husband and a potential younger lover.[13]

Brigitte continued her film work—still as a pert redhead—with a putative comedy made by Michel Boisrond and Vadim, *Cette Sacrée Gamine* (*That Naughty Girl*). Dancing is one of her main contributions in this movie where a constant effort to be funny, including via slapstick, makes one realize why the French idolized Jerry Lewis: *they* could make fine soufflés, haute couture, and wines, but simply couldn't get his anarchic brand of comedy right, or not then.[14]

Bardot also returned to Rome to work in a film called *Mio figlio Nerone*, or in English, *Nero's Weekend*, a multilingual product, where she was one of the crazy Roman emperor's mistresses. Gloria Swanson plays Agrippina, Nero's supposedly incestuous mother, and Vittorio de Sica is Seneca. Bardot has to pare down here, including for an authentic milk bath, and in real life, had a brief fling with an Italian crooner while there.

Back in Paris she began shooting in February 1956 on another Allégret-Vadim flick, *En Effeuillant la Marguerite* (later called in English the nonsensical *Mam'selle Striptease*). The film is pleasant enough, and the many lines Bardot was given show how much harder she worked than is generally understood.[15] However, disrobing was the part of the film that again got attention, though at this point Bardot was still no household name internationally. At least she now rated her own *maquilleuse*, Odette (nicknamed Dédette) Berroyer. And though this is pleasant enough fare, with Bardot her usual unaffected self, she is not yet the star here of something that might astonish the world.[16]

She was, however, on the eve of a hugely transforming breakthrough, of the kind all famous figures experience in their careers. This breakthrough, making Bardot a household name everywhere and leading to much unanticipated misery, would come as a by-product of her next screen effort, the Vadim–Raoul Lévy project of 1956, *And God Created Woman*.

As a kid of about 11 I remember the moment—when as noted, things European were still far out and risqué. I remember my father furtively reading a copy of *Lady Chatterley's Lover* at our rented summer cottage, and I couldn't understand why a normally outdoors fellow would hole himself up inside all day, when the sun was shining and the water beckoned.

Vadim's idea was to shoot a heuristic vehicle, allowing Bardot to be more or less herself on screen.[17] Along with her husband, another true character was behind the project, its producer Lévy. A Belgian of Russian-Jewish background, and a navigator for the RAF in wartime, who once landed mistakenly in Germany instead of Dover, Lévy was an inveterate high-roller. Supposedly ruined five times to the point of bankruptcy, he nonetheless had a lot to do with seeing what Bardot had and catapulting her to fame. Even if he lacked an imposing

A glamorous young Brigitte Bardot, but not yet the blond bombshell of world fame.

track record in the film world, Lévy at least possessed an adept sense of the new. As the gambler he was, he decided to bet on the young Vadim and his beautiful wife, and on *Et Dieu créa la femme.*

In a white heat Vadim wrote a draft for the movie, but finding money for such a treatment was a problem for the two men. To have a chance of scoring with the film, Lévy felt it advisable to hitch their wagon to the bright American star of the '50s. Columbia Pictures had deep pockets and Technicolor capability which *might* give the movie a chance of attaining wider success; but its American executives had little familiarity with this French screenwriter and director, Vadim. In order to make their pitch to Columbia unassailable, Lévy and his younger sidekick felt they needed star bait to dangle, and got the idea of wooing Germany's Curt Jurgens for an as-yet unwritten role in the picture. That suave actor was already known to American audiences and studio moguls; so Lévy and Vadim hopped a train to Munich, where Jurgens was then filming, took an expensive hotel room to impress the actor, stocking it with caviar and vodka—all beyond budget—and Lévy also got Vadim a hooker, whom the latter used for higher things. Over the next couple days at the hotel the lady typed up a new part in the picture for Jurgens that Vadim was busy scribbling. Inviting Lévy and Vadim to his lakeside Bavarian villa, the German actor looked at the project and somehow accepted a leap into the unknown. Columbia then came on board with its cash, color, and clout.

In some ways this was the most crucial change in the film's conception and story-telling, helping to make it such an important cultural phenomenon. It turned out that Jurgens would perfectly incarnate his cinematic role as the practiced, cynical, older businessman-playboy. He would play a man who had seen it all and who normally resisted attachments, but who nonetheless was able to call on reserves of generosity when it counted.

Owing to Jurgens' tight schedule, *And God...* had to be shot rapidly, so Bardot soon found herself at work on the Riviera in May–June 1956, with a then unknown actor, Jean-Louis Trintignant, cast in the film as the bumbling brother of a hunk (Christian Marquand), and both after Bardot's Juliette. By then her marriage to Vadim was starting to totter, and at first it appeared that an elegant warhorse like Jurgens might turn Brigitte's head, not an unknown like Trintignant. In fact, Bardot was initially repelled by this seemingly provincial French southerner, who was perfect for his role in the film. The earnest Trintignant in turn disliked Brigitte's prima donna petulance on the set, and she *was* difficult, especially on viewing daily rushes, crying about this or that unflattering shot, and needing constant reassurance from her director, "Vava."

After three weeks on the beach at Saint-Tropez, the cast finished things off in the studios of Nice, and a surprising love meanwhile had been growing on the set. Daily proximity facilitated it, and also the fact that Trintignant was easy to underestimate, possessing more depth than was first apparent. Having come up to Paris from the South of France at the outset of the '50s, he had worked hard to smooth down his Provençal accent when interpreting Molière or Corneille. He was also a demon poker player, able to bore in psychologically on others' weaknesses. Finally, before the end of shooting Vadim realized that Brigitte and Trintignant were feeling off screen what they were portraying on celluloid. The sultry actress did translate emotions on having two men in her life into a form of art here, albeit not of the highest variety, but which nonetheless helped render the film appealing.

My own first view of *And God...* was of the censored Anglo version with dubbing, and not a very good film; the original in French is much better. With suggestive cha-cha music by Paul Misraki impelling the watcher through credits dominated by Bardot's name, the movie opens with a view of the Mediterranean at Saint-Tropez, where a debonair businessman in sports car and shades (Jurgens) has decided to build a hotel and casino. Getting out of his convertible, he comes upon Juliette Hardy (Bardot), sunning herself in the buff on a terrace hidden by clothes on a line; she then dons a shift, but remains the village bad girl, and the movie retains its then scandalous tone all the way through.

The film of course became Bardot's rocket launcher, and also launched the career of another French star—Trintignant. And it did anything but diminish Jurgens' large screen reputation of the time. Dialogue in the original French comes out of the Left Bank Vadim knew so well, and even young cinematic luminaries like François Truffaut saw something truly original here, not least erotically.[18]

But at a layout of some $600,000 the picture at first didn't do so well with French audiences, debuting on December 4, 1956, in a theater on the Champs-Elysées and garnering mostly indifferent reviews.[19] This portended another financial bust for Lévy, an eccentric who would eventually end his life in 1967, shooting himself in the stomach over a woman. But it wasn't yet time for Lévy to pull the trigger. Even though the British

Brigitte as village bad girl Juliette Hardy, held by Michel Tardieu (Jean-Louis Trintignant) in *Et Dieu créa la femme* (*And God Created Woman*), with Michel's jealous brother, Antoine Tardieu (Christian Marquand, foreground), looking on. The movie launched Bardot's career and a deep relationship with Trintignant. (Iéna, UCIL Cocinor, 1956)

censored the film more severely, perhaps due to their enhanced puritanism they also gave it more critical and popular acclaim than the French. However, the full avalanche would only occur via *America's* response to the movie, and that would be deferred through most of 1957.

Before the deluge, Bardot's still rather restricted degree of celebrity is seen by perusing *Paris-Match* for that year. Along with a number of other actresses she is seen from time to time advertising Lux soap (as in the January 12, 1957, issue). But *Match* gave much more play to Princess Grace and her babies, or to Queen Elizabeth and Prince Philip, than to Brigitte. In the February 16, 1957, issue there was a spread on Vittorio de Sica and other celebrities at "le Bal de B.B.," part of the Munich Carnival. Clad in Dior dress the young Bardot was guest of honor at this dance given by a Munich newspaper. One sees pictures of her dancing with her "partner" in *And God...*, Jurgens, and with the handsome Italian, Raf Vallone, with whom she would one day have an affair. But really there wasn't much more on Bardot through that year; again, full celebrity would only be launched from across the Atlantic.

In the U.S. the premiere didn't come till later in 1957, and constituted a real shocker for that period. The movie opened at New York's Paris Theater on October 21, followed the next day by a Bosley Crowther review in *The New York Times*, predictably emphasizing its racy quality.[20] A poster of a partly unclad Bardot would now look down on passers-by in Times Square. But despite religious and other protests in various American cities, the film was to make Bardot a top name and star in the U.S., symbolic of a piquant European sex appeal; eventually, profits from *And God...* ran to over four million dollars.

A plethora of articles on the Bardot phenomenon began hitting the American press in November 1957, crescendoing through 1958. A *Life* magazine piece of November 18, 1957, reflected the sense that Europe was ahead of the game both erotically and mentally, and that Brigitte mirrored both trends. As they noted, "The intellectual French see something very special in the towel-draped figure of Brigitte Bardot.... To the people of Paris, Brigitte Bardot is less girl than she is an exciting philosophical attitude ... a symbol of the eternal woman in rebellion, who finds that life unfortunately is sometimes sad and frequently futile." Meanwhile, "Americans, less cerebral about movie stars, are smashing foreign film box-office figures at a New York theater to make up their minds about Bardot.... She also has a tendency to remove large parts of her clothing and show much more than American audiences are used to seeing...."[21] *Time* stressed Bardot's child-like face and demeanor. From the neck up "she looks about twelve years old, and bears a striking resemblance to Shirley Temple at that age." But the writer conceded that "her movies have smashed attendance records ... and Hollywood has bid high for her services." The week before this issue came out "Bardot's most notorious film [was] doing record business in Manhattan...," and another would soon open. *Time* notes of that latest film (opening in the States after *And God...*) that it doesn't have much plot or decent dialogue; still "she's a fetching little hussy, and the language she speaks can be understood without subtitles."[22] In a review of that film, *The Bride Is Much Too Beautiful*, *Newsweek*'s writer declared: "Talent or no ...[in] the U.S. during the sixteen weeks that four of her movies have been shown, there have been signs that she might well be taking over from Marilyn Monroe." But they too damn with faint praise, noting that "Bardot on screen looks and acts like Peck's Bad Girl and, according to her friends, she is. She has the naïveté and temper tantrums of a child."[23] The *New York Times Magazine* (November 10, 1957) also pondered "whether she is the 'grown-up child' some of her friends call her...."

Emboldened by America's unexpected response to *And God...*, Lévy brought out a second release in France, and the picture went through the roof there, too. The result? By the late '50s Brigitte's charismatic beauty would become a tidal wave around the world, and she began coming of age as a celebrity—meeting Winston Churchill, invited by Picasso to his place above Cannes, etc. Almost single-handedly she helped popularize Saint-Tropez and the entire Riviera. Here was the region that had once been a magnet for dyspeptic Brits who needed to convalesce in a fine environment—Smollett, Lord Brougham (inventing the carriage of that name), Robert Louis Stevenson, even Queen Victoria. In the '20s came the Fitzgerald era, and of course his *Tender Is the Night* is shot through with the Riviera's ambiance. But more than any single figure, Bardot helped "make" the Côte d'Azur both in France and internationally, bringing it to the ken of the masses.[24]

Not that she lived for such things. Despite her own approbation of what she deemed her best cinematic endeavor to date, she was quite indifferent to the first waves of publicity and the dawning of stardom. For something that would always be more important to her had surfaced: love. Bardot found herself truly moved by this serious, earnest Trintignant, so different from Vadim, who had really become a best friend in recent years of their marriage. To be sure, while starting up with Trintignant, Bardot *was* still married, as indeed he was—to the actress Stéphane Audran, though they were supposedly separated. The press (before the full *And God...* explosion) blessedly granted the new couple a reprieve, and for a time the affair remained basically private.

At first the two could see each other only in a Paris hotel room, then, separating from Vadim, Bardot would later redo her apartment and Trintignant moved in, cooking, putting on classical music, and reciting poetry. Bardot was a woman who would always inspire the artist in men. They had no TV, no radio, no newspapers, and a nicely skewed sense of time vividly lived, uncounted via the clock. The journalistic calm was, however, the calm before an imminent earthquake!

There were already portents, as when Bardot made the mistake of ruffling the important feathers of one Jean-François Devay of *France-Soir*, arriving a half hour late for an interview. Though a friend of Vadim's, Devay grew so angry that he vowed to destroy the young actress of the moment, which he would sedulously try to do in future articles!

Separations wrought by the demands of Bardot's trade constituted another severe problem lurking on the near horizon, given that movie contracts now poured in to the office of her all too willing agent, Mama Olga. As if the prospect of shooting elsewhere weren't enough to threaten Bardot's deep love for Trintignant, she was also depressed by news that French military authorities were calling him into service, initially at Vincennes at one end of Paris. Despite his proximity, Bardot could only see her beloved on Sundays, his permission day, so she took little joy while still shooting *La Mariée est trop belle* (*The Bride Is Much Too Beautiful*) with Louis Jourdan. (Here Bardot plays a photographer's model, and Jourdan the editor of a magazine dealing with her professionally, but ignorant of her growing love for him.) Inside Bardot was dying with fear that Jean-Lou might be sent to the hellhole of Algeria. This was far from impossible, since Algeria, more than Indochina, was the French equivalent of America's Vietnam War of the '60s, claiming by conscription hundreds of thousands of soldiers in a long, dirty, and ultimately fruitless struggle to hold onto the nation's last showpiece colony, inhabited by some 1,000,000 French-speaking Europeans.

Her troubles with Trintignant intensified, for he was next sent to a military garrison in Trier, Germany. The frantic actress tried using a connection with her friend Christine Gouze-Rénal, whose brother-in-law was the politician François Mitterrand. Mitterrand helped procure Bardot an interview with a high government official, who might presumably extricate Jean-Louis from the draft. With hope in her heart she went to see the man in Paris, but doubtless aware of her screen persona, the distinguished official came onto the star in his office, letting her know that if she did right by him, Trintignant *might* get the pass. This sort of thing predictably disgusted her, and she soon found herself taking the first of a series of mournful train trips out to Trier, arriving tired out at the dingy hotel in fog and rain.

The balance of life and career began careening out of control for Bardot. Mama Olga had the power to commit this growingly famous name to movie after movie, taking her 10 percent cuts. These contracts would keep Bardot occupied for years to come, wreaking havoc on her personal life. They did, however, put money in her pocket, and with some of it Brigitte procured a new apartment on Paris' Avénue Paul Doumer in the usual 16th *arrondissement*. But she rapidly found her life discombobulated and less and less her own. Interviews, scripts to read, functions to attend quickly multiplied.

To see the Queen of England at one such function she took an onerous boat-train trip, forgetting her vanity case, which then put her in a funk. She had obtained a Balmain gown for the event, but was terrified she wouldn't be pretty enough in it. The vanity case was sent in by plane and picked up in London by Raoul Lévy, then relayed to an anxious Brigitte, panicky in rehearsals with celebrated American and British actors and actresses. For the ceremony Bardot wasn't allowed to wear black, so her coat had to go, then her dress revealed too much for the time. In a hysterical fit she nearly returned to Paris, but Mama Olga got a lady in the hotel to sew some camouflage on the suspect parts of her garb; and somehow Bardot did fine with the Duke of Edinburgh, Princess Margaret, and the Queen, who posed anodyne questions in French.

Bardot also had one of the defining moments in her young life here, by chance meeting in the ladies' room a goddess of the American and really world cinema of the time, Marilyn Monroe. In Brigitte's recollection Monroe reeked of Chanel, but though they only encountered each other for less than a minute, the French actress was impressed by the natural, fragile quality of her American counterpart. It was the only time she met her, but Bardot would be greatly saddened by Monroe's death. Did she have an inkling that her own career would soon spin out of control in much the same fashion?

For a brief moment there was, at least, a delightful pause, before the onset of celebrity pressures that would eventually overwhelm and nearly kill the sensitive young French actress. Over Christmas at the end of 1956 Trintignant received a "permission," and the couple escaped to a rustic cabin at Cassis in the South of France, belonging to Bardot's new friend, the photographer-painter Ghislain ("Jicky") Dussart. Night and day she and Jean-Louis burned pine branches in the fireplace, and they took baths in water warmed up by the burning wood. Jean-Lou grilled dinners, using Provençal herbs as seasoning, and for ten blissful days they lived an anachronistic, simple life of the type at least part of her would always desire, but too rarely get. There were no lights, only candles; no car, so they did their shopping on foot. On Christmas Eve they attended midnight mass. It was a luffing of sails before the tempest, and in retrospect, she calls this perhaps the happiest swath of time she would ever know.

Might this Trintignant love have made it for Bardot as a lasting domestic situation? Anyone who has seen him in films like Eric Rohmer's masterpiece, *My Night at Maud's*, not to mention those that resonated most with American viewers like Claude Lelouch's *A Man and a Woman*, or political films such as *The Conformist*, can feel the ponderous solidity of the man, and how much he seemed to have feet planted on the earth. Directors almost uniformly loved working with him, given his sincerity, industry, and the subtle complexity with which he informed characters he played. But unfortunately, Trintignant's relationship with Bardot had many strikes against it. One was the very nature of the film business—constant separations that would so often be difficult for Brigitte, compounded by that demon of military service which soon reclaimed Trintignant, sending him back again to his garrison in West Germany, which he took very hard. Another was the invasions and distortions about to be visited on her in growing proportions by the press.[25]

For now, Bardot returned to Paris, busying herself in the new year of 1957 with decoration of her Paul Doumer apartment—one she would have for the next 15 years. But in the near future the place would turn into an intermittent prison, with the full repercussions of *And God...* around the corner, and a wave of paparazzi assaults on her private life about to start up in earnest.

Vadim? The feline one whom military service never seemed to touch, and who had had so much to do with creating the Bardot phenomenon, would still direct her in a number of movies, but finally end their marriage formally in December 1957—a divorce by mutual consent. Vadim would say that Bardot was his last real heartache—and that he never allowed himself to go through that again, despite later involvements and marriages with feisty, beautiful actresses named Deneuve and Fonda. At least Brigitte and Roger remained friends after the split, and from time to time, when Bardot traversed one of many personal crises to come, he would be one of the few confessors and confidants she could really trust. (That is, until he published memoirs in the 1980s!)[26]

3

The Era of High Celebrity

IN 1957, BARDOT HAD BECOME a super-hot commodity, which begs the question: in what ways did she differ from her Gallic predecessors on the silver screen? The answer is that she now incarnated the femme fatale she would so often play, the saucy strumpet (sometimes with heart of gold)—and was therefore nearer to America's Monroe than any prior French screen actress could be. None of those predecessors, even with hair bleached Hollywood blond, made it internationally as sex symbols—and with good reason.

One was the aforementioned Michèle Morgan, and whether one watches her in the fall of her career in *Grandes manoeuvres*, or in its springtime as a prim, brown-haired, raincoated girl opposite Jean Gabin in Marcel Carné's brooding masterpiece *Le Quai des brumes* (1938), she is no authentic siren on screen. Nor is Arletty, most known to foreign audiences as a 19th-century courtesan in Carné's *Enfants du paradis* (1945). These actresses *play* such roles, but don't quite persuade. Nor do a celebrated trio appearing in Max Ophüls' *La Ronde* of 1950—Simone Signoret, certainly prettier here than the later wrinkled bourgeoise holding forth ideologically with Yves Montand; Danielle Darrieux, often looking startled and proper on screen, though undoubtedly a serious actress; and Simone Simon, coming nearest to this *appelation contrôlée* of femme fatale.

On the edge of Bardot's stardom Signoret appeared in the popular and critical success *Les Diaboliques* (opening January 1955), and though letter-perfect as the devilish mistress, there was enough reality in her fatigued, "been there, done that," husky-voiced portrayal to make her almost a foil for the fresh, earthy Bardot. Something similar may be said for Darrieux, appearing in a film version of *The Red and the Black* in that same era just before Bardot made it big. Again, she was well cast as the unhappily married *bourgeoise* opposite Gérard Philipe's Julien Sorel, but too one-dimensionally chaste and physically ordinary to offer anything like a comparison to Bardot.

One must finally mention the French actress who more than any other Bardot putatively dethroned, Martine Carol. Here was yet another woman who was mostly a blond, but anything but a Lana Turner. Carol's career crescendoed after her role in *Caroline chérie* of 1950, including quite a few historical films—*Lucrèce Borgia* of 1953, *Madame du Barry* the following year, *Nana* based on Zola's novel, and Ophüls' *Lola Montès* (both 1955)—too many on the stately past to be present internationally. In *Lola* Carol's hair is jet black, but here she is another one-note samba on screen—invariably sad, sublime, and wistful in flashbacks prodded by a circus ringmaster (Peter Ustinov). She is no convincing femme fatale in a role requiring one, and the film does not wear well. Carol's private life was characterized by instability and depression, and she was finally found dead in her Monte Carlo hotel room in February 1967, having been eclipsed a decade earlier by Bardot.[1]

Some might argue that Bardot's *différence* was also partly a matter of advertisement, and it is true that placed against other posters for movies of the '50s, those for hers sometimes verge on elegant pornography for that era. Tight red dresses falling off the bosom, blond hair entwining Brigitte *au naturel*, or her tanned body prudently covered in parts only by bold print announcing a film: such advertising undoubtedly affected potential spectators when other movies were promoted more prudently, and before the sex revolution hit the mainstream.[2]

But obviously the star herself had little to do with this publicity machine, and in that breakthrough year of 1957, press distortions and outright lies about her private life and personality began to shock her—it was the debut of finding herself in a celebrity fish tank, with ever-famished sharks of the Fourth Estate always peering inside. Increasingly, the press started tampering with her life, especially concerning the Trintignant affair. Journalists and photographers began laying siege to her place at Paul Doumer, and strung tight with tension, Brigitte responded with a cold sore, the first of a series, and particularly disconcerting when an actress known for pulchritude had to start shooting a new film.

In March 1957 she was indeed slated to commence work on *Une Parisienne*, with Henri Vidal and Charles Boyer, who would admire the young Bardot's poise. But at the outset the newly famous actress was clearly nerve-wracked, not only due to her lip problem, but because Boyer seemed larger than life to her. The newspapers that helped cause these shameful blemishes played up her disfigurement as a cost to the film companies. Deeply ashamed, Bardot took vitamin C shots, stopped answering the phone or having guests, and avoided reading newspapers which might be vilifying her.

In addition to studio work in Boulogne-Billancourt, she had to go down to the Riviera to film with the suave Boyer. En route, prefiguring her animal obsessions of the future, Bardot picked up a donkey and ultimately had to keep him in a garage, which the papers seized on as well. Shooting was mainly in Nice, and the film's producer, Francis Cosne, wanted her to appear at the nearby Cannes Film Festival; but Bardot kept saying no, fearing and even threatening another cold sore. Instead the Cannes journalists would have to visit her![3]

Despite the beginnings of these trials by press, *Une Parisienne* was a comedy Brigitte would be proud of, one of her rare films she fully endorses today. Bardot and Vidal made good partners, though the film is less humorous than farcical and at the same time, oddly serious. This is partly due to the solid, sober mien of Vidal. He seems right here as a handsome heavy in his thirties, collecting mistresses, then forced into marriage with Brigitte by his boss, who is the French president and Brigitte's father (she bears her real first name in the picture). A prankish Brigitte ruins her hubby's former amorous life, then makes *him* jealous by coming on to a visiting prince consort played by Boyer, who flies her down to Nice for a day in a borrowed fighter plane. There they take a dip in the sea, run into gangsters, and catch cold; but he can tell she only wants to irritate her husband, and nothing serious results. However, back home their telltale sneezes show that husband that she really did make it away with the visiting dignitary, and a more solid marriage results. There is a modern scat-jazzy score in this Technicolor Michel Boisrond-Cosne production; but though apparently up-to-date, the movie is also in the tradition of French plays from the 18th century, and both insightful dialogue and the deeper sadness of the eternal fidelity problem again make it more serious than a plain comedy. Bardot enjoyed working with Vidal, and there was hope for more of the same in a future film.[4]

Tenderly holding a dog in *Une Parisienne*, Brigitte's love of animals is already evident. (Les Films Ariane, Cinétel, Filmsonor, Paris, Rizzoli Film, Rome, 1957)

The summer of 1957, however, brought a family tragedy—news that her great-aunt Tapompon's only son and hope, Jean Marchal, who had become a doctor, was killed in a suspect auto wreck. The death bothered Brigitte deeply, especially when she heard from her mother that it was really a suicide, in reaction to his wife's announcement of wanting to live with his best friend. This was no Marivaux farce when at 37, Jean crunched his car into a tree, devastating an entire family— Boum, who felt he had lost something of a son; Anne-Marie, herself an only child for whom Jean was a brother-figure; and especially Tapompon, who felt she had lost everything. And indeed, no sooner was Jean buried then his widow married the best friend! Very sensitive about death, and with intermittent suicidal feelings of her own, Bardot would long remain affected by this sad event.

To compound her woes she now had to go over the frontier to shoot a Vadim-directed and Lévy-produced film in Spain, *Les Bijoutiers du clair de lune* (*The Night Heaven*

Charles Boyer as the visiting "Prince Charles," and Bardot as Brigitte Laurier, daughter of a French politician, in a scene from *Une Parisienne* (the two had flown to Nice for a day).

Fell), with Trintignant not allowed even to visit the set. How stupid, she recalls, to leave the love of her life (to that point) for a film shoot of several long months in a faraway location! She hated being alone for any length of time, and stuck between the easygoing contemporary attitude of loving the one you're with (to cite Stephen Stills), and the forbearance of an older generation, she had no easy time emotionally. Too, she was already considered by many as a home-wrecker. Trintignant might call himself separated, but his wife wouldn't grant him a divorce, so Brigitte was the clichéd other woman, confirming her cinematic look.

From the beginning the whole Spanish episode was a trial to her. Not knowing the language, she tried out home-baked Italian, but found that despite common Latin roots, it didn't work at all in this country. She also had a demanding role in the movie. Finally, despite her hatred of flying, she took a first weekend flight back to Paris to see Jean-Lou, but the little plane terrified her, and 24 hours with her loved one was too short a time.

Against all odds she tried her best to hold onto the love she had that steamy summer in Spain. But on Monday morning at seven sharp Brigitte had to be back at a job she didn't really enjoy—a life of constant waiting, constant redoing, of people talking at her on the set, when all she looked forward to was a bit of nocturnal peace.

At first those nights were unexciting ones spent eating fruit in her room and trying to connect long distance with Jean-Lou. To a woman who felt that she was made for love it was a depressing existence. Rare nights out only came after the insistent prodding of friends involved in the film. In spite of herself Bardot began to enjoy drinking sangria and dancing barefooted to flamenco guitars. The Spanish dubbed her "Guapa" (pretty girl), but the pretty girl paid for these late nights by finding early wake-up calls onerous, along with scoldings for missed lines or makeup alterations. Still, the flamenco sounds she heard brought her a new hobby. Buying a guitar, she managed to learn some chords and soothed herself by strumming. She also saved and adopted a little dog almost hung by Spanish kids, and this "Guapa" would become a longtime fixture, starting out in her room against hotel policy, and later following her back to France.

Trying to be a good girl and with no Mr. T. around, Brigitte slept with Guapa, teaching the dog not to relieve itself in the room and sharing meals with the animal. She still flew up arduously for Parisian Sundays, but found herself happy to regain her hotel room and her pet, realizing then and for the rest of her life that unqualified animal love would never play her false.

After two and a half months in Madrid, the cast migrated down to then peaceful Torremolinos on the Costa Brava for more shooting. From there it was more difficult to call Jean-Lou, but Brigitte felt happier ensconced in a bungalow by the sunshine-bathed sea and sand, with smells of oranges or bougainvillea in the air. Odette had also brought along French Camembert, fouling her bags in the process! Bardot continued fighting the good fight, trying to reach an increasingly hazy, far-off Trintignant, putting up with 12-hour waits to get through via poor European phone systems of that era. To console herself, she swam off a then empty beach, where only the odd peasant and donkey came by. Odette badly missed her hubby as well, but Jeannine, another friend on the set, *didn't*, and again, Brigitte found herself sailing somewhere in between two relationship shoals, the Charybdis of fidelity, the Scylla of procuring quotidian enjoyment in this brief gig on earth. She finally got through to Jean-Lou, but being surrounded by a knot of 30 people and hardly able to make out his voice didn't help. Jeannine, who at the time was Bardot's aide and married to her lifelong friend Jicky Dussart, slept with a Spanish actor in the cast who spoke no French, pointing the way to perdition. Doing what for her came naturally, she got herself pregnant and would remain in Spain.

The first time Bardot went down a similar path, hurting her deep relationship with Trintignant, was apparently with a widower working on the film, Gustavo Rojo. Though Bardot was anything but the faithless, frivolous slut of press legend, this was also no woman to be left alone for long periods of time. Was the "donna mobile"? Potentially of course she was. In Bardot's life to come there would often be the lure or threat of fresher male pastures, and she certainly had no liking for extended separations.

For her birthday celebration, taking place a little late that year in October, she received a baby ass from Raoul Lévy, and the animal got to live as well in the beautiful woman's hotel room, though Guapa became jealous. A big storm blew out electricity and for several days, the telephones, causing much damage and many deaths; plus the cemeteries were ruined with bones strewn everywhere. Terrified, Brigitte begged for a return to Paris. She was also scratching constantly, due to plentiful fleas attracted to her

The future animal protectress in a scene from Vadim's Spanish-set drama, *Les Bijoutiers du clair de lune* (*The Night Heaven Fell*). (Léna Productions, UCIL, Paris, CELAD, Rome, 1957)

animals. Coming down with a fever, she reluctantly gave her donkey Chorro to a peasant. The trip on the road back up to Madrid felt difficult as well.

Finally safe and sound back in Paris, Brigitte found Jean-Lou legitimately worried about his loved one's fidelity all those months. She also had a heap of bills to pay—bills the men in her life would rarely take care of—and an old dog, Clown, who couldn't get along with the new one, Guapa. There was also the sad death (for her) of a cow in the movie, given an injection on a Paris set, where they were finishing up the picture. There would always be plenty in life to bother Brigitte Bardot!

And yet, this Franco-Italian production with Vadim at the helm is a wonderful cinematic surprise—sharply plotted, gorgeously shot in sumptuous country by the sea and in arid mountains, and benefiting from a fine score by Georges Auric, Columbia's color, and well-cast acting. The tone works from the beginning, when we are presented a sadistic nobleman who owns the village where his niece, played by Bardot, debarks (from convent school). The man seemingly rapes at will here, and soon comes an act of retaliatory violence. Bardot's Ursule then goes on the lam with the suspected killer, Lamberto (played creditably by Stephen Boyd), who had acted in behalf of his defiled, dead sister.

The film is better than *And God...* because it doesn't try to impress by shock; nor does it try to be the kind of wan comedy Vadim would sometimes hatch with his ex-wife.

Instead *The Night Heaven Fell* is as deep and ponderous as those fiery Spanish villages of the time, and little is done here without the dignity of verisimilitude—from the black-veiled funeral procession for the lecherous count down to the end (with the possible exception of Bardot and Boyd finally having to embrace in full love while dirty and starving—something she rarely enjoyed anyway in movies).[5]

The sought-after actress now started right into another shoot at Paris' Joinville Studios, beginning in November 1957. *En Cas de malheur* was directed by Claude Autant-Lara, based on a Georges Simenon novel, again produced by Lévy, and starring a hallowed name of the French cinema, Jean Gabin, making Bardot anxious all over again. As was often the case, the theme was erotic—Bardot cast as an amoral strumpet defended on a robbery charge by the lawyer Gabin and paying with her favors, then seeing something like love bloom on his end. In reality divorce with Vadim was closing a chapter of Brigitte's young life. Her revulsion with the downsides of French film-making and celebrity was growing, and she also had a morbid, unreasoning fear of being too ugly opposite Gabin!

And yet, this was something of an apogee for her. Gone definitively was the darker-haired *gamine* of the era before *And God....* Brigitte was now a mature, beautiful, leggy blond, and in cinematic garter belt or other forms of *déshabillée*, as fetching on screen as the era could offer. Being back in Paris and with the influence of Trintignant still in her and on her face—these things were undoubtedly a part of that. *En Cas...* became a good film, with Bardot in the same league here as Gabin, the strong, older man driving his Cadillac, rivaled in searing jealousy by a young student and industrial worker (by night), the latter zipping a motorbike, and equally devoted to Bardot's character. Her dramatic force, her switches from tears to come-on babyishness to adult sophistication—it all adds up to an actress of *far* greater adeptness than commonly known. Bardot was something here, too, that few young stars in today's cinema are—an authentic femme fatale. Equally rare in the age of middle-aged women attending rock concerts in tee shirts is the type incarnated by Gabin's elegant 40-year-old film wife (played by Edwige Feuillère), sleeping apart for birth control, giving into his affair with fatigued tolerance, and a legitimate fear that it would carry away their upper-bourgeois solidity—as when pregnancy comes into view, and the final paroxysm of a young lover's jealousy intervenes, it nearly does. The film, however, saddens, as Bardot was then on the edge of descent into a series of grave personal problems.[6]

"BB" had become an ever hotter, more controversial property in France, and that would be reflected in a mixed critical and audience response to her film with Gabin. Some in movie houses booed, others vigorously applauded, but the picture would certainly do well at the box office. One critic called it a kind of Rolls-Royce that negotiated its way elegantly even through difficult curves; others thought Gabin's character too ambiguous, or out-glittered by Bardot's. Gabin himself had almost nixed the role, worrying that his children might watch an immoral movie featuring their father. He also made sure that this was his last "love" picture, though on the whole he had enjoyed working with Bardot.[7]

With a difficult year winding down, Brigitte was contacted by Gilbert Bécaud to participate in a TV show, slated to air for New Year's Eve, 1957; and her meeting with the star *chansonnier* was the beginning of an ill-considered, draining *coup de foudre*, given that he was married, if peripatetic in his concert-giving lifestyle. Né François Silly, Bécaud was a Provençal of modest origins, who after attending the Nice Conservatory and starting out classically, had come up to Paris, become a piano accompanist for various *chanteurs*, then charted his own course as a singer and songwriter, aided by three poetic lyricists, including a prefect, Louis Amade. An exciting performer dubbed "Monsieur One Hundred Thousand Volts," Bécaud had a growly, poetic, semi-spoken style that was all French, despite jazz influences from the U.S.; and some of his co-written work would eventually make it big in English (as "Let It Be Me" and "What Now My Love").[8]

When Bardot started lying to Jean-Louis, Vadim's view rang true—that she would always suffer when she had two men in her life. (Eerily parallel to *En Cas....*) If it weren't the glare of publicity generally ending the secrecy of such affairs, then it was the maladroitness of the lovers themselves. Early on, Trintignant received a lucky confirmation (for him) simply by breaking in on Bardot and Bécaud, then in a manic heat, packing his clothes at BB's "Doumer" and driving away in a new Austin convertible she had given him. Crawling like proverbial serpent, Bardot would get Jean-Lou back for a time with professions of good faith; but the powerful Bécaud also retained a spot inside her body and soul, and Trintignant would finally leave for good, sad for Bardot, given that this represented the departure of one of her great chances for enduring stability. She had adored Trintignant, but also wanted freedom, and as the English say, one can't have it all ways. Nor did Jean-Louis look back; having admired Brigitte's underestimated intelligence, and always sympathetic to her ordeals with the press, he would go on to a glittering film career and to a domestic life with a new wife, Nadine, spent in homes to which they migrated around France.[9]

Meanwhile, as in the later Rohmer film *Full Moon in Paris*, Bardot found herself stuck with full moon and empty arms on lonely nights, cuddling her dogs Clown and Guapa, while a triumphant Bécaud on tour would wake her at three or four in the morning after completing a concert somewhere in Europe. Answering the phone in a daze, Brigitte listened to his recitation, knowing she had to rise early the next morning for her own shoot. She found it sad coming home each night with nobody there to share *her* day's events. Christmas Eve was a true "other woman's" night—Brigitte at 23 ultra-lonely, and thinking obsessively of the departed Jean-Louis, while aware that Bécaud was with wife and children near Versailles. The next day she cried on Papa's and Mama's shoulders, managing to obtain some comfort. Bécaud visited her that night, but set his alarm for a two a.m. departure—far from the ideal life scenario for a needy, loving, and beautiful woman.

On New Year's Eve she still found herself alone, but by now, the press had zeroed in on the affair, and paparazzi began invading in panzer-clustered force. Headlines splashed out on Bardot and Bécaud, and the married singer became gun-shy of seeing her now, isolating Brigitte even more. At the beginning of 1958 she tried concentrating on her film work, but the journalists kept pestering her about this relationship with the crooner-composer. Brigitte's loneliness and shattered nerves now took a toll, as she learned the reality of being both a sensitive person and a star under sweeping media searchlights.

Bardot as the gorgeous criminal Yvette Maudet and Jean Gabin as her lawyer, André Gobillot, in *En Cas de malheur* (*Love Is My Profession*). (Iéna, UCIL, Paris, Incom, Rome, 1957)

The result was another suicide attempt—a very serious one indeed. This was another where she used gas, but also pills, and in his version Vadim had a premonition that made him call her father in the nick of time to save BB. (Pilou simply rushing over on foot from the nearby Rue de la Pompe.) In hers Bécaud had called her long-distance to Paris from Marseille, where he was then appearing; and receiving only a garbled answer, phoned a doctor in the capital, who found Bardot in a coma, and promptly pumped out her stomach.[10]

Remaining in a semi-coma, then wired up to machines and submitting to hospital injections, Bardot reluctantly endorsed a "What will the Joneses think?" story concocted by her mother, involving a plate of bad mussels as the reason for her hospitalization. The show, as always, had to go on, and barely able to sign, a weakened Brigitte scribbled out more acceptances of movie contracts.

Recovering, but enfeebled, Bardot went out briefly in the Tout Paris atmosphere she would always distrust, replete with people who praised her to her face, then gossiped behind her back, sometimes gaining her confidence only to sell stories to the press. The look-before-you-leap paranoia of a DiMaggio, an Artie Shaw, a Princess Di was becoming evident in her. Guapa meanwhile had puppies, presumably by Clown, and Bécaud wrote and cut a song for his intermittent loved one; but her loneliness at the top persisted.

With *En Cas...* wrapped, a present seemed in the offing, when she was enticed to Geneva by Bécaud in February 1958. There she registered at a hotel as Mademoiselle Mucel, waiting in a room for her lover. Growing bored, Bardot descended to the bar for a tomato juice and was of course recognized. Flimsily disguised, she then went to hear Bécaud sing, but was kept in his private dressing room like a true mistress, with the singer's wife also in town! Brigitte heard songs she loved, but remained disconsolately cooped up, smoking her brains out, until finally chauffeured to a restaurant, where at two in the morning of a snowy night she still awaited the resplendent arrival of her paramour. The press, however, ferreted out the rendezvous, came down heavily on her, and the next day Bardot left Bécaud forever. Her love life would never be an easy one, and perhaps that was what the ultimate conversion to animal protection would partially be about—finding more stable objects on whom to lavish great stores of care and affection.

Numerous letters meanwhile poured in to the lonely French icon, some pornographic, and off in alpine Cortina for a week's relaxation with her double Dany and her sister Mijanjou, Bardot was also besieged by paparazzi, in the country where they had gotten their name. Dany, "Mija," and Brigitte slept in the same large bed; it wasn't much of a life. Bécaud kept calling, but Bardot perhaps recognized the veracity of Napoleon's old saw—that the only victory over love is flight.

A better and deeper friend was "Jicky" Dussart, who impulsively took Brigitte down to the Riviera where she was looking to buy a vacation place and establish roots. With that artistic pal, every moment seemed magical, but the press, still hyping the Bécaud liaison, also made false allegations about this friendship.

Back home in Paris she visited a hospital and held hands or touched the faces of French soldiers wounded in the Algerian war, then at its most vicious, but in some ways, oddly idealistic apogee.[11] Through Christine Gouze-Rénal she also met again that Italian theater actor, Raf Vallone, exquisitely polished and cultured, and had some glorious, violin-accompanied restaurant meals with him. After one of his theater gigs (he was appearing in an Arthur Miller play), he came to her bed for the balance of the night. Vallone taught Bardot to appreciate Paris' fine Russian eating spots, literary works she hadn't read, and the music of composers like Vivaldi. For Brigitte the opposite sex was always a great source of education, starting with her father and continuing with her lovers and husbands.

But her nemesis remained abrupt separations from newly formed routines, which was exactly the nature of the movie business. Reluctantly, she said yes to her next flick, *La Femme et le pantin*, to be shot in Seville, Spain. More emphatically she kept saying no to the siren call of farther-off America. For in the spring of 1958 Bardot and a huge American name, Sinatra, were almost teamed in a Lévy-Vadim film project, *Paris by Night*. Vadim spent a week schmoozing the American crooner in Miami and Chicago, and enjoying himself, thoroughly at ease with the colorful company Sinatra kept in such places. Both Bardot and Sinatra were intrigued by the possibility of working together, but Bardot wouldn't fly to the States for four months of shooting, and Sinatra wasn't about to forsake his home turf for several months in Paris. So the project fell through.

Bardot as Eva Marchand dances provocatively and feigns happiness in a scene from *La Femme et le pantin* (*A Woman Like Satan*). (S.N. Pathé-Cinéma, Gray Film, Paris, Dear Films, Rome, 1958)

Bardot, however, was hardly an unemployed actress; in only a half-dozen years her film resumé had reached the prodigious number of 22 movies.[12]

The journalists thankfully remained on Bécaud's scent, not Vallone's, but leaving was still difficult for Brigitte. Spain was broiling, she had to get used to a new double, Maguy Mortini, replacing her friend Dany, and it was the annual time of "féria" in Seville, when crimes of passion soared, and Bardot in horror witnessed her first bull run and sanguinary killings of those animals. Men exposed themselves to her, and in sum, the shoot for *La Femme et le pantin* was anything but marvelous, despite a saucy title English distributors gave it—*A Woman Like Satan*, though only *The Female* in the U.S. (In this truly bad film Bardot dances provocatively and feigns promiscuity, but resists the advances of an affluent bull-breeder, who smashes up a nightclub in frustration.)

Back in Paris to complete the shoot in a studio, as "Bardolâtrie" continued sweeping France and the world, the unsnobbish actress received a bum on the set whom she had once met in the streets, and who repelled everyone else by his presence. The tattered visitor declared that he had been a musician and had been ruined by a woman. Taking her chance, Brigitte led him to a piano, and in front of everyone he played a beautiful sonata, then disappeared forever. Among great cinematic stars, perhaps only Brando would have the kind of democratic humility of a Bardot.

Viewing *La Femme et le pantin* today is hard for one who knows Bardot's sad life of the era. After her suicide attempt, and the split with Trintignant, she looks anything but fresh here. There is saucy guitar music, the film is shot in Technicolor (making one long for the black and white of better predecessors), Bardot snaps heels to flamenco and is supposed to be seductive and lighthearted; but the mask wears thin for those aware of the chaos in her existence.[13] What a cash machine, a beast of burdens she had become for Mama Olga! The ruin of married men was becoming the ruin of herself.

At least her decidedly snobby mother finally located her daughter a suitable spot in Saint-Tropez; and in May 1958, with the Fourth Republic dying amidst Algeria's chaos, and de Gaulle about to bring on a Fifth, Bardot bought her soon famous spread there, "La Madrague" on the Baie des Canubiers—then removed from the main town, now quite near as huge villas spread along the coastline. A month later her beloved grandfather, Boum, now skin and bones, passed away.

Going down to La Madrague to distract herself with other things, she found a situation like Tom Hanks' and Shelley Long's in *The Money Pit*—tree roots had stopped up the septic tank, ruining the plumbing, so pungent odors made a powerful welcoming committee indeed. Repairs were urgent, and Bardot got to them; for a supposedly pampered star, she would always take care of daily realities such people generally delegate.

Brigitte found herself still longing for a true relationship, and providentially, a handsome young man soon came to the rescue—the singer-guitarist Sacha Distel. Bardot had met him once in Paris and asked him to stay in touch, and suddenly, here he was. Distel's father (like Vadim's) was a Russian who had fled the Bolsheviks for Paris, then lost his heart to a Jewish girl at a ball. The courtship went on six years, and the couple finally married over the objections of her parents, won over only by the birth of Sacha in 1933. Distel grew up in a musical milieu via his mother and his uncle, the bandleader Ray Ventura. At a young age the boy could sing all of Uncle Ray's tunes. Then came the war, and the same words in the air like "Dunkirk" or "exode" that had mystified the young Brigitte. Sacha remained confused when his mother had to sew a yellow star on her jacket; and then in February 1942 two policemen came to their apartment and despite the boy playing piano for them, took her away. She was fortunate to end up in Paris on the site of a former furniture business, where her job was to classify confiscated goods destined for Germany. These included her own paintings, and furniture belonging to Sacha's grandparents. The boy meanwhile was packed off to Catholic boarding school in the West of France and given a backdated baptism. The Normandy invasion led to hasty burnings of Pétain pictures in homes of the region, and the Americans arrived with Coca-Cola that fizzed in Sacha's nose.

Back in Paris the guitar became Sacha's instrument after the war, and his inspiration American jazz players. As he grew older, he spent entire nights in Saint-Germain and sat in with gods like the saxophonist Lester Young. After barely slipping through baccalaureate examinations, he left school to work in Ray Ventura's music editing company. This allowed him to meet top French crooners like Trenet and Chevalier, travel to New York when Charles Aznavour was living on hot dogs there, and gig at a dingy Harlem bar with "Bird" Parker himself. Nights back in Saint-Germain he would bump into rising stars of the French cinema like Truffaut and Godard. Distel also broke his heart a number of times, including with Juliette Gréco and Jeanne Moreau, the brunette actress who would also affect Raoul Lévy, among others.

In sum, Distel was already destined for a significant musical vocation, and though it is certain Bardot's name would help, this is not why he came calling on her. He too was on the rebound—most recently, due to a *bourgeoise* whose parents had a place in Saint-Tropez. Down there to overcome their aversion to him, which didn't work, he met a reporter from *Match* who was supposed to write on Brigitte and couldn't get into La Madrague. Blithely, Distel brought her there, and with no thought of staying himself; but Bardot's earlier invitation in Paris was on the level. (In her version her double Maguy found this human catch of the day in a local nightclub. Maguy had to leave for Paris, and Distel ended up at La Madrague.) In good French style Sacha soon brought a retinue of singing and strumming *copains*, vying with Bardot's own support group, preeminently, Jicky Dussart. For a few weeks there was much music-making and dancing at La Madrague, and Bardot managed to have a summer romance without press publicity. But that kind of respite could last only so long, and Distel was, like her other paramours, entirely unprepared for the impending onslaught.[14]

For in this summer of 1958 "Bardolâtrie" was at a white-hot point, both in France and across the Atlantic. In an article of June 30 that year *Life* signaled the continuing "Bardot Boom" in the U.S. According to them, "not since the Statue of Liberty has a French girl lit such fires in America.... One of her films, *And God Created Woman*, has played for eight months in one New York theater ... and, with her four other current films, has jammed art theaters until people complain they are clogging up culture...."

Paul O'Neill's more discursive piece follows in the same issue, again reflecting that moment when Europe still provided models for both the impending sex revolution and the intellectual revolution to come. Yet reciprocally, America's hunger had also reinforced the Bardot phenomenon in France. This was of course the U.S. of the '50s, with its meat and potatoes stability. "Like the European sports car," O'Neill declared, "[Bardot] has arrived on the American scene at a time when the American public is ready, even hungry, for something racier and more realistic than the familiar domestic product. American actresses, like American four-door sedans, seem to have grown more and more standardized in styling." O'Neill found Bardot films bracing, partly because importers

Sacha Distel and Brigitte in Saint-Tropez, 1958. (SIPA/NewsCom)

of foreign films could evade the American film industry's self-censorship, not to mention that of organizations like the National Legion of Decency. Due to incomprehensible dialogue, wan subtitles, and presumably smaller audiences for most imported product, censoring boards were more latitudinarian than with domestic fare.

O'Neill goes on to say that Bardot's walk and look were being emulated by many young American women. And quite correctly, he notes that "Brigitte ... has not lifted a finger to achieve publicity. In fact, she treats all reporters like net men from the pound." Meanwhile, "owners of art theaters have discovered that they can pull truck drivers and mourners after the vanished burlesque houses in off the sidewalks to see foreign language films if Bardot's name is on the marquee."[15]

In France Bardot made the cover of *Match* on May 3, 1958, while shooting in Spain. An article on the Cannes Film Festival (in the May 17, 1958, issue) observed proudly that she was outdoing Hollywood stars in their own backyard. In good part thanks to her, French cinematic profits had been growing steadily as well.[16] After a time-out for heady events in Algeria and de Gaulle's return to power, *Match* came back on July 26, 1958, with an article on the downside for Bardot of this American-French popularity surge: a tidal wave of paparazzi assaults.

By this time the launching of the Côte d'Azur was also in high gear, another phenomenon in good part due to *And God...*, and Bardot's own residence there. So that July 26 article is titled "BB: Vacation for a Tracked Animal." With accompanying pictures the piece describes an "offensive des photographes," mentioning reporters disguised as fishermen, surfacing by sea to shoot at the renowned actress, who sometimes replied with stone-throwing and insults. There is a picture of her looking sad and tense from behind the grillwork of "her sunny prison," where any swimmer might be a "photographe camouflé." The frequency of Bardot articles in *Match* had increased, allied to this Saint-Tropez craze she incarnated. So one of their articles of August 16, 1958, notes how "the old fishing village has become the kasbah of summer visitors," full of foreigners, fast cars, and numerous women aping the Bardot look. Like Bardot, herself from the Paris bourgeoisie, "the 16th in Paris also provides its contingent of young women...." Another article in the same issue by Guillaume Hanoteau treats this Tropez phenomenon in more depth. He notes how 40,000 crush for only 360 hotel rooms in summer, clogging the nearby beach of Pampelonne. But there is indeed a "style Saint-Tropez," where one dresses the part, has the right drinks, etc. Here one might bump into Vadim arriving by motorboat, or some other star in blue jeans emerging from an Aston Martin. Above all, there is Brigitte Bardot. "People fight to see her. In the cafés she is the subject of all conversations." Vacationers find themselves overcome by an ailment neologistically described as "sainte-tropie," and having started with a hotel room, they then want to buy a second home.[17]

Bardot was indeed getting overwhelmed by all the "Bardotistes" coming through the paved pass, and it would make her personal life difficult at least until the mid–'60s. At home she helped turn a sober France trying to pull up national socks (after the debacle of 1940) toward the country of *yé-yé* and materialism in the coming decade. In America she and what was perceived as naughty "Europe" helped erode a longstanding puritanical heritage. In sum, the Bardot phenomenon wrought a number of major influences both in her country and abroad, and not least, in her own life!

That life during this summer of 1958 found her in what would become a typical predicament: a two-man situation, at least in her heart. Hearing Distel's songs composed for her, she kept thinking of the more mature musical efforts of Bécaud. Nor was she really over Jean-Lou. She did, however, enjoy the handsome young Distel's company, though like Vadim, he found her attention needs a bit too constant. He was also put off by her prejudice against marriage and children, which he says he was looking for at the time.

When they went off to attend the Venice Film Festival in September to present *En Cas...*, the breathtaking trip across the Alps in his Austin-Healey was a balm to the spirit; but in Venice an explosion of paparazzi besieged the couple, and she hated all the star imagery she was forced to project. Every gondola ride, each walk was wrecked by these journalistic hordes. Yes, they were and are "the nightmare of stars," says Bardot.[18] Some would continue arguing that Distel had Bardot's name to thank for getting an invitation to sing on Ed Sullivan's American TV show, significantly, on September 28, 1958; and for the fact that his career was on an upward arc, even as their romance ebbed in the coolness of a Paris fall.

That autumn Bardot voted for de Gaulle as first president of France's new Fifth Republic—the man whose face resembled the map of France, and who seemed to incarnate his country's destiny better than anyone. Bardot had to put up with a Distel recording of his "Brigitte" song that left her cold, and with a jacket photo of them together at La Madrague. She much preferred his private guitar renderings of Django's "Nuages," or visits to jazz clubs in Paris, where he still jammed with the likes of Stéphane Grappelly or Miles Davis. Distel wanted Bardot to come to Paris' Olympia music hall to hear his public version of "the song," but she not only disliked the record, she also hated crowds. Meanwhile, her biggest enemy in finding lasting fulfillment in the personal realm remained the cinematic life itself—both the constant, uprooting apartness that always hurts relationships, as well as the white-hot glare of see-all, tell-all publicity.

The man who would follow Distel became another, but more tragic bleached bone along the well-watered desert of Brigitte's chaotic intimate life. Jacques Charrier was born in Lorraine of a solid army family, but his father was sent to Tunisia when the boy was six months old, so that sun-splashed part of the French empire in wartime was the scene of his formative years until May 1945. At war's end the family migrated to Paris, and unlike his brothers, the boy was drawn to the arts: drawing, ceramics, music, and above all, acting. Charrier appeared in classical plays, and was in revolt against his father, a colonel, and his brothers, who were also in the service. He loved bohemian Paris of the '50s and read Henry Miller, dug jazz and Léo Ferré, learned to jitterbug in the Cartesian French manner. Bardot's version of how they met has Raoul Lévy putting him in her next movie, *Babette Goes to War* (*Babette s'en va-t-en guerre*), and the young man touted as the new Gérard Philipe falling in love with her on the set. Charrier's version is that Bardot had already seen him act in the theater, then met him at a party in Paris, danced with him, and asked her to drive him home, where he left her at the building's front door. Two days later, he says, he received the screenplay for her latest film.[19]

In it Charrier played a French officer who goes gaga for Babette, enrolled by the British in London and the French Resistance to seduce and capture a German general in France, and to foil his plan to invade England; but as was often the case with Bardot,

Jacques Charrier as a Free French officer of World War II, Lieutenant Gérard de Crécy, and Bardot as a ditzy secret agent for the Resistance and England, Babette, in *Babette s'en va-t-en guerre* (*Babette Goes to War*). (Iéna, Films Ariane, 1959)

cinematic fiction and reality began to blend.[20] They worked on the picture in Paris and in London, where she stayed in the same hotel as Charrier. However, the romance was a gradual thing, and according to him, it began with him as an ear for an unhappy actress at the top. And yet again, the same story of the man she was progressively leaving and the man with whom she was starting up unfolded in a curious dialectic. During the day she saw Jacques all day on the set, increasingly appreciative of his sensitive qualities; but Sacha was still in the picture, too. Again, she felt divided, but with Distel away on tour, Charrier received an invitingly clear path to his loved one at her apartment. Bardot hated being alone, so she needed to be furtive when answering Sacha's long-distance calls in another room at Paul Doumer, whispering appropriate "I love you's," while Charrier chafed. Jacques was no fly-by-night lover; he had come from deep roots and even more than Sacha, wanted to put down some himself. He was in love and by God, he desired marriage with a hesitant Brigitte, already plenty man-singed!

One night things came to a head with Bardot in bed with Charrier, and Distel making a surprise appearance, coming up the apartment elevator, calling out from the hall, a furious Jacques hustling on pants, and Brigitte frantically locking the door. The scene (in her memory) continued with Distel banging at the door, Charrier demanding the key so he could open up and throw punches at his rival, Bardot running to a window and impulsively flinging the key down into the street, the dogs barking, Sacha and Jacques yelling at each other from both sides of the door like original cavemen both after the same woman in skins; and finally, Distel audibly slamming doors and taking off. At two a.m. Bardot had to call her concierge to go down in the street, pick up the key, and unlock her door.[21]

This bad night wrought by romantic turbulence made Brigitte's eyes visibly red for the next day's shoot. With Sacha gone, she felt abandoned and blue. A last footnote to the short Distel affair seems in order: Sacha would also for a time romance Annette Stoyberg, Roger Vadim's second wife.

Meanwhile, Jacques, unhappy with her Paul Doumer residence, took a hole of a flat on the Rue Legendre, named for a Jacobin butcher of the French Revolution. He now beseeched Brigitte to spend nights there and to eat poor café food for dinner—mainly, starchy *croque-monsieurs* and beer dragged back to this coop. Against her better judgment Bardot complied. She would start out the night at Doumer, ringed by a squadron of photographers, then sneak out to this pad lacking blinds, pillows, or table, and of course felt approximately like *merde* on toast next day at the studio! A diet of beer and cheese-laden bread made her gain weight, and it became an unromantic routine to wash Jacques' dirty underwear and socks in his miserable sink. She now missed her smiley Distel—something of a Gervaise out of Zola's *Assommoir*, Brigitte didn't get over men easily.[22]

The papers meanwhile were playing up the Distel-Charrier tussle in full force. Photos of Distel connoted the poor jilted lover, Charrier was depicted as the manly conqueror, and Bardot was the slutty bitch who inspired such human messes—the "bouffeuse d'hommes" (or man-eater)! If only they could have seen her washing socks in cold water, she recalls ruefully. But the papers would say anything they pleased, and telephoto lensmen hunted her as zealously as guests had once chased that deer at the chateau of the Loire.

Inevitably, the paparazzi nosed out Jacques' *pied à terre*, so he took to visiting Doumer in the middle of the night, then rushed out like a rat at dawn, joining bleary espresso sippers at stand-up bars just opening their shutters. One day Bardot hugged her father near Doumer, and a picture of that got splashed in the papers, too; why, she was into older men as well! A terrible anger festered inside her, and although later in life she would have topflight lawyers retaliate with lawsuits, for now the young actress could do nothing. How she envied one French actor who cornered the author of a piece of trash on him, literally making him eat his words!

If it weren't the press, then it was the public assaulting, and that might include maniacs trying to rip off a piece of Bardot's celebrated hide. When her double Maguy had an appendicitis attack in April 1959, Bardot went to visit her at a Paris clinic on an outwardly peaceful Sunday. Going up the elevator, she found herself stuck alone with a supposed nurse carrying a lunch tray for a patient. Suddenly the woman started screaming obscenities at Bardot, to the effect that she was a whore taking all the men, and leaving none for honest women like herself! Declaring that she would like to puncture Brigitte's eyes, the nurse suddenly began attacking with a fork. Screaming, Bardot parried the attack, getting the fork stuck in her coat sleeve, and with the lady still hurling insults, managed to escape at the fourth floor, while her attacker continued upward. It turned out that she had been confronted by a phony nurse. Here too was another movie scene, and in fact Louis Malle would later adapt it for his film *Vie privée*, featuring Bardot.

At least when Brigitte's parents got wind of Charrier from the papers, they uncharacteristically approved. Their daughter seemed finally to have found someone socially suitable. En route south to shoot exteriors for *Babette*, BB also stopped in Montpellier to meet a cooler Colonel Charrier and his wife, both well up on her scandalous reputation and not very forthcoming.

Jacques now began imploring Brigitte to have his baby, telling her that it would give her life stability. She herself nervously counted days of the month, and in her memoirs divagates a bit on all that terror, but on the beauty of love too that has been lost in an era of routinized birth control. Bardot, however, was still afraid of maternity, and not living a sane enough life, she felt, to contemplate adding a child to it.

Nature took its course when she was stuck with Charrier in a snowbound chalet at Chamonix, that April of 1959, and got herself pregnant. At first she didn't tell him the news, instead deciding to discuss her fears with Vadim. After her vacation, they met furtively in Paris near the Bois de Boulogne on a rainy night, and then drove around in Vadim's Ferrari, while she talked. Bardot was no stranger to abortion, but with his feline, gossamer intuition, Vadim could see that this Charrier thing was for real, and he pushed her to have the baby. Her friend Christine Gouze-Rénal was more favorable to the idea of an abortion, but a top gynecologist in France refused—on medical grounds; while the Swiss clinic with which Bardot was already familiar said she was now so famous she would bring them adverse publicity. So they said no as well. What a baby has to do to get born in our century—much as from a salmon climbing all those ladders to reach home, bruised and battered, simply to spawn! For indeed Bardot now tried by other means to abort, taking a series of injections, with Charrier still in the dark on all this.

Perhaps the embryonic baby inside wanted to live, for Brigitte continued to vomit regularly, nauseated by odors like that of cigars that hadn't previously bothered her. Finally she spilled the beans and Jacques was overjoyed, putting his foot down for both child and marriage. In her memoirs Bardot says that honor is now one of those outmoded words that still meant something in 1959 (witness, for example, that all three of Charrier's brothers were then serving in France's growingly futile Algerian war). To preserve her family's honor, as well as the Charriers', she decided to accede to the offer of marriage. Her parents looked forward to a first grandchild, but Bardot knew that Charrier was unrealistic, and that she would have to worry about the apartment, a new film in the works, and how to have the baby safely away from the press! She also wondered how deeply she loved Charrier and whether it would last; and if it did not, would she ever find another suitable man as a divorcée with child?

Jacques then cut a song for her in Paris! Bardot thought with a queasy stomach how many men had been inspired to compose and warble for her. Seeing her probably competitive sister, Mijanjou, pranking about openly with a recent conquest named Distel did not improve the pregnant Brigitte's disposition any.

Meanwhile, finding a place to run the marriage away from the media took a good deal of homework and deception, and it almost worked. Their Schlieffen Plan was to hold the wedding at the Louveciennes town hall, where the mayor primed with hush money was to perform a very private ceremony on June 18, 1959. That paid-off official was supposed to avoid leaking any mention of the Bardot-Charrier union, but somehow *Match* got the news—the mayor having undoubtedly double-dipped; and then of course came the full flood, in the form of hundreds of photographers stampeding and flashing at a flustered, angry couple, and journalists from around the world frantically scribbling on pads. The pregnant Brigitte was freaked, going through with a marriage that in her heart and soul she didn't really want. Through rent dikes the photographers came in like the ocean itself, breaking tables and knocking the *mairie*'s bust of Marianne to the floor. Only Colonel Charrier's and Papa Bardot's quick military thinking allowed them to barricade the couple and family in an office, while organizing a *sortie* like those seen during the siege of Paris in 1870.

Finally police arrived, fighting a losing battle with these snapping hordes, while Bardot in tears and a greenish Charrier, as she recalls, went through with the ceremony in that shaky office. To this point the windscreen of her life had often, too often been streaked with rain.

But at least something in the planning process worked—a secondary deception, whereby two friends disguised as the couple enticed marauding journalists to one exit, while the real couple eluded the hordes, managing to race away unscathed to the Gare de Lyon. There they hopped a train, exiting Paris in relative peace for a ten-day honeymoon at La Madrague—where of course they would inevitably be blitzed by another army of telephoto lenses!

Looking for quick solutions, Bardot was persuaded to get herself a guard dog there, Kapi, who would presumably scare off intruders. Instead, he bit her friends and even a postman. The dog would, however, permit thieves and other unwelcome people to enter the place unscathed.

On their return to Paris things continued to go unsmoothly for the newly married couple. Journalists still prowled in Pattonesque force, and the film company running her new production, *Voulez-vous danser avec moi?*, a murder mystery, demanded a pregnancy test, which if positive, meant they could not get insurance. So the inventive Bardot made her Dada urinate in a jar, which she willingly did for Brizzi, and using a rabbit as well, the results were negative, and the company received its insurance.

Relationship prices people rarely see ahead on the horizon inevitably became acute in Brigitte's case, and the marriage with Charrier was no exception. The old nemesis of separation loomed, with Brigitte in Nice to start work on her new film in mid–July, and the press predicting and prophesying marital disaster. To avoid that separation, Charrier gave up a good role of his own in another film. Then news of the pregnancy got out among cast and technicians. Tension between a future papa hanging around the set on furlough and Mama Olga and Moussia, Bardot's house lady, became acute, and Charrier exploded, pleading a feeling of being left out. In private, things ended up physical between him and his wife, with blows, slaps, and kicks coming from both sides in an altercation that nearly caused a miscarriage. In a silent funk Bardot stomped away, then the couple made up. By the fourth month fitting clothes over her protuberant belly became painful, and she had a persistent fear of producing an abnormal child, due to all the stress she had been experiencing.

She then received the synopsis of an Henri-Georges Clouzot film (to be produced by Lévy), *La Vérité*, a movie she would ardently love; but a furious Jacques ripped it up, and to retaliate, Brigitte started whacking her own stomach in the bedroom! Deciding to down a bunch of pills to commit suicide, she then hovered for a terrible week between life and death; and Jacques kept coming and going in a huff, while Dédette, Moussia, and her male secretary of the era hugged her bedside. Weak as a lamb, Bardot still inked a contract for *Vérité*. Jacques eventually reconciled, but Bardot now realized they were doomed. For a woman terrified of, yet so often courting death, the weakness of her 25-year-old co-star Sylvia Lopez and her ensuing death of leukemia just before the end of the current shoot constituted another sad shock.

Bardot and Charrier: from screen bliss in *Babette*... **to uncertain relationship and marriage in real life.**

Brigitte's foundering marriage received further blows—an appendicitis operation for Jacques, and the old card of military service hitting the table, when he was informed that he would be called up for two years, starting in the fall of 1959. With more and more apprehension Bardot approached her due date. It seemed that *she* had to be the adult in the marriage, working for the two of them.

When an apartment opposite hers at Paul Doumer became vacant, she grabbed it, redecorating for a nursery and an office to keep Jacques occupied. But on September 20, 1959, Charrier went off to his army base, and returning for a weekend, fasted and took pills to make himself a psychiatric mess and thereby elude the service that had been so central to his family. His nerves were more than usually rattled, and again he slapped his wife, knocking her to the ground. Vulture photographers hovered outside, and to take a walk, Bardot resorted to wigs, but with little effect—her balletic gait was simply too distinctive.

Back at his base at Orange in the South of France, Charrier found himself terribly ragged, and began going *truly* crazy. When he finally wangled a three-week pass, Brigitte was shocked to find her husband skinny as a rail and stammering from tortured nerves. Afraid to return to the army ordeal, Charrier had a full-scale breakdown, and in hospital—shades of his wife—tried cutting his wrists. Perhaps out of competitive sympathy Bardot then took morphine injections! Drama, drama, and more drama; nothing on screen could compete with Brigitte's real life of the era. Then in December 1959 her male co-star on *Voulez-vous danser avec moi?*, Henri Vidal, with whom she enjoyed working, died of a heart attack at 40. After Sylvia's death and Vidal's the superstitious Brigitte felt hers might just make a hat trick.

That film, however, was a kind of testament to how well Vidal and Bardot had worked together, and how she was able to surmount personal difficulties to shine in a movie that remains enjoyable today. This Cosne-Boisrond murder mystery has Vidal, a dentist, married to Bardot, his nurse. After several months of marriage they quarrel, and he goes to a club, where he runs into a smooth talker and dancer, inviting him to her place for a brief drink. There a blackmailing buddy played by Serge Gainsbourg snaps photos. This Anita Florès then takes the photos to Vidal's dental office, urging him to visit the Florès dance school with cash on hand. When Anita is murdered, the dentist is in a pickle, and on finding out, Bardot's character infiltrates the school as an instructor to locate the real killer. The movie is light, and shot in bold Technicolor, yet one wants to hang in to find out "who dunnit." Whatever she was enduring in real life, Bardot again delivers the goods here both as an actress and dancer.

As 1960 and a decade of intense change dawned, the ordeal of an imminent, celebrated birth in France loomed. At least Jacques was finally released from the army after three months under the colors. But the paparazzi remained at their surging worst. Stuck in her apartment under siege for several days before the birth, and unable to get out even to visit the doctor, Bardot thought she would die from this ordeal. There was a menacing division of journalists camped in the streets below, and police also had to fight off almost revolutionary crowds of an ultra-curious public. Ersatz deliverymen tried to get into the apartment, even photographers garbed as nuns; and set to deliver, Bardot was within an ace of a breakdown, compounded by a urinary tract infection giving her terrible kidney pain. She couldn't emerge for necessary X-rays, and her doctor finally had to install a birthing station right inside. Albeit that it provided her a cushy material life, cinematic fame had ended anything like private normality for her.

Jacques, however, was happy with the birth of his somehow healthy seven pound, four ounce son Nicolas on January 11, 1960; and so were many Bardot fans, for umpteen Nicolases were soon christened across France. The birth was a national event. Christine Gouze-Rénal, who had never had children, became the child's godmother, and a journalistic mogul and friend of Brigitte, Pierre Lazareff, the godfather.

Life after the birth wasn't, however, any easier than before. The press continued reporting the couple's every move, including Bardot's preference for using a bottle to feed, rather than the breast. Brigitte decided to escape to the mountains with her hubby, leaving her son with the woman who became his most enduring mother, a Slavic lady, Moussia. They then moved the child down to La Madrague, though it was still cold there, and Bardot planned an addition to accommodate him. Jacques was perhaps getting high on the drug of idleness, hanging out with pals and drinking, and discussing films he might make. An idea that now possessed him was to produce Brigitte in a Charrier-conceived project. She retorted that her cinematic card was full for the next two years, and essentially, that Olga was her boss. An angry Jacques stomped off into the night to sip with his buddies—which was fine by her. She was soon back to the reality of a new movie shoot, slated to begin making La Vérité only three months after having the baby. Back in Paris other aspects of reality assaulted her, including piles of bills awaiting her signed checks. Plus the "help" was anything but reliable. The latest maid wanted to leave, and Bardot's secretary Alain was now smitten with a male singer. Only Guapa—Clown having retired to the country with friends of Brigitte—provided any real solace. Jacques came up to the capital, but talk of the new movie, with the magisterial,

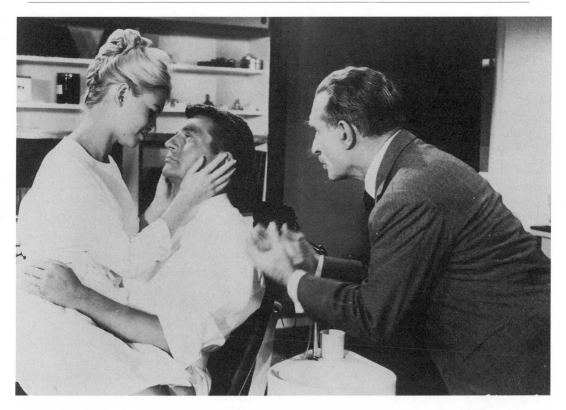

Bardot as the nurse Virginie Dandieu, embracing her husband, Hervé Dandieu (Henri Vidal), in a scene from the lighthearted murder mystery *Voulez-vous danser avec moi?* (*Come Dance with Me*). Her father, Albert (Noël Roquevert), meanwhile seeks attention! (Francos Film, Paris, and Vidès Films, Rome, 1959)

demanding Clouzot as director, and with Olga constantly on the scene made him more depressed, and he took calming shots from a doctor. Bardot felt she was carrying everyone on her back, not least, her husband. The doctor counselled trips out to the nearby countryside, so she would take Charrier around to fields and stay in inns, and at night it was brother-sister now, she says. Trying to work in a new housemaid was a trial, too, and her secretary was more and more absent.

Invited to Lisbon for a screening of *La Femme et le pantin*, Bardot then got scared on the plane and began hemorrhaging, slopping up her skirt and, when standing, whatever her friend Christine and Jacques could snatch to absorb the liquid—Christine's scarf, Jacques' jacket... Later on in a Mercedes crossing Lisbon, Bardot had to sit on the jacket of Christine's future husband, Roger Hanin, afraid she might soil the car seats. A gynecologist was summoned, the inquisitive press doped it all out, and Brigitte remained in her room, groggy from multiple needles taken to calm herself. Trying to get up for the premiere of *La Femme...*, she found herself still bleeding profusely. But the cream of Lisbon society was on hand, so she attended.

Again, much the way a hounded DiMaggio felt safe only on the diamond, Bardot was quite happy to begin work on *La Vérité*, starting in early May 1960. The story involved a woman of easy virtue who rebels against a respectable upbringing (shades of Bardot), and ends up obsessing on a sensitive piano virtuoso and conductor, ultimately paying a big price. The first problem involved a perfectionistic Clouzot making Bardot do try-out scenes with possible romantic leads. The young actors chosen for a look-see included newly famous ones, such as Jean-Paul Belmondo, whom Clouzot, however, found too cocky for the role. Jean-Pierre Cassel wasn't hunky enough, and Clouzot rejected *her* choice, Jean-Louis Trintignant; and on it went, until they located Sami Frey, requisitely tender, yet a bit distant and mysterious. To a demanding Clouzot Frey seemed right for the part, and he turned out to be correct.

According to Alan Williams, Clouzot in the film world was a famous but "isolated figure—the victim of bad health, a controversial past, and his own misanthropy." He was also "the unofficial film community spokesman for the fear that trusting someone— anyone—can be a very dangerous thing to do," which he showed best in his film *Les Diaboliques.* Among those he failed to trust were his own actors, whom he cajoled by a variety of heavy-handed methods into doing exactly what he wanted. Why had he chosen an independent-minded Bardot for this role? The main influence was apparently his wife, who had herself helped make *Diaboliques* a masterpiece by her sensitivity on screen, and obviously noted the same quality in BB.[23]

Bardot as Dominique Marceau and Sami Frey as the classical pianist-conductor Gilbert Tellier in a passionate street scene from *La Vérité (The Truth),* directed by a demanding Henri-Georges Clouzot. (Iéna, Paris, CEIAP, Rome, 1960)

The producer of *Vérité,* Raoul Lévy, placed Bardot's name at the top of the credits, and the tone was set from the outset by somber piano music and black and white photography. The story line is partly courtroom drama, partly flashbacks. Dominique Marceau (Bardot) is charged with murdering her lover, the classical pianist-conductor Gilbert Tellier, played by Frey; and the real "truth" is whether the crime was premeditated or not, premeditation meriting the death penalty. The film is psychological, with a heavy dose of sibling rivalry—Dominique's sister is the model child growing up in Rennes, while Bardot's character is a bad girl who liked boys and trashy novels, and was expelled from school there. Both were then after the same man in Paris, but Sami Frey's Tellier fell deeply for his apparently trashy opposite.

The court part nears its paroxysm with a classic sibling boilover, when Bardot's Dominique avers passionately that her sister never loved and was never loved, and what did *she* know of life? In the climactic scene, the accused prosecutes the prosecutor and others in their robes—they too haven't known what life is and are merely disguised in bourgeois raiments.[24] Pure Daumier, and some existentialism here, too; but worst (and saddest for a viewer) is how eerily close all this came to the star's existence, in her first authentic dramatic role, complete with final cinematic suicide attempt in prison with shards of cut glass opening her veins, followed by death in hospital.

Bardot's real-life vicissitudes certainly helped make this the masterpiece it remains. How better to portray or purvey than from the gut? For while shooting transpired, Charrier languished in a private clinic; Alain, who had once organized Bardot's life, was frequently gone on love leave; the new housemaid was a disappointment; there was much unanswered mail growing spore-like all over the Paris apartment; and Moussia took round-the-clock care of Nicolas, zealously, even jealously so. No one was protecting Bardot—or so it seemed.

Shooting made greater and greater demands, and anyone who thinks Bardot was simply a light actress ought to take note of her high standards here. But after long, arduous days on the set, she had to visit Charrier at night in his clinic, and later in his home bedroom, feeling more like a nursemaid than a wife. *She* needed to do the nurturing; again, there was no one to nurture back.

Then came a bombshell, one of many acts of treason friends and acquaintances armed with potentially lucrative information would perpetrate on her. Alain, Bardot's secretary of four years or so, had sold a memoir of daily life with his famed boss to *France-Dimanche* for 50,000,000 francs! Pierre Lazareff, the newspaper's editor-in-chief, informed Bardot of the deed, and she was thunderstruck. Alain had been spending nights away with no phone number given, and returning in the mornings. When he came back the next day, he was hit by a tirade. At first pleading ignorance, he then confessed that his loved one had pushed him into this meretricious deed. Bardot took away his key, telling him curtly to leave for good and kicking his butt as he skulked away. She was then informed that she could not stop the memoir from appearing; the best she could do was read it line by line, a torture, striking out what was clearly false. The articles came out each week for several months on end, detailing her arguments, birth scene, suicide attempts, how much she paid in taxes, and so on.

To get away from the pain of all this she bought a farmhouse outside Paris at Bazoches-sur-Guyonne, which also meant getting away with Charrier. At least there was the movie to preoccupy her, and on the set Clouzot proved to be a great director, partly because he was such an unchained tyrant. This was why *Diaboliques* had so persuaded with its grisly sadism and human evisceration, influencing the work of Hitchcock. Desiring certain emotions from an actor or actress, Clouzot would, as usual, go to any lengths to provoke them. One day he required Bardot's tears for a dramatic scene and told her every awful thing he could think of, which only made her laugh. Finally Clouzot slapped her twice, Bardot impulsively slapped back, and then she stomped on the Napoleonic director's feet. A fuming, hurt Brigitte decamped, informing Clouzot that she wouldn't return to the set until he apologized.

At another point in the shooting, when the character tries to commit suicide, Clouzot wanted Bardot heavily perspiring and salivating. She had to redo the scene and asked for aspirins, so Clouzot slipped stronger pills into her water. The scene was a great one, but Brigitte became so groggy it took her a couple of days to emerge from the daze; and her father was all for suing this tyrannical film-maker. Raoul Lévy forced his associate to write and sign a letter to the effect that he would never do such things again.

All those years, in other words, Bardot, who seemed to have it all, was in a war, or really, a series of wars—the paparazzi wars, the director wars, the man wars, all intensified by the delicacy, flair, and distinctive beauty that had first brought her into this trade. And she often attracted men who were themselves *grands sensibles*, including Charrier, who was prone to jealousy of her romantic leads. And in fact it turned out that he had something real to be jealous about this time around.

At first the handsome 23-year-old Sami Frey, a fine actor, but distant, inward, and slightly jeering, had intimidated Brigitte. They were very different in cinematic styles— she liked to do things at one fell swoop, he wished to repeat scenes ad infinitum. She couldn't quite figure out this human conundrum, though she knew he had a girlfriend, Pascale Audret. But one day she came to the set palpably hurting from her problems with Jacques, and before going on to do their scene, Frey consoled her, gently taking her hand. From that moment the bridge of distrust between them was blown, and only tenderness remained. Brigitte's life would again be played in the incomparable key of love. And inexplicably, she became an easier commodity for Clouzot to handle on the set.

Fortunately, this growing interest in Frey was masked by Clouzot's sadistic interventions, her husband's first object of jealousy and the main target of press rumors as well. But Frey had that subtle complexity which so often appealed to Bardot. Meeting secretly, the couple took their tentative time getting to know each other, and her returns to Doumer became ever more painful.

Toty now hired a new secretary for her daughter, one Madame Malavalon, a distant relative dubbed "Mala," who took special interest in pornographic letters Bardot received, and which she opened. Moussia had meanwhile virtually taken over Nicolas, keeping Bardot away by pleading a fear of germs reaching the little boy! Brigitte was sweet to Guapa, and Jacques griped about her lack of sweetness with their own child. It was a Catch-22 home situation, and anything but enjoyable.

Sami then decided to rent a bachelor apartment on a bottom floor near the Parc Monceau, a depressing place, but the only way for the young actor and Brigitte to find solitude together. There they listened to classical music—shades of the film; and there she grew to love his depth and warmth, wishing she had met him earlier in life. But because she kills him off in the film, he left for a few days of August vacation with Pascale Audret. Then Bardot *sans* makeup had to do that paroxysmal scene in the box of the accused, faced by judge and jury in a stuffy studio courtroom, reeking on the set of cigarettes, hot rubber, and sweat, while outside ordinary people who fantasized about her life and even dressed like her could prank about freely in the summer sun. Suddenly the scene seemed like *her* trial—of *her* life, frivolity, immorality, yes, of a woman who had had too many loves. They pointed the finger at her, and Bardot had the last word— a very emotional monologue. And she really got into this one, one of those epiphany moments in acting. At the close she flopped her head down into her hands, totally exhausted. Clouzot yelled "cut!" and cast and technicians erupted in vociferous, heartfelt applause. There was no need for another take. Bardot herself knew what she had, and the final, awful suicide scene, where she tearfully cut into herself, came easily as well. *La Vérité* would be one of her favorite films, and what she considered her first truly serious cinematic product.[25]

In real life she was having a heavy effect on Sami, for his vacation with Pascale Audret had predictably turned sour. As the French say, "on ne badine pas avec l'amour" (you don't fool around with love), and on his return, coinciding with the film's end, the real cat began emerging from the bag. A *déception sentimentale* settling into the beleaguered Charrier's psyche made him this time desire a fine death as a paratrooper in Algeria (still in vogue among certain parts of French youth). But he never managed to get there.

As usual, Bardot was pulling away from one human port to moor at another that would be anything but storm-proof. Her penalty for falling for men younger than herself was the old nemesis of military service, and indeed Sami was to be called up by the end of September. She just couldn't win for losing. Jacques was mostly away from home now, but used Moussia, the nursemaid, and Madame Malavalon as spies, and Bardot was no Fort Knox personality. Dany, Bardot's loyal double in *Vérité*, gifted her apartment on the Boulevard Saint-Germain for Brigitte's rendezvous with Sami. In Bardot's estimation Vadim hadn't been jealous enough, but her second husband more than made up the shortfall in that department. At one point the anguished Charrier followed Bardot and got in a photographed fistfight with Frey on the Boulevard Saint-Germain. Sami managed to whack him one in the jaw, then each man tried to pull away Brigitte, and a dozen photographers were there to "machine-gun the scene," having a field day. Bardot dropped a purse containing Sami's letters, her identification cards, and money, and Jacques eagerly scooped them up. She then ran to the car, and Jacques punched at Sami through the open window, and it was all another film, the film of her life! Paparazzi flashes made a crepitating racket, and a big crowd gathered to watch Sami bleeding profusely from one eye.[26]

The two lovers like huddled refugees of the media wars got away, arriving late that night at Yves Robert's and Danièle Delorme's country cottage, where they were fed and cared for, and given a bed. Death was starting to look good to both! Sami said that if he didn't get a reprieve from the military he would indeed kill himself, and Bardot responded in a Shakespearian way that she would follow.

Back at Doumer she felt severely depressed, owing to that September call-up; but her mother whisked her down to a place on the Riviera owned by family friends, Jean-Claude and Mercédès Simon, near Menton. There, Bardot continued to lie in bed, feeling low; but at least she felt safe—the only possible spy a deaf old gardener. But when spotted dining at a restaurant in Saint Paul de Vence, she had to race back to the villa, with a Keystone Cops brigade of journalists now at her heels. Brigitte announced that she would *die* from all this unwanted press attention and pressure! Hounded for being a married woman and a mother, yet carrying on with Frey, who wasn't even around, bobbed her in a sea of guilt. She had a lachrymose consultation with her old confessor, Vadim, but even that failed to alleviate her runaway anxiety.

To compound matters her 26th birthday was slated for September 28, and she had never much enjoyed that milestone. The family friend Mercédès was to take Brigitte to

From *The Truth*, Bardot's paroxysmal scene in the box of the accused, beside her lawyer M. Guérin (Charles Vanel).

another friend's place for a celebration. At six or so that evening they had a champagne toast before setting off, but the romantic victim of French military service let tears fall into the glass, announcing that she had no stomach for food. Instead, she wanted to be left alone, she said. Lacking a telephone—still a luxury item in France—Mercédès decided to drive and inform her friends of this latest development, then return home. She was plainly worried, but Bardot assured her that she would be fine. After the lady's departure, however, Brigitte finished her champagne with a pill at each gulp, ultimately taking a whole bottle of narcotics. She had had enough of this life, went out into the sweet night air, feeling sorry for herself, and walked toward a peaceful sheep pen. She heard the animals bleating, then for good measure opened her veins with a razor blade. Life was this time imitating, but as was more usual in her case, outdoing art. Mercédès meanwhile had been having a drink with her friends—for one always had to "prendre un pot," nothing more French.

Returning home too late to prevent the deed, she couldn't find Brigitte, and frantically organized a search party to fan out in the darkness. This time Bardot very nearly succeeded in her death wish, and had it worked, a lot of animals on this lovely earth would have been the losers. The person who fortunately found the moribund Bardot lying on the ground was a 13-year-old boy who lived in a neighboring house and had fallen asleep outside, watching the place where the famed actress was staying. The teenager then began running home, scared his dad would punish him. En route he came upon a woman sprawled in the garden, already in a coma a good 45 minutes, with deep cuts on right and left wrists, and copious blood splashed about. In another 20 minutes she would surely have been dead. Good luck came in for a welcome landing; but even so, some photographers almost helped finish her off, making the work of the ambulance whizzing to the scene doubly difficult. Bardot was then taken with alacrity to St. François Hospital in Nice, and had her stomach pumped in the nick of time. Her suicide note discovered at the Simons' villa pled a deep, insoluble case of the blues.

Of course all this made the French and world press fire up again, with headlines about Bardot, Charrier, Frey, and Clouzot. Some writers even had the gall to describe the suicide attempt as a publicity stunt!

Two days later at the Nice hospital Brigitte began coming back, with wires in her again, and shrinks having used restraints, fearing she might try once more. Mama too arrived in the prison-like room where her daughter was locked up, and where there were bars on the windows. She was the only visitor allowed. Outside, the hospital was ringed by photographers, waiting patiently for their wounded prey. Nurses near the room blithely flitted *France-Dimanche* or *Ici Paris* to this front-page news. Some apparently whispered that Bardot should have succeeded in her suicide attempt—same-sex hatred and jealousy at its most overt. Bardot had wanted to flee an imperfect world; was she completely wrong about that world? Even as she convalesced, it was busy confirming her worst expectations.

Raoul Lévy and the producer of her upcoming film, Francis Cosne, eventually escorted her out of the clinic. Uncertainly balancing herself on "Fran-Fran's" arm, Bardot was glad to leave this prison behind. Barely able to stand, she found herself sympathetically viewed by the public, but again was flashed heavily by the world press. Lévy drove her and her mother down to Saint-Tropez, and her mother shared Brigitte's bed that night, fearing another suicide attempt. But soon the upper-bourgeois lady returned to character, bringing in other rich, gossipy ladies to keep her company during the vigil. The latter enjoyed opening Brigitte's mail, reading out certain items also in favor of a successful suicide, noting, for example, that Brigitte might try jumping from the high building on Doumer next time! From her bed Brigitte heard their discreet laughs, still felt very alone, and began wondering why she *hadn't* died. These women were driving her crazy, and of course photographers remained on round-the-clock duty outside.

On the plus side Sami received his release from the military, and when Jean-Claude Simon got down to La Madrague, he hijacked Bardot over the cries of her mother and pals, driving her up to a country house near Paris rented by Frey's impresario.[27] Due to his time in the service Brigitte's loved one was himself skin and bones. She was far from solid either, her wrists still bandaged. Left alone, with no telephone, and several miles from the nearest village, Bardot had one of those blessed interludes that she so relished—a wood fire, classical music spilling out, and Sami finally unfolding the story of his childhood.

As noted, ordinary people generally hail from happy backgrounds, and ordinary Sami wasn't. A Bach violin concerto accompanied the recitation of his life by the fire's glow. It was 1941 in his recollection, though from a historical standpoint 1942 sounds more likely for the great Nazi roundups in Paris. The scene was the Jewish section of the Marais, and the child, Sami, no more than three or four, was playing on the apartment floor, while his mother was busy cutting cloth. A noise of heavy boots resounded in the stairwell and quickly she hid her boy in the pile of cloth, telling him this was a new game and that he was not to move or speak until the game was fully concluded. Dutifully, he complied, while he heard rapping at the door, then those boots clomping in and alien voices shouting instructions. He remained immobile under the pile of cloth, while his mother assured the men she was getting her coat and that she was alone. Furniture was overturned, then the adults left, the noise of their boots and voices becoming more distant as they descended the stairs. Sami remained in his hiding place, falling asleep there, and when he awoke in the middle of the night, now hungry and tired of this game, he tentatively emerged, looking around for his mother. Timidly, he opened the front door, and alone in the dark stairwell, began crying. Hearing these sobs, a neighbor appeared, and Sami's wartime childhood passed with those neighbors, as well as with cousins, and with farmers in the country. Like many other Jewish children of the time he was baptized a Catholic. Here then was where that delicate inner beauty came from, that sensitivity one can't fabricate. Protective and sympathetic, Brigitte fell more deeply in love with Sami, then went on to read other Holocaust testimonies.

Each time she fell in love she hoped of course that she was at an endpoint; but that endpoint seemed hard to find. She had gone from Vadim to Trintignant to Distel to Charrier to Frey, not to mention shorter, but vivid dalliances along the way. None had been close to forever...

The baby, meanwhile, bearing a nickname of "Dimple" and resembling his dimply father, was growing, and segments of the French public were definitely angered by the way Bardot approached her maternal responsibilities. As if to confirm their anger, she would blurt unfortunate half-truths, such as: "I am no mother and I won't be one."[28]

She was also increasingly repelled by the film world, wanting out from the time of her suicide attempt. Yet she had contracted for more pictures, chaining herself to the trade that perhaps represented her only constant in life. Sequestered in her safe nest with Frey, she knew she still had to honor the commitments of that other world. After not hearing from her star in a while, Olga brought her back to reality, telling her of the need to do "synchro" for *Vérité*, then of the imminent beginning of her next film shoot for Cosne, *La Bride sur le cou* (*Please Not Now!*, among other titles in English).

Back at Paul Doumer after six weeks away, Brigitte found Moussia still taking obsessively good care of Nicolas, "Mala" still trying to run things, but using up the actress' savings in the process, and the latest housemaid clearly incompetent. There was the usual heap of bills to pay, a broken vacuum cleaner, a bidet that overflowed, and neighbors complaining of the to-and-fro between her two apartments. In addition Bardot's new country place at Bazoches had been broken into, and Jacques wanted a divorce!

Sami stayed at his impresario's apartment in Neuilly outside Paris, and Brigitte went there at night with Guapa to keep her love going. *La Vérité* came out in November 1960, and wonder of wonders, the critics finally took Bardot seriously![29] She and the movie won prizes, and mail flooded in, and she tried to treat any supposedly sincere missives seriously. Of course one couldn't always tell. One letter accompanied by a photo of an

18-year-old handicapped fellow in wheelchair mentioned the high cost of an accordion he coveted as a Christmas present. So open-hearted Bardot stomped around Paris with Mala to locate an accordion, finding the cost of a new one plus case exorbitant. Finally a friend who worked in a museum got them a nearly new one that was cheaper. Bardot dutifully sent it out, and the "handicapped" scam artist wrote back, noting how cheap she was, and that to make amends Bardot ought to send his mother a new washing machine! Plus he wasn't handicapped at all—he had only sent that photo to see if her renowned avarice was really true, as the papers had informed him. Sobbing and depressed, Brigitte began to despair of ever trusting humanity again.

To get away from such sadness she tried to see Nicolas alone over Christmas, but Jacques kept hanging around them. In January 1961 Bardot started shooting *Bride...*, coinciding with the debut of a love affair between her good friend Jicky and a younger woman named Anne, taking care of Bardot's residence at Bazoches. The couple made the place homey, and Brigitte and Sami would go there on non-shooting Saturday nights and Sundays, enjoying the change of pace. She wasn't crazy about her current film director, Jean Aurel, and still fancied working with "Vava" on this comedy. As a favor to her Vadim did take over the project from Aurel, teaming up with Cosne. But it was tough to redo the movie and change its tone, and they took to doing improvised shtick right on the set. It also failed to cheer Brigitte that Vadim had a 17-year-old girlfriend in tow, whose real last name was Dorléac, but who would soon be known to the world as Catherine Deneuve. Some of the movie's winter scenes needed to be shot up in the mountains, in a spot reachable only by cable car. After the actors' ascent, a snowstorm blew out the electricity up there, as well as the telephone, also canceling any possibility of an imminent return by cable car. Stuck in primitive alpine simplicity, Bardot worried about Sami and his possible jealousy at being unable to get through to her. Actually, it was one of those nice reprieves, where Brigitte played checkers and other games, and passed the time in a simple manner.

Back in Paris for the finishing shots, Vadim pried a nude dance out of his old protégée to spice up a sorry film. Sami was now installed at Doumer, but the place remained chaotic. Bardot tried an Italian couple there as help, but they would watch her every move, eavesdropping on conversations, until she finally got rid of them. Sami had to leave by the service entrance, but kept bumping into Jacques, who used the same one to come up and see his child!

Blessedly, there were more weekends in the country at Bazoches with the curative Jicky and Anne. Brigitte and Sami loved the getaway, and despite an old French apothegm that one must never return to where one was (even moderately) happy, Bardot also had the impulse of whisking Sami and her friends off to the mountain retreat where she had recently been stranded. Stopping at a hotel en route in Bourg-en-Bresse, famed for its chicken, Sami signed in as Camillo Guapa and gave as his profession "Spanish dancer." Jicky used his real name—Ghislain Dussart—but made his profession that of high-wire artist (*funambule*). The next day the local paper mentioned Bardot spending the night in Bourg accompanied by Camillo Guapa and the celebrated *funambule*, Ghislain Dussart.

Arriving without further mishap in the mountains, they left their car below, took the gondola ride up cum dog, cat, and bags, and found themselves alone in their hideaway, and loving it. But another snowstorm came blowing in, and fearful of being stranded, Brigitte finally opted for a descent on foot! That took two or three awful hours, with the cat's claws stuck into Jicky's bloodied neck; but somehow, they made it. Stopping in a bistro, the group cleaned up as best they could, and drove all night back home to Bazoches. One of those plans that didn't pan out, fish that weren't caught—many such in Bardot's life...

Endorsing de Gaulle as the latest father-figure to the French, now busy extricating them from the North African morass and anchoring a firmer Fifth Republic, Bardot entered the go-go decade of the '60s still ahead of the pack as an international sex symbol. The bitter end of the Algerian War, including O.A.S. bombing threats in Paris, sent her packing for La Madrague in the South, where she soon got sick of everyone's nitpicky ways—Sami overly careful about food and more and more of a downer; Dédette, her makeup artist, eating too *much*; Moussia covering Nicolas and keeping him out of the sun and away from the ocean (for who knew what health reason?)—it all began to grate on Bardot's nerves. When Sami returned to Paris to act in a Brecht play, she was happy to stay put without him and check out the port scene, finding male company there in the form of François de l'Esquinade. Her friends Christine Gouze-Rénal and Roger Hanin came down, and along with de l'Esquinade things cheered up for Brigitte. Sixteen years her senior, François was the first man in a long time with feet so firmly on the ground that he could take care of Bardot in a consistent way—doing the cooking, etc.

Back in grayer Paris Brigitte missed this vacation love affair down in a more outdoorsy Midi. She now had to do a brief, week-long film part with Alain Delon in *Les Amours célèbres*, but at that time found Delon (universally called a "pretty boy" in France) not her cup of tea. In this historical film, Delon plays a Bavarian prince, Albert, who marries a peasant girl on the sly, played by Brigitte. Accused of being a witch, she is drowned, and Albert comes home a bit late, drowning himself in the same river out of grief. It was not a memorable film, and as for *Bride sur le cou*, the movie Vadim had supposedly "rescued," it ended up perhaps the worst Bardot flick ever made! There Brigitte plays a rather down-at-heels Paris model, with a boyfriend who leaves her for a rich American heiress. Via scenes of crazy driving in Paris, go-karting, room-changing on a train, bobsledding in the mountains, and a phony swami's help, Bardot's character aided by a male pal tries to make her ex-lover jealous and/or exact revenge. The movie isn't funny, interesting, or diverting even for one minute.[30]

But in June 1961 she was to start shooting in one of her most idiosyncratic projects, and under a celebrated, innovative director, Louis Malle: *Vie privée* (A Very Private Affair), based loosely on episodes of her own chaotic life. Malle, later known to Americans for films like *Murmur of the Heart*, *My Dinner with André*, and *Atlantic City*, and for his marriage to the actress Candice Bergen, had come off an affair with another French screen siren, Jeanne Moreau. He had also been the lover of Bardot's sister, Mijanjou, who seemed to trod on her older sister's pathways.

Arriving for the shoot in Geneva, Bardot found this director both tough and tender, but not quite open enough for her taste. She didn't look forward to her work schedule with him, and as for Malle, he had to overcome what he had heard about Bardot as a prima donna. But François de l'Esquinade arrived by pleasant surprise, and he and the star occupied a romantic lakeside villa belonging to a Swiss playboy. Again she had to take telephone calls furtively, this time from Sami. The Swiss public became censorious of the French icon and her lifestyle, and a first night's film work in an old part of Geneva opposite Marcello Mastroianni (who tried to pull out near the beginning of shooting) was a debacle—a pot of geraniums was dumped down on Brigitte, then came tomatoes and panfuls of water, accompanied by insults like "whore," or "get out of Switzerland!" François whisked her away from the shoot, but back at the villa she continued crying. Christine Gouze-Rénal, the producer who had first interested Malle in this "Brigitte" idea, and Malle himself tried to reassure her, and a local doctor was summoned to give calming injections.

In July the cast was back in Paris for interior studio shots, and again, Bardot felt envious of people on the outside, cavorting in the sun. Twelve-hour days, including Saturdays, became onerous, and even in the old elevator attack scene, adapted for the movie, she didn't quite put her full self into it. This would be no *Vérité* for her. But Malle found her work convincing, and echoing others, Peter Haining would call the finished product "an intriguing and revealing film, one of the most crucial in any study of BB and her life."[31]

Bardot was glad to be back in the capital with Sami, her "husband" of the era, though they were only briefly together before he had to migrate down to the Côte d'Azur to start work in a new film and she to Spoleto, Italy, in order to finish up the Malle shoot. It was a reprise of things she hated—suitcases and airplanes—and she understands in retrospect why the life of showbiz couples has so often been a bumpy one. In Spoleto Malle got the chief cast members a lovely house, and he took the main and first floors, with Bardot on the second. From below she could hear the director's parties. The paparazzi of course began stalking in D-Day force, and Bardot wanted badly to exit her fortress. But to do so meant being "machine-gunned" by thousands of flashes emanating from surrounding roofs.[32]

After shooting, everyone else could go out for a meal to a cozy trattoria, while Brigitte had to lock herself up behind thick curtains, eating cold chicken. Malle worked all this mayhem into his last scene, where Bardot's Jill falls victim to the paparazzi—a photographer's flash, surprising her, makes her tumble from a rooftop (where she had been hiding) to her death.

On Sundays everyone migrated to a nearby lake to cool off and relax, but again, Brigitte remained stuck inside. One Sunday she decided to disguise herself with scarf, shades, and an old shirt. Somehow making it to the water unscathed, after drying herself off she encountered a full-scale invasion. She screamed, and Christine's husband, Roger Hanin, punched some of the pursuers, while Brigitte clumsily pushed two photographers into the lake. One hit the water along with all of his equipment. Out of reach, the telephoto brigade compulsively photographed the entire scene, as Roger too fell into the water, locked in an embrace with a photographer he was still trying to pummel. Making a run back to the car, Brigitte was spat at and kicked in the face, but continued throwing punches of her own. Finally she fell face down on the sand—the film within a film continuing.

Hurrying to Spoleto to comfort the shut-in and shaky actress in her room, Sami prepared at the end of August to drive her away from this horrific atmosphere. But there was no easy way to protect a star many considered pampered anyway. Getting out of Italy was therefore difficult, and hordes of telephoto lenses remained omnipresent. Bardot's nerves were close to shattering again. Any time their car had to slow down, crowds invaded, so avoiding stops for food, drink, or washroom needs became a necessity. On an impulse the besieged couple zipped up toward Switzerland, finally locating an isolated mountain chalet, where only big, tranquil cows surveyed them with little interest: safe at last.

Malle's completed movie, perhaps too consciously trying to be a masterpiece, seems tongue-in-cheek and superficial in its first fifth or so, especially in a frantic Paris setting; but it then gets better and better, partly due to a superb, mostly classical score, and also from the way it was made. The screenplay wasn't finished when Malle began, and improvisation with his sometimes prickly collaborator, Jean-Paul Rappenau, and a more relaxed feel by the time they reached Spoleto made the film basically several in one. Yet despite a number of bad reviews that then greeted it, the movie may indeed be a masterpiece. It is certainly an invaluable primary source on the life of a star viciously pursued by media and public. Bardot's character Jill (from Geneva) gains fame as a model in Paris, and then as an actress who eventually wants only to get away from the mobs. Among the smothering hordes is the ranting cleaning lady in her apartment building who besieges her in that elevator scene drawn from life. Jill returns to Geneva and looks up an old friend, Fabio (Mastroianni)—a magazine publisher, playwright, and impresario freshly jilted, and looking splendid in fine Italian suits.[33] The two are drawn to each other, and she cannot leave him alone for two weeks when he mounts a huge production of a play to take place in Spoleto's main square. Marvelous music, the barrage of a surging public now interested in both character-celebrities, Jill crawling up on a roof to watch this impresario's play unfurl below, then the flash making her tumble blissfully, and in an oddly peaceful, dove-like manner to a death that releases her from all torment: here are Malle and Bardot at their best together. And again, it needs to be reiterated, and not out of gratuitous revisionism: Brigitte is so natural that she makes acting seem easy in this complex film. Hence she was, and continues to be underrated. But clearly the awful invasions of her life helped make this a precious cinematic work (perhaps the best scene being an earlier mass trampling in Paris where she faints and is borne aloft to recover).

Revenue for the movie, however, failed to attain the level of Bardot's previous dozen films, and that was perhaps partially due to events in the wider world.[34] For when it came out, French Algeria was in its last and saddest year. The Bardot tragedy simply couldn't compare to Europeans and Muslims alike going out in Oran or Algiers, and in great numbers, having throats cut at bus stops, or being beaten to death, or shot, or falling victim to numerous bombings. The word "terrorism" was splashed all over newspapers of that era, and to Malle's credit, he did not just sign simplistic petitions from faraway comfort. Rather, like Camus before his death, Malle wanted to know all sides of the thorny problem, traveling to an unsafe Algeria in its colonial death agony, where he listened, watched, snapped, and scribbled. Ruthless members of the FLN (Front de Libération Nationale) had long promised either the coffin or valise to a million Europeans there, and soon those who could fled with nothing; many Muslims who had sided with France would remain behind to be gruesomely tortured and killed by other Muslims.[35]

The model and screen star Jill (Bardot) and publisher-impresario Fabio (Marcello Mastroianni) in Louis Malle's *Vie privée* (*A Very Private Affair*), based on Bardot's own frantic life as a celebrity. (Progefi-Cipra, Paris, CCM, Rome, 1961)

Bardot meanwhile returned from her film-making travails in Switzerland and Italy, regained French homes, and continued to experience much public and press intrusion. At La Madrague a forest of telephoto lenses lay in wait, making the star angry and guarded. Her nerves were knotted, and she became ever more paranoid and reclusive. Her memories of these press invasions come thick and fast. She remembers, for example, some American woman in flowery bathing cap swimming toward her shore and towing a wooden case. Jicky, Anne, and Sami were taking the sun, when suddenly the intruder stood up in shallow water, quickly extricated camera equipment from the box, and "machine-gunned" the star point-blank with her topflight equipment.[36] No American, or woman for that matter, this was a professional French photographer in disguise. Bardot started empathizing with animals trapped in zoo cages or tracked by guns, empathy that perhaps unconsciously was leading her toward another kind of life.

The intrusive public kept coming at her from the sea, over her fences, even clambering onto the roof at La Madrague. Many times she remembers discovering humans on the swing outside, on the chaises longues, even in her bathtub. She often had to get rid of them with a kick in the pants, a broom swipe, or a call to the police. One day a busload of German tourists descended on her supposed haven, promised a tour of La

Madrague by someone from Club Med, who had taken off with their money. Instead of seeing Bardot, they encountered Jicky exposing himself! Another time visitors were met with a hail of firecrackers—Bardot lobbing them at every head or camera she could see.

At the beginning of 1962, the year she and the father of her child were definitively divorced (with Charrier getting custody), she was up to here with the celebrity's life. But though she had been talking of retirement, she soon started filming *Le Repos du guerrier*, with a clutch of movies to follow.[37] Many young women worldwide still imitated the Bardot look (as in the Malle film); and she still found herself in high demand on the silver screen.[38] But her private life kept mingling and interfering with her professional one. A letter putatively from General Salan of the O.A.S. terror (or counter-terror) group tried to shake down Bardot, as it had other celebrities, for contributions—or else... The asking price was 50,000 new francs, and her fellow apartment dwellers at Paul Doumer were terrified of being bombed. But where other stars would appease and pay up, a feisty Brigitte fought back with an open published letter, hiring guards to patrol outside the apartment. For a while she was scared of all packages that arrived there. The O.A.S. later tried to pressure her father for the 50,000 francs, menacing an acid job or bombing of his daughter. Police and politicians seemed pusillanimous in response, though de Gaulle, himself an artful dodger from assassination attempts, admired Bardot's pluck.[39]

At the beginning of 1962 she had also made the acquaintance, first via a fan letter, of a 64-year-old woman hospitalized with throat cancer, and partly due to the star's encouragement, gifts, and friendship, the woman would somehow hang on another 20 years. This too was the year that Bardot really began her work on behalf of mistreated animals, starting with the powerful French slaughterhouse industry. A 20-year-old acquaintance, Jean-Paul Steiger, procured a job in one of Paris' abattoirs, and kept phoning Brigitte daily about what occurred inside, as well as taking secret photos. Bringing the shots to her apartment, he showed the results of his three weeks in the slaughterhouse, and she cried and was utterly sickened by them, and unable to eat. A few days later Bardot got on TV, faced by three tough-looking slaughterers weighing in for the meat industry, and the debate reduced her to tears. Finally she pushed for a meeting with Roger Frey, Minister of the Interior, even carrying pistols to his office that she thought ought to become standard issue in abattoirs, i.e., to render doomed animals unconscious, instead of permitting suffering that ensued from gradual bloodletting. (Random beatings of animals screaming with pain were also common among butchers.)

Arriving on a freezing winter day with her three heavy firearms, she was nearly ejected from Frey's antechamber; but then the minister cordially invited her in to see him, promising to consider changes to the industry, that is, when the O.A.S. and other problems of the era gave him respite. In fact it would take ten long years for the *pistolet* to be adopted by law in licensed French abattoirs; unlicensed ones, however, would remain beyond that law.

Le Repos du guerrier, made by Vadim and Cosne, started into production that February of 1962, with Bardot as a bourgeois heiress who dumps her "normal" fiancé in favor of a Dostoyevskian bad boy, played by Robert Hossein. After foiling his suicide, she puts up with his odd ways and bibulous cynicism, and becomes more at one with him. Finally, he grows into the weak and needy one, proposing marriage, and she attains a final strength of character.

Despite some depth to this Vadim adaptation of a Christiane Rochefort novel, the movie drags, with its boiled-over existentialism preached too repetitively. Hossein's Renaud in the end begs Bardot's Geneviève to make him join this "stinking human race." Crying out for her to marry him, he utters a climactic line right out of Sartre or Camus (Hossein had in fact begun his career in the play *No Exit*): "Force me to live!"[40]

Little wonder that the idea of retirement still appealed to Bardot, particularly given the serious beginnings of her "animalian" consciousness. At the studio cafeteria she felt alienated from others working on this film, blithely munching their *steak-frites* at lunch. In the evenings she came home from shootings tired and depressed, but as usual, nothing and no one was there to soothe her, for Sami was invariably leaving to do a late-night theater gig. She thought of her pals and their conjugal happiness—Dédette, her makeup artist, with good marriage, friends, and regular department store expeditions, unmolested by paparazzi; Dany, her double, also solidly married, and with many friends, and a well-slaked fondness for restaurants and movies; Mala, her secretary, married to a retired naval officer, and enjoying middle-class pursuits like bridge; Olga, her agent, also happily married and giving frequent dinner parties; Jicky and Anne... and on it went.

In the spring of 1962 cast and crew of *Repos...* moved to Florence to shoot the movie's bucolic Italian scenes (featuring James Robertson Justice as a sculptor urging Geneviève to stay strong in the face of Renaud's infantile vicissitudes). Florence entranced Bardot with its art, architecture, and vistas on the river. But this was again the country where the paparazzi had gotten their name, and they were still plentiful.

Back in Paris she found herself across a growing emotional divide from Sami, their frequent separations obviously no aid to the relationship. Bardot had too often gone for sensitive men, and was thereby forced to take care of time-consuming mundanities like bills, broken appliances, and housemaids. However, she still loved Sami, and enjoyed driving down with him through Burgundy and into Provence en route to La Madrague. His favored music was stately 18th-century fare—Mozart, Haydn, Vivaldi—and maybe Bardot in part was made for the Old Regime, both as aristocrat and peasant.

Down in La Madrague they joined Jicky and Anne, their housesitters, and it was there in August 1962 that Brigitte heard of Marilyn Monroe's death, news that affected her deeply. It made her wish even more desperately to get off the film treadmill, and for a while she did get some rest, with a bit of non-taxing television work and a visit to Méribel the coming winter.

In this era Mijanjou was married to an actor, Patrick Bauchau, and they would soon give Bardot a niece, Camille, born on February 24, 1963, a girl she would ardently love. But inroads on her time continued to be made. The formidable intellectual director Jean-Luc Godard now enrolled Bardot for a movie project *Le Mépris* (*Contempt*), based on an Alberto Moravia novel she had read and enjoyed. She duly signed on, and in April 1963 she and the rest of the cast and crew pushed off for Italy to begin shooting. Her co-stars included the legendary Fritz Lang as a film director, Michel Piccoli as her screenwriter husband, and a baffled Jack Palance (suffering from no French) as a money-obsessed, know-nothing American producer. Bardot says quaintly that she doesn't

The director Jean-Luc Godard (holding furled paper) and from left, Brigitte Bardot (Camille Javal), Giorgia Moll (Francesca Vanini), Jack Palance as the exploitative American producer Jeremy Prokosch, and Michel Piccoli (Paul Javal), Bardot's screen husband, in *Le Mépris* (*Contempt*), in which Godard also plays Fritz Lang's assistant. (Les Films Concordia, Rome, Paris Films, Paris, Compania Champion, Rome, 1963)

like warming up old soup, but Raf Vallone, a face from the past, came down to keep her company on the Isle of Capri, and then in a more frenzied Rome.

Rome was obviously *the* paparazzi lair, and keeping determined types at bay there became nothing less than an art. Toty and Pilou visited, but to leave the hotel and try out some of the city's excellent restaurants was well-nigh impossible. At first Brigitte's mother couldn't believe how bad things were outside, so to show her, Bardot placed one of her wigs on a stick, lifting it up near a window, and it produced a cacophony of crackling flashes. Horrified, the dignified Toty decided to imitate her daughter's crawling on all fours in the hotel room to elude the snappers! Finally a friend of Anne-Marie's disguised herself in a Bardot-type wig, and wearing black shades, got into a Mercedes reserved for the star, drawing away "the screaming crowd of imbeciles."[41] The maneuver allowed Brigitte and her parents a night on the town.

Godard's earnest manner and mien, symbolized by a stodgy hat always on his head, did not really agree with the French starlet. He was of course iconic in the film world, and superbly intelligent, at least on the psychology of daily existence (if not on currents in world politics or science). But Patrick McGilligan in a biography of Lang shows why the earthy Bardot would find it hard to feel at one with this director: "Godard was the Bertolt Brecht of the nouvelle vague: an impossible, mercurial man, a piercing critic-filmmaker whose writings and films were increasingly marked by an uncompromising raised fist of chic aesthetic and political radicalism.... With his first feature film, 1959's *A Bout de Souffle* (*Breathless*), he had leaped to the front ranks of nouvelle vague experimenters, and with subsequent films he became the movement's enfant terrible—increasingly trenchant, cold as dry ice, confrontational."[42]

In fact *Le Mépris* does not wear well, showing how ephemeral that early '60s avantgarde has become. Yet in this case it was *big budget* avant-garde—a film that cost plenty, and with heavy hitters like Carlo Ponti and Joseph E. Levine behind it, while itself disserting fictionally on the big-budget process. Godard's first wrap mainly pleased Ponti, but didn't seem commercial enough for the Americans, who forced him to add footage with Bardot unclad.[43] Palance is truly a caricature as the American producer Jeremy Prokosch, trying to steamroller an artistic director, Lang, into a modern version of *The Odyssey*, aided by screenwriter Paul Javal's forced rewrite. The shattering of the latter's marriage with Camille (Bardot), impelled by the prostituting morality or non-morality of Prokosch, who feels his money can buy anyone, and by Javal's apparent masochism—all this material seems passé, and the dialogue is ultra-pretentious. At one point Palance is given a line to the effect that when he hears the word "culture" he reaches for his checkbook. Godard then feels it necessary to say it used to be a revolver, tipping his hat to the original Goebbels quote. An earnest translator keeps putting all of Palance's English lines (after he utters them) into French. Even the music is ponderous. The film went over budget, came out in different versions, and pleased nowhere but in the intellectual sectors of France, and with certain critics in cities like New York. However, Martin Scorsese, sponsoring the movie's re-release in the late '90s, acknowledged its influence on him. And as in Malle's film, *Contempt* did incorporate the paparazzi nuttiness to which Bardot had repetitively fallen prey.[44] This was again art drawn from life, *her* life of the era, before everything began changing in a big way all over the western world.

4

Waning Stardom and
the Rise of Sachs

WITH HER SAMI FREY RELATIONSHIP beginning to evaporate—there had been talk for a while that she might convert to his Judaism à la Liz Taylor, but it came to nothing—Bardot met a handsome playboy named Bob Zagury at the Cannes Film Festival later that spring of 1963. Born in Casablanca to a Brazilian father and French mother, Zagury loved to dance, and his penchant for the bossa nova rapidly began edging out Frey's heavier strains of Vivaldi or Mozart. After what seemed a fairly prolonged down cycle, life became vivid again for Bardot. Zagury came over to La Madrague with some of his Brazilian pals, Brigitte played guitar and relaxed, but of course it hit the papers, reaching Sami, who was working in Paris. The frank Bardot says she often wanted her cake and to eat it too, but that remained difficult in the celebrity fishbowl.

At La Madrague she found herself plagued by doubts and indecision, crying and throwing herself around in front of Dussart and Anne, who had witnessed this sort of thing before. At one point she was set to take off for Paris, but Bob's talk of Brazil and of a long future ahead soothed her, and they went out for a laugh-filled double date, lasting till the wee hours. The new, pervasive odor at La Madrague was of expensive cigars.

In October 1963 Bardot had to go to London for a new shoot on *Une ravissante idiote* (the simplest translation being *A Ravishing Idiot*). This Cold War comedy co-starred Anthony Perkins as a klutzy Soviet agent, with Bardot as an unworldly English seamstress to an upper-class lady, whose husband is trying to foil these Russians and their plot to snare important information. Old *Get Smart* fans might enjoy this light-hearted flick, and Perkins with his accented French works well with a thinnish Bardot, who falls in love with Perkins' character. In the end she turns out herself to be working in the counter-espionage branch (among other surprises), and love wins out.

Bardot as Penelope Lightfeather and Anthony Perkins as a bumbling spy, Harry Compton, co-starring in the Cold War comedy *Une ravissante idiote* (*A Ravishing Idiot*), in a scene where they flank her menaced screen grandmother (Hélène Dieudonné). (Belle-Rives, Paris, Flora Film, Rome, 1963)

Bardot brought along her new boyfriend for the London shoot, and Zagury was astonished, like his predecessors, by the paparazzi surge there, wondering about the price to be paid for a relationship with such a star. It was not just Bardot's zenith before an inevitable descent in popularity; but also the last era when movie stars were still larger than life—before TV won out, and rock singers or sports figures began bringing film actors to earth as only one part of a growing celebrity crowd. Brigitte certainly welcomed this demythologizing, but it would have to wait a bit.

The Westbury Hotel off Bond Street where they stayed became a daily mob scene, with fans far outnumbering the press and Bardot very fearful. Outdoor London was simply too bumptious for shooting, and the cast hightailed it back to a French studio, with sets constructed to resemble English streets and locales.

But a return to Paris also meant a return to daily reality for Bardot. The latest housemaid was scandalized by her change in men and gave notice. A new secretary, replacing an ill Mala, seemed a poor choice. In the papers Brigitte read that Sami had moved on to a new fiancée, and she experienced pangs of jealousy. At least the harried actress found a loyal, together new maid in the form of "Madame Renée," as she would call her for the next 15 years. Zagury also located a better secretary, and enhanced organization at home resulted. He smoked cigars procured from Davidoff in Switzerland, played poker more and more inveterately, and to a despairing Toty and Pilou seemed like another bohemian con man in their daughter's life.

That same October of 1963 Anne de Miolles married Ghislain Dussart, filling Brigitte with emotion. She comments that she had always loved the idea of marriage, and really wanted to marry every one of her loved ones. Bob now became her Saturday night–Sunday vacation consort with Jicky and the pregnant Anne—at Bardot's near-at-hand retreat of Bazoches. But in Paris the racket from a new building going up opposite her apartment on Paul Doumer upset her, and despite her aversion to flying, Zagury began entrancing her with the idea of a real vacation in Rio.

Bardot was in fact *often* getting away, which included being well apart from a son now growing up at the Charrier villa not far from La Madrague, with a new stepmother the boy liked, though unfortunately she didn't last. The boy would attend an expensive private school, and while Brigitte saw him infrequently, she was always very protective of him, due in part to the possibility of a kidnapping.

In January 1964 Bardot duly made her first crossing of the Atlantic with Zagury; but jetlagged in Rio, was met by the same old racket of flashes there. Hordes of photographers then followed the couple in a brigade of cars. The pair somehow made it to Bob's apartment, but found themselves stuck in with a bunch of his friends who shared the rent and spoke only Portuguese. Bardot became volcanically frustrated, wanting badly to leave. She was holed up almost a week in a kind of hostage scene, looking out at the lovely bay of the Jobim-Gilberto era. A blithe "girl from Ipanema" she could not yet be; for in the streets lurked the usual army of media hounds, and exiting would create a stampede.

That week Brigitte cried continually, flying off the handle at Zagury and repetitively demanding a return home. Instead, he decided to pack up a VW bug with cans of food, bottles of mineral water, and other provisions, and the couple made their escape, driving up the coast to another Brazil.

They arrived at a fishing village, Buzios, on an isolated swath of the coast, taking a cottage on the surf, with no electricity, and no fridge or telephone, only long beaches, sparkling sea, and in the backwoods, marvelous birds aplenty. Here people blessedly didn't know her name (though Buzios would later become a tourist trap, partly because of Bardot's sojourn there). A cat lived in the vicinity, and the smell of bougainvillea and the splendid sand for bare-footing by the ocean calmed her nerves. Miraculously, the press hadn't located the couple in this paradise. Under mosquito netting at night Bardot read Simone de Beauvoir's *Second Sex*, recalling this interlude as one of the finest moments of her life. All she had ever wanted, she says, was a relatively simple existence; but in no dependable fashion—given her trade, personality, and fame—could she obtain one.

Professional obligations, including two days of shooting in an American movie, *Dear Brigitte*, with Jimmy Stewart, called her back to Paris. The movie involved an American boy who writes Bardot a fan letter and pushes his professor father (Stewart) into a meeting with her in France, featuring the true article for about five minutes of the picture. Bardot in a relatively happy era comes off as gentle and believable here—sweetly maternal with the Norman Rockwellian lad, to whom she offers a puppy as a gift.[1]

In that period Brigitte also cut a bossa nova record, an increasingly popular kind of music. Then Mama Olga, along with Malle, came to La Madrague with a new project, again traceable to Bardot's friend Christine Gouze-Rénal, and which would take her back across the Atlantic. This was Malle's *Viva Maria*, with Jeanne Moreau to be cast as Bardot's fellow music hall performer and eventual revolutionary (both named Maria).[2] Brigitte enjoyed the pages that Malle showed her, but her instincts told her to eschew the project. She feared that Moreau would become a rival, and also that her French homes would suffer from lack of needed attention. Reluctantly, however, she ceded to the pitch.

The world press made a big to-do of Bardot turning 30 on September 28, 1964, in a period of great transformation that was starting to pace ahead of her. To celebrate, she quaffed a quiet champagne in a Paris restaurant. Minus Nicolas and Moussia, now with Jacques, she found her apartment difficult to bear, and a new pet, a baby ass named Cornichon, didn't really fill the emptiness. With Bob out at night playing poker, then returning at dawn, either laden with money or busted, she was getting antsy here. Over and over she had kept falling for interesting, yet flawed men.

Mama Olga set up a meeting of the two reigning Gallic beauties, and Bardot found Moreau to be pretty well what she had expected—outwardly warm, devastating to men, but tough inside. Leaving for Mexico was the usual mishmash, with Guapa yowling and Brigitte wanting to stay and play with the dog. At Bazoches she left Cornichon and a sheep, "Nénette," and was pushed into allowing the place to be modernized during her absence. Guapa remained in Paris with Madame Renée. So with ten suitcases full of clothes, and Bob and Jicky accompanying her, she was off by plane—first to Rio, where this time she was more used to Bob's apartment, enjoying the city's antique shops and music she sang and played on guitar. Her own bossa nova record was heard everywhere here, and people rushed up in the streets to kiss her. Bardot found she was starting to like the happy, insouciant ways of these Brazilians. Then with Zagury she spent Christmas of 1964 up at Buzios, this time at the vacation home of an Argentinian consul and his wife, and her happiness remained intact.

Flying from Rio up to Mexico was, however, a jolt, for there were stops along the way, and it was a difficult trip. In Lima the mayor asked what the French movie star wanted as a gift, and she asked for a handful of Peruvian earth, which she has kept. In the high and thin air of Bogotá in Colombia, she gazed around with fascination at Indian faces. Then came Mexico City, where the old journalistic mayhem returned to assault the couple. Her terror of crowds went into high gear, and in her latest hotel-fortress Bardot cried continually again, consoled by Mama Olga and Dédette, who met her there. She was earning more money than Moreau, but the brunette actress was astonished to find that she actually liked the supposedly finicky Brigitte, if not her hangers-on.

With lots of Mexican personnel on hand, and polyglot orders flying out in French, Spanish, or German, filming began at the base of Cuernavaca in January 1965, and Bardot fell in love with the country. Despite the rigors of working here, she would really see Mexico on an extended stint—its beauty and misery alike, including wild animals, poor peasant kids, and skeletal dogs lacking food, to whom she continually brought victuals. Even on Sundays off she went out to feed them. Paparazzi invasions diminished,

Brigitte Bardot listening to the director of *Viva Maria*, Louis Malle. (Nouvelles Editions de Films, Productions Artistes Associés, Paris, Vidès Films, Rome, 1965)

and in almost six months here she grew to appreciate this country more than any she had seen.

Moreau meanwhile was living in higher style, with champagne and truffles jetted in from France, while Bardot's entourage was into bare feet and guitar singalongs. Journalists made sure to embitter relations between the two stars, alleging all sorts of quarrels, while rivalries were fed as well by the stars' respective staffs. And Malle wasn't quite above the battle, having been Moreau's lover. His "Mexwestern" shot in sun-scorched sameness or thin mountain air became an intermittently tension-filled experience, and Malle wished in retrospect that he had made the film in English, featuring two less well-known stars (at that point)—Julie Christie and Sarah Miles. The journalistic hordes bothered a man who liked to shoot in isolation, and his big budget was never big enough—either bigger or smaller would have been better.[3] Weather and time constraints made it hard to film at the right part of day, sickness also affected schedules, and the moviemaker once more found it hard to settle on one tone. Malle would finally feel that he had bitten off more than he could chew here.[4]

At Easter Mama Olga awarded her star client two baby ducks, one of whom survived—

eating and sleeping with Brigitte, bathing in the swimming pool, and requiring a "duck baby sitter" during shoots, provoking mirth among the crew. People would joke about wanting to cook the chick in a casserole! Even when they went off to different locales, including the mountains, the duckling came along. Its droppings in bed with Bardot and Zagury did not amuse the poker-playing playboy.

Papa Bardot also came to Mexico armed with guidebooks, and father and daughter together got a feel for the country's history. Her outings with Pilou constituted enjoyable breaks in the action, a going home that sometimes works out later in life. Meanwhile, there were Brigitte's ducks, donkey, rabbit, et al., to worry about, and her feeling of inferiority to Moreau's Comédie française acting background. There were also hazards on some shoots, and Bardot had the more difficult and dangerous roles of the two Marias. At one

Bardot in her *Viva Maria* period, relaxing as usual with an animal in her arms.

point she sat on a rock, and the crew began gesticulating wildly; under the rock was a family of scorpions! At other times actors shot in rivers full of crabs and bloodsuckers, and even in shark-filled salt water, where one technician lost a leg. Deadly snakes, large spiders, crushing heat, the lack of potable water, forcing tooth brushing with Coca-Cola—these were some of the realities here.

At the end of shooting Bardot knew she couldn't take her duckling back to France on a plane, so she left it in a kind of hotel zoo, where it got itself whupped by rivals, ripping its "mother's" heart in two. That in turn provoked jealous attacks on the part of Bob—"me or the duckling" became his refrain. Minus the pet they finally flew back to Paris, which after Mexico, Bardot found gray, small-minded, and too chic. Guapa, however, was crazy to see her.

Off to Bazoches, she couldn't believe the redecorated results, including a swimming pool whose sketch she had sent from Mexico, modeled on one she had seen at Cuernavaca. She thought sadly of her "canard" and how it would have loved swimming in it.

Coming home also meant returning to painful thoughts of her growing but mostly absent son. Realizing he couldn't raise Nicolas in a proper manner, Jacques had decided to turn him over to his sister Evelyne, who had a large brood and was supposedly a good mother. She was, however, located rather far away, near the old family homestead outside Montpellier. Bardot found herself sickened by the move. Could they not have given the child to *her* mother? But of course there was ambivalence there, and Toty was already the caretaker of niece Camille. Bardot said on a number of occasions that she would have loved to be a mother, but knew that one couldn't change lovers so often, forcing a child to adapt to a kaleidoscope of home atmospheres. So she reluctantly agreed with Jacques' idea, knowing, however, that Nicolas would grow up deeply wounded.

Another surprise was the fact that her parents were in this era unceremoniously ejected from their Paris home at 1, Rue de la Pompe after 23 loyal years there. So Bardot procured them a new apartment on Avénue Paul Doumer at a whopping price, but still located near hers. The demi-ogres of her bourgeois youth turned out in old age to be wizards of Oz, harmless and powerless once pried out from behind screens that had given them their power, and with old repressions beaten back by a surging youth revolution.

Grandma Mamie was also installed on Paul Doumer in a main-floor apartment, where she could spy Brigitte's comings and goings through her blinds. She had long kept Dada as a quasi-slave, but due to her rheumatism, the old Italian *bonne* often dropped things, with Mamie barking in *Odd Couple* fashion that she would dock her pay for whatever was broken! In tears Dada confided her troubles to Brigitte. Somehow, she was stuck, having no social insurance for retirement at 65. So Bardot ended up killing with kindness, procuring Dada a studio apartment with TV, and Mamie her own place on Paul Doumer; however, bereft of the tonic of daily wrangles, each withered on the vine, and soon after separating, both passed away.

Bardot was at least more faithful to her elders than a mere sex kitten could be. When La Big, her one-time governess, began dying miserably on the Rue Legendre, Brigitte brought the feverish old woman to the apartment she had taken opposite hers at Doumer, empty since the departure of Nicolas and Moussia; and she cared for her for several years until her death in 1972. She also brought Great-Aunt Tapompon to the same quarter of town, the lady who had lost her only son.

Meanwhile, at La Madrague Bardot finally got real barriers installed, including walls protruding out into the Mediterranean, which had cost her much lobbying and provoked media protest about her supposed privilege. She says, however, that without them she would surely have left.

At La Madrague Jicky, Anne, and their son Emmanuel lived and thrived, and Jicky enjoyed painting there in the tonic air, and with verdant, hilly vistas over the bay. But then they decided to find a new home of their own, another disruption to Bardot, in a life replete with them. Jicky, more than Bob or her other lovers, had always been a kind of human guard dog, able to repel invaders attempting to snare under things on the line or enter the house. One was a jailbird whom Jicky patiently talked off the premises at four a.m.!

For the American premiere of *Viva Maria* Bardot found herself pushed into a first trip to the U.S., something she wanted to avoid. But Moreau was otherwise engaged, so it was up to Bardot to spread the publicistic magic. In December 1965 she left—with Bob, Jicky, Dédette, and Olga along to provide moral support. Arriving in New York for the first time can be memorable, but Brigitte was met by a battalion of journalists and an American public still quite mad for her. The crowds made her queasy, cameras flashed, questions flew out in English, and she wondered if she could stay the course here. Pasting an invariable smile on her face, she coached herself to be the sexy blond image people expected. Responses to questions at her first press conference still make good reading. Who was the stupidest person she had ever met? "You, for asking such a stupid question," replied Bardot. Favorite film? "My next one," she answered blithely.[5] Barricaded in a suite of the Plaza Hotel, with the telephone ringing off the hook and her agent Olga answering, the actress' nerves felt unsteady again.

Next day, while the rest of the group toured New York on foot, she had to stay in her room, where a supposed electrician came in, really a journalist. The day after, she went out to visit the Astor Theater, and crowds in the Times Square area seemed overwhelming. It all felt dangerous, and became exactly that when a photographer's flash exploded only inches from Brigitte's eyes, detaching a retina. This was her right eye, now bandaged in black, and since in her left one she had had only limited vision since birth, Bardot bestrode this New World colossus nearly blinded!

In Los Angeles, where dark glasses were more the norm, things improved a bit—she shook hands there with some American stars—but by and large still didn't see much. One moment she enjoyed was at the old hatchery of sirens like Lana Turner—Schwab's Drugstore. Then she, Bob, Jicky, and Anne made a clandestine getaway to Puerto Rico, with a decoy "BB" plane for New York confusing pursuing journalists. However, Puerto Rican misery, combined with an air-conditioned hotel room where one couldn't even open a window, failed to relax her. Back they all flew to New York, then came a quick change of planes, and on Christmas day, they were en route to Paris.

At home the French press made much of Bardot's putative conquest of America. As for her, she was happy to be back in the relative peace of Paul Doumer, with her Guapa, and a Christmas tree procured by her mother. But for New Year's it was off to Bazoches, and more turmoil. Here was the handsome French actor, Alain Delon, speaking seriously of euthanizing his German shepherd Charly, since he couldn't take him away on a day's plane ride. Feeling sorry for the animal, Bardot adopted him, but Guapa went crazy with jealousy. In the same period Bardot matched Moreau's Rolls with a new one of her own, but parking tickets on Doumer mounted precipitously. Then, off to ski in January at Méribel, with Madame Renée, Bob, Jicky, Anne, and their child, plus Charly, she met a politician on the slopes by virtue of the dog's penchant for biting skiers. Bardot found it odd that she ended up slathering mercurochrome on the bare leg of one Valéry Giscard d'Estaing; but it launched a solid and important political friendship, particularly given her coming transformation into a protectress extraordinaire of animals. In the late '70s Giscard would help Brigitte ban the importation of baby seal skins into France, and also stop the use of baboons being thrown at walls to test seatbelts. The friendship would only cool in the '80s due to their radically different positions on hunting.

It was now the heyday of the Beatles, with the counter-culture explosion around the corner, and Bardot starting to wane as a world commodity. The western masses found that sexiness could become part of everyday life, quite apart from Hollywood or Paris cinematic lifestyles. And while *Viva Maria* appealed to a number of French critics, and did well in Europe, it made less of a splash in the U.S. In my own case I remember going to it then, and rare in those days of still dependable mainstream flicks, found myself somewhat bored. Watching it over 30 years later was a different experience—Malle's marvelous attention to costumes and battle scenes, and to music of different varieties, truly admirable, compared to what we now generally get. In the 21st century the movie is watchable much of the way. One savors even the satirized soldiers serving a growing techno-capitalism (automobiles and such only for the rich) and dictatorial repression. Not to mention sober-costumed priests losing sway over peasants, defecting in droves to the two revolutionary Marias. The movie's most problematic quality is the way it falls somewhat between the stools of comic spoof and serious yarn.[6]

From this point on Bardot's film career gently wound down, even as her love life and attire were becoming at one with an increasingly liberated, risqué culture. Yes, one got engulfed in such tidal waves, rather like the Beatles, first blazing a path through the passes, only to find a throng jostling one off paved highways later in the '60s. And after a pretty good run of several years, Bardot's relationship with handsome Zagury began tottering as well.

Between Zagury and Brigitte's next serious relationship there was a short fling with her Paris dentist; but as the go-go '60s got into high gear, it was almost appropriate that her next real beau was a tenured playboy, Gunter Sachs. This shift came against the background of Zagury becoming a TV producer, including of Bardot, smoking cigars, setting up meetings, and beginning to bore her more of the time.

In May 1966 a brother-figure, Philippe d'Exea, drove Brigitte and Guapa in her Rolls down to sunny Provence, while Bob's sister followed in another car. With classical music, plus Beatles and Stones tunes filling the car, Brigitte soon grew happier. Arriving at La Madrague, she and "Phi-Phi" went off to dine at a restaurant they liked in the hill town of Gassin, occupying a table near a group of gorgeous young women and loud roués, among whom was Sachs. Here was the quintessential jetsetter, but also with deep roots in a more sober Central European tradition. Gunter's grandfather, Ernest Sachs, was a German engineer who around 1900 had invented the freewheel bicycle, allowing bikes to go downhill without the pedal winging away. Son Willy, Gunter's father, took the freewheel business and built up Fichtel and Sachs, branching out to more lucrative motorcycles and car parts. He also married Eleonore von Opel, cementing an automotive dynasty. But Willy and Eleonore split in 1935, and Gunter's mother sold off her Opel shares to General Motors, taking son Gunter Sachs von Opel to live with her in Switzerland. Here again was a mixed-up childhood—there as well in the cases of Vadim and Frey, in the sore thumb artiste of his family, Charrier, and in the cosmopolitan upbringing of Zagury. As usual, Brigitte eschewed caste-faithful, predictable types.

Gunter had studied math and art history at Lausanne University and learned to speak several languages well. He learned too to be at home everywhere and nowhere. In 1955 he married an Algerian French "pied noir," but during a routine back operation his wife developed a problem with the anesthetic and passed away—at 26. Gunter was left with a son, and an inheritance approaching 100 million dollars. A good businessman (he would diversify from the family's automotive concerns into both a clothing chain and film production), he was also a hedonist, and very eligible. He did all the things a noble playboy would do, especially showing a carefree attitude toward death. This was manifested in his taste for fast cars, motorboats, and bobsleds. He was also a zealous photographer, particularly of women. Perhaps he had come by his daredevil attitude honestly, as his divorced father ultimately committed suicide.

Bardot as Maria II and Jeanne Moreau as Maria I in saucy *Viva Maria* garb: from cabaret stars to revolutionaries!

Sachs was devotedly peripatetic, with sumptuous pads in London, Paris, Gstaad, and Lausanne, not to mention an estate back where it had all begun—in Bavaria. He knew the rich and famous, including the Kennedys (mainly Teddy). He had been seen with women like Tina Onassis, Marina Doria, a world water-skiing champion, and Persia's ex–Queen Soraya. The '60s word "jetsetter" seemed minted for him. You could find him one day in Manhattan, and the next in St. Moritz or Monte Carlo.

Now down in Bardot's bailiwick yucking it up with pals, Sachs and his noisy retinue got the attention of the adjoining table. Brigitte noticed Gunter, he noticed her, and it was the proverbial *coup de foudre* once again. Philippe d'Exea smoothed introductions, and Gunter came over to their smaller table, whisky in hand. Bardot liked his noble, tousled look, and his ways. She had been cut up in relationships and had done her share of gutting, too; but here she was, and here he was, and Gunter would soon romance her theatrically and outlandishly, in a unique way she had never known, and would never know again. On that very first night they went off to dance at a club till dawn, each driving a Rolls. Back at La Madrague Bob's sister was suspicious, and with reason.

Soon after their initial meeting, Sachs blew in off the ocean, and drove away a man with whom Brigitte was chatting. Other days he dropped myriad roses from a helicopter onto her property. Bardot recalls gathering them for hours from the bushes! His large yacht (*Dracula*) and fine cars were mobilized for the campaign. In Brigitte's home he would sometimes end an evening by shooting out the candles with an air rifle. A courting artiste, Sachs was perpetually gilding the lily in this domain. On one occasion he took Bardot to a restaurant where the owner had idiosyncrasies redolent of certain rock stars. For favored customers this proprietor would toss a few pieces of furniture into the fire. However, for the new couple this one romantic evening, he threw pretty well everything he had in there for kindling.

On another day in this over-the-top courtship Gunter sailed Brigitte around the Riviera on his yacht, then decided on a dress-down incursion into a Monte Carlo casino. The couple arrived tattered, windblown, barefooted, and in jeans, flouting dress codes. But who could refuse entry to such a pair? In several throws at the roulette wheel, Sachs pulled in a pile of lucre, though he was angered when the take was diminished by the house cut. A bit drunk, but ahead by over $100,000, the two rich bohemians left the casino.

Their Rabelaisian dating continued. Courtships generally involve men showing baubles, brains, brawn, soul to women—in whatever order. After a stint in Paris Bob arrived back down south with cigars stocked and TV shows planned, and Gunter gave Brigitte three days to make a choice between men. Bardot signed her television contract and Bob received his walking papers, returning to Paris for good. At a dinner party soon after, a triumphant Sachs offered the beautiful actress three platinum bracelets—one bearing 50 red rubies, a second with 44 of the finest diamonds, a third with seven blue sapphires, these hues all blending into French tricolor. He also offered three rings from Cartier and that night at La Madrague, asked for Brigitte's hand in marriage, which she accepted, as in a trance.

To dodge the media for such an event, Sachs thought of Vegas, where the great French singer-composer Charles Aznavour married his third wife in that period. Gunter's idea was to do it fast, and on the patriotic date of July 14, 1966. How could Bardot say no? She hadn't been with her man long enough to see any negatives! With no more than a month under their belt, one of the great female symbols of France patriotically assented. (Some would consider this an example of Franco-German cooperation at its finest.) But inside, Brigitte was a bit apprehensive. Sachs certainly planned like a German, but really, how well did she know him? His entourage of playboys and their playgirls, even when attenuated, also disquieted her.

Before taking their flight, the couple stopped at Gunter's sumptuous Paris apartment on the Avénue Foch. Here pictures of lovely women adorned the walls and vague perfume smells still scored the inside air. There was also an ersatz fire, and false book spines covering a bar. Was this really her genre? Was the woman who had searched all her life for simplicity going to find it with this man? The avuncular Vadim, still an intermittent advisor, had his doubts.

On July 13 Philippe d'Exea drove Bardot in her Rolls to Orly Airport, while Gunter and his pals took their own. From France it was 14 hours to Las Vegas in those days, but on the flight Bardot simply put her head on Sachs' shoulder, while he kept talking of his plans, including a honeymoon in Tahiti.

The plane landed in LA in the dark, but there was nonetheless a crowd of photographers to greet their arrival. Sachs put them all on the wrong path, giving the Beverly

Hills Hotel as the couple's destination, which it was—but not that night. The press corps waited patiently there, while Bardot and Sachs flew on Ted Kennedy's Lear jet to Vegas.

In a judge's chamber at 1:30 in the morning, July 14, 1966—the city of course had no normal sense of time—the celebrity couple exchanged "I do's," though Gunter later reran the ceremony for his friends' cameras! Nocturnal Vegas with its burping signs ushered them to the Hotel Tropicana, where they dined with friends and dropped coins in the slots, before retiring at four a.m. The European press went crazy. One journalist figured out that Bardot had gotten married every seven years—Vadim in 1952, Charrier in 1959, now Sachs in

Brigitte Bardot and Gunter Sachs, at the time of their hasty Las Vegas marriage of 1966.

1966. And the declining French Catholic Church found strength to critique Bardot's frivolous view of marriage.

The actress wasn't much impressed with her stay at a Beverly Hills Hotel bungalow, nor with Hollywood celebrities they met. As for Tahiti, she arrived there with something of the enthusiasm of a Bougainville, loving the smells and the gentle women she encountered. The Gunter magic was still working. They then traveled by seaplane to Bora Bora, wading into the water with valises on their heads. Here Sachs and a German-speaking owner of a hotel bungalow nattered into the night in a language Brigitte could never master, nor enjoy. As her new husband spent time drinking and playing chess with this fellow, she began realizing that he would always need male company, and that for him women were to a degree mere ornaments. Another eggbeater plane flight scared her, taking them to some atoll; then she shared a room with a half dozen of Gunter's hangers-on, cum insects! The honeymoon was spoiled as well by Brigitte's foot grinding into something sharp on the beach—coral or sea urchin—as well as by French paparazzi.

They next flew back to civilization in Acapulco, where photographers and journalists again abounded; and Bardot started hearing a sickening story that Gunter might have married her simply to win a bet. She began believing it, confiding in her friend "Phi-Phi," with the latter counseling a quick divorce in Reno. Brigitte cried; she still wanted Sachs desperately, which seemed to push him ever closer to his pals.

Brigitte returned with her husband to marital as well as career reality in a Paris that now felt a downer to her. The city soon enough became a backdrop for the couple's irreconcilable differences. Sachs liked the high life—big, brassy restaurants and night spots—while Bardot favored tried, true, and above all, simple bistros for intimate evenings, not to mention the simplicity of animals. He wanted her to move into his Avénue Foch apartment, and she demurred—only with a complete housecleaning of all feminine vestiges (photographs, intimate apparel, odors) would she even consider it. She never received a key to the place. They soon migrated down to Saint-Tropez, with his eternal posse of six buddies on hand, the ones who had made part of their honeymoon so cramped. Her *amazones* (Bardot's term for girl-pals) at La Madrague had to make room for these playboys. There were henceforth two Rollses parked in the driveway, and Gunter's chauffeur on the premises as well. In came his crystal—he wouldn't drink wine out of anything else—and white porcelain dishes. Kapi, the guard dog, kept nibbling at humans, while Guapa hid under armchairs. A partially rustic ambiance here suddenly became too glitzy. The telephone rang continually as though this were some Hollywood agency—calls that were almost all for Sachs.

At least an aged Louis Bardot finally got to meet his new son-in-law and try out some German with him. The snob in Toty was also gratified at the cachet of Gunter's lineage; here was someone finally on Brigitte's level.

But a playboy Gunter inveterately remained. On August 13 he set off for Paris, putatively to do business in a city that shuts down that month, while its occupants by the millions loll in the countryside, or by the sea. Alone on the Riviera Bardot had to suffer this touristic invasion, and the whole next day found herself highly irritated. In the evening at a restaurant in Phi-Phi's company she kept dialing Gunter's Paris apartment, failing, however, to reach him. She tried to have a good time, imbibed a good deal, but calling even in the wee hours produced no answer. A business meeting after midnight in a Paris August? Something didn't compute here.

Returning to La Madrague at dawn, she and Philippe decided on the spur of the moment to motor to Nice, then grabbed a seven a.m. flight to Paris. Arriving at 8:30 and taking a taxi to 32, Avénue Foch, where they paid and got out about nine, the manic Brigitte and Phi-Phi hastened upstairs and leaned on the doorbell. An astonished *maître d'hôtel* let them into the place. Brigitte marched directly to the bedroom, with Phi-Phi following—not only was it empty, but the bed was perfectly made, and there was no toothbrush or razor in the bathroom. Samir, Gunter's Lebanese secretary, put on a robe and tried to soothe his guests, and they decided to cool their heels. At ten a.m. a key turned in the door. Luckily Gunter arrived with no woman on his arm, but he was plenty tousled, and there was a telltale toiletry bag under his arm. He used what "business" alibis he could summon up, but Brigitte wasn't buying. She and d'Exea took the midday plane back to Nice, her brother-figure again broaching the idea of a quickie divorce. Having swum with one of the big sharks, Bardot now felt good and bitten.

But from that moment on she nursed the idea of revenge inside. Here was the time for Gunter to arrive back at La Madrague in ultra-theatrical style, descending to the ocean in a helicopter, throwing his valises into the water, then jumping in himself and wading ashore. From the start he tried to level with Brigitte, to the effect that he and she were adults, not of common clay. Protective Philippe steamed back at him, and perhaps even Gunter realized that it was time to try and "get real"—if only temporarily. He conceived the idea of removing his wife from tourist-ridden Saint-Tropez, in order to convey her up to the cool valleys of his family domain in Bavaria. She would then see where her husband had come from, and particularly, meet the one person around whom he had to toe the line—his authoritarian mother. Armed with his knowledge of German, Papa Bardot was also invited, along with two of Brigitte's girlfriends, and they all took a flight from Nice to Munich.

Despite being disgusted in Bavaria by all the hunting trophies she beheld on the walls—slain deer looking eerily alive—Brigitte found this area different from any she had ever visited; it made her feel very peaceful inside. Sachs' mother was a tough cookie, speaking no French, only German and some English. The day after her arrival Brigitte was fitted out in Bavarian Tyrolian garb. And around Mama her son became a little boy! The estate was huge, and as its lord, Gunter spent days combing hundreds of acres, checking on practical matters, and conversing with peasants.

As for Pilou, he was happy to wander about in pure country air with his daughter, all alone, and without Toty to offer her frequent two cents' worth. Being here with her father seemed to put Brigitte in touch with her past and roots.

But a long-distance call from Mama Olga brought her back once again to the film world. The biggest killer of her relationships would return to haunt the couple—the plague of apartness, endemic in a union of movie actress and jetsetting businessman. For Bardot was to start work in Scotland on *A Coeur joie* (*Two Weeks in September* and *Head over Heels* in English) on September 10, 1966. At the end of her Bavarian visit she watched lederhosen types slap themselves, and she quaffed beer, little realizing that this would be her last visit to this peaceful environment.

A quick trip back to La Madrague for its seasonal closing was followed by a short, unsatisfying stay in Paris, before departure with her friends Monique, as her movie double, Carole, also given a small part, and another, Sveeva, as her photographer—all to keep her company. Her last evening dining on the Avénue Foch, with Samir running the place, and female photos still adorning the walls made her anxious. Gunter asked Brigitte to stay over, but she was happy to regain Doumer, getting up at dawn for the departure. Phi-Phi drove her in the Rolls up through lush Normandy countryside to the boat, and away from a man he still considered beneath her. She and her girlfriends crossed the Channel, the English countryside stirred her senses, and then came an increasingly rugged northern landscape en route up to Scotland.

At the hotel there she met the movie's producer, Francis Cosne, and her agent, Olga. A telegram arrived from Gunter, and at one point he came up briefly, but left barely a day later. The filming wasn't much to remember, but Scotland gave Bardot pleasant feelings. However, back down in London for part of the shoot she saw a gorilla going crazy in a zoo cage and became depressed. She also had a brief affair there with a handsome Austrian-British singer, actor, and film critic, Mike Sarne, playing the role of her photographer in the movie. Sarne was devastated by Bardot and wrote about her—she often seemed to inspire men's words, songs, drama, or outlandish acts.

Back to Paris she went, where a truly outlandish Gunter now felt she shouldn't remain at Doumer anymore, scenting her ability to be swayed by others. Bardot left enough clothes at his Avénue Foch apartment so that she could spend one or two nights a week there. Demanding studio work on *A Coeur joie* was still going on, so she preferred to regain her own apartment at night, luxuriating in a bath, drinking champagne, lighting candles, hugging Guapa, and chatting with Monique, La Big, or Madame Renée.

Bardot as the model Cécile in a London scene from A Coeur joie (Two Weeks in September). (Francos Films, Les Films du Quadrangle, Les Films Pomereu, Paris, and Kenwood Films, 1966)

At Gunter's Foch pad there was often a formal dinner party, and after sweating at work all day, Brigitte found she disliked getting dolled up again, then listening to the crème de la crème sound off (Gunter's acquaintances ran from Dalí to the Rothschilds). Complications arose too when Monique, one of *her* team, fell for Samir. Her double now became a mistress of the house where she ought to be!

Consciousness of others' suffering often outbids one's own, and the suicide death of Raoul Lévy early in 1967 at age 44—a reaction to being dropped by his model girlfriend, Isabelle Pons—got to Bardot, now in her early thirties. So did further meetings with Jean-Paul Steiger at the studio, this time describing conditions at the Paris Humane Society. One day he showed her those conditions directly, and she cried and cried, impulsively opening up cages, letting a mob of dogs and cats stream out at her, then stuffing her "Noah's Rolls" with some en route for Bazoches. A half-dozen dogs and ten cats filled the luxury vehicle with their stink, and at her country place Bardot turned them loose. What a cinematic scene it became—cats climbing trees, testing their legs, and dogs yelping with joy. Bardot would soon be off on a crusade, publicizing Dickensian horrors of the S.P.C.A. (or in France, S.P.A.). It all presaged her final cut with the world that had given her such money and fame.

Finishing her shoot on *A Coeur joie* at Paris' Billancourt studio now seemed secondary, and indeed she had the S.P.A. ship a truckload of animals there, placing just about each one with a new owner. The last two dogs included one that reeked to high heaven, but a man working on the film reluctantly said yes, and would keep the pet another 15 years. Due to her media campaign on the S.P.A., adoptions went up generally in France, and Bardot also pushed for a more salubrious locale for the Paris branch. She herself took one limper out of a cage to La Madrague—another animal that would have a decade and a half left in him! This was the beginning of a new life—of making a difference when it came to the world's creatures in pain.

But Bardot was no more finished on screen than the Beatles of that time were on records. Just as they followed their "Yellow Submarine" era with classic rockers like "Back in the U.S.S.R.," so Bardot in *A Coeur joie* (1967) surprisingly shows herself at the top of her powers as an actress here. The script, Serge Bourguignon's direction, the production of Francis Cosne and one Bob Zagury, the casting of Bardot against Laurent Terzieff, a young man smitten with her in the film and threatening her boring but stable screen marriage—from start to finish, this movie (except for a plunk-a-plunka score featuring monotonous bass and xylophone) comes off as tasteful, if upstaged by *The Graduate* or *Blow Up* of that era.

A la *Blow Up*, Bardot's Cécile regains her intermittent trade of fashion model, with two weeks in London spent away from her publisher husband, a good but dour Parisian. The film then does what the French could do best then—dissects love and marriage in suitably aphoristic fashion. Played admirably by Terzieff, the smitten geologist seems both laconic and off the wall. The movie is truly romantic, and never would one hear Bardot's French more savorous, and of the earth, easily comprehensible to anyone with high school French. For a contemporary viewer, this Franco-British production will be a surprise, right up to the movie's conclusion at a London airport. As much as in any film she made, Bardot makes acting seem invisible, seamless, and easy here.

Her real life, however, remained a dissonant one, with nights in Paris spent at both Doumer and Foch, and with Monique now top female at the latter venue. Brigitte seemed ambivalent about this development: on one hand she found it galling that a provincial girl, formerly a fisherman's wife, had o'erleaped her to this social pinnacle; on another she was reassured having a pal of hers there. In the same era she made new friends of her own, preeminently Jean Bouquin, who threw her into a kind of a hippie mode that gained more French emulators.

Over the Christmas holidays of 1966-67 there was a trip to Gunter's Gstaad home, with Samir, Monique, and Guapa on hand; but Bardot preferred less fancy Méribel in the French Alps. At Gstaad the old demon of loneliness clung to her, as Gunter attacked ski hills from early in the morning, and of course had to be an expert at that popular '60s sport. They toasted New Year's at a chalet where deer ranged nearby, then began a year when the world seemed to be changing faster and faster around the celebrated actress.

Her dream of making Bazoches a kind of outdoor humane society got an early, rude puncture with the poisoning death of one of her adopted dogs, "Barbara." It sent her into a depressive spin full of tears and anger at the human race generally. Over the ensuing years, hunters and others in the area would gradually knock off the rest, though many more happy days remained to the dogs than would have been the case in cages.

Bardot (Cécile) and Laurent Terzieff (Vincent) on an impromptu screen trip up to seaside Scotland.

She also added two goats pried by Steiger from the abattoir. Bardot learned how intelligent goats were and started to figure that if people actually had to kill each animal they consumed, there might be a lot more vegetarians.

From Bazoches, which she departed with difficulty, it was back to Méribel in February—there had been a kind of contract with Gunter for half their alpine relaxation to transpire on his turf, half on hers. But the gulf was growing between the two, and it was not all his fault. For at Méribel they met eminent French rockers Johnny Hallyday and his wife, Sylvie Vartan, and when the latter announced her pregnancy, Gunter immediately wanted Brigitte to go that route as well. Instead she kept working the calendar to avoid having a child, probably thankful her husband was so often absent! She was emphatically against the baby idea, so Gunter ran off in a huff to another Swiss ski town he enjoyed, St. Moritz. By the end of February '67 Brigitte was back in Paris, with

Mama Olga having concocted a new screen project for her, a film adaptation of Poe stories called *Histoires extraordinaires*, one of the three to be made by Malle, and with the participation of Alain Delon. Shooting was to take place in springtime Rome on this film to be released in Britain as *Tales of Mystery*, and in the U.S. as *Spirits of the Dead*.

For the shoot Gunter impulsively rented the perfect apartment in Rome, where the couple could lavishly entertain. He loved the new and unusual, and given the wanderings of his childhood, found it easy to uproot on a regular basis. He enjoyed having Brigitte hobnob with the likes of Prince Rainier and Princess Grace. Too, he was now à la Zagury getting into showbiz, fancying himself a film-maker. While his wife was working on her part of *Histoires...*, Sachs was putting together a deal for *The Bet* with an American, Harry Matthews. In that film a playboy, played by Sachs' brother-in-law Patrick Bauchau, would seduce a covergirl, featuring Bardot. But it never happened.

In Rome Bardot learned again why she loved Italy, but Gunter wanted to advise on the present film as well—feeling that an eminent American actor of the Peck or Lancaster rank ought to be inserted alongside Delon to pep it up. Brigitte did not relish such interventions. The death of Catherine Deneuve's sister, Françoise Dorléac, in a car accident made her see the fragility of life, and she took a little revenge on Gunter with a young man named Pierre, involved in the Malle film. (It happened when Pierre was designated to drive Brigitte back to Paris.)

Her deal-making husband next wanted his wife to present one of the films he had gotten done at the May 1967 Cannes Festival. Sachs threatened divorce, and she was unmoved. Her personal life remained an unsettled jumble. Meanwhile, Jicky and Anne had had a second son, and Phi-Phi was in love with her married friend, Sveeva; and the entire western world was shaking aplenty.

Bardot then saw Zagury in conjunction with the TV show she had promised to do for him, and wondered now why she had moved onward and upward. She cried on Bob's shoulder and he came out to Bazoches for a poker weekend with Phi-Phi, Sveeva and the gang, while Gunter was off somewhere in Europe.

In the department of exes, Jacques Charrier remained in the picture, renting for a time within four kilometers of Bardot's Bazoches menagerie, and placing Nicolas sadly near her—sadly, because when she approached, she found a son who neither knew nor wanted to know her. To her chagrin she kept finding out that she wasn't part of his world, nor he of hers.

With her personal edifice crumbling, Brigitte now decided to give in to Gunter's ultimatum, for the alternative seemed to be more loneliness. She knew he saw other women, and though some of his best friends liked her, she realized they would all make poor substitutes. So she attended the Cannes Festival, where, as she had predicted, his film *Batouk* was not well received.

With Gunter life was becoming a succession of intermittent dates, such as on July 14, 1967, for their first anniversary. Count Sachs used the day for both a celebratory party at Maxim's in Paris, but also to publicize a group of his new boutiques! Bardot then accompanied her husband to Munich for the opening of an art gallery, and thence to Gstaad and St. Moritz for other business-pleasure ventures. A bit of summer remained at La Madrague for visits from Nicolas, who at least told his mother how beautiful he found her, and from Rolf, Gunter's son from a former marriage.

On September 28, 1967, Bardot turned 33, and was finding less and less enthusiasm for her métier. She liked singing better, cutting records not only in Paris studios, but in Spain and England. In Paris the boozing, poetic composer, Serge Gainsbourg, phoned her with material, and they got together and drank champagne, then made a record of her singing his song "Harley Davidson," went to dinner afterwards, took each other's hands under the table—and suddenly here was more than a spiteful little act of revenge. For Brigitte required the tenderness a helter-skelter Gunter hadn't time to give, and again, she fell deeply. Gainsbourg composed a racy song for her called "Je t'aime moi non plus," along with others. The two would then date all over Paris, with her dressing outlandishly. They hit Russian restaurants and even Maxim's, plus dance spots, and it was all bracing for an incurable romantic. Sitting close to each other in the studio and singing together, they cut "Je t'aime moi non plus." But when it came time to release the song as part of an album, an angry Gunter forced his wife to phone the record company at the last minute and have it deleted, something she would always regret doing, especially as the song later became a hit in other hands.[7]

On November 14, 1967, Bardot met Sachs against her will for his 35th birthday party at the Avénue Foch pad, relishing her delirious affair with Gainsbourg by comparison. But of course that love would also be doomed by the nature of the business to which she was still reluctantly committed. For Brigitte had signed on to do a western titled *Shalako* with the huge James Bond star of the era, Sean Connery, and shooting was set to begin in January 1968 in hill country around Almeria, Spain.

Gunter was still, however, trying to impress her, presenting her to bigwigs, and there were few she admired more than France's second-term president, Charles de Gaulle. She and Gunter were invited to the Elysée Palace on December 7 to meet le grand Charles, and instantly Bardot was slain—she found him authentic *vieille France*, redolent of her grandfather, Boum Papa, an orderly, rooted, strong man who was unique, yet iconically French. That night Brigitte was happy with Gunter on her arm and de Gaulle in rare form too. Yet again, she found herself torn between two lovers in the form of Gunter and Serge, two very different personalities, each with pluses and minuses.

Having gotten "Je t'aime moi non plus" off her new album, a jealous Sachs now pushed Brigitte to abandon her beloved Doumer apartment for a new one nearer to the Avénue Foch. Again, he gave her an ultimatum, threatening divorce, and Bardot essentially told him to go fly a kite.

Her Zagury-produced TV show airing January 1, 1968, and with an appearance by Gainsbourg, was a success—Brigitte needed no man telling *her* how to make it in show business. But a few days later it was off to Spain to work on *Shalako*—another brutal change in routines. In tears she beseeched Olga to extricate her from the project, but her tough agent retorted that the contract was signed and could not be cancelled. At the last moment before departure, Serge met Brigitte at Doumer as she was hastily doing up bags, they cut fingers together, and in blood she wrote "Je t'aime," with him adding, "moi non plus." Then they kissed, and she did not want to realize that this would be the end for them, leaving only tender memories.

Bardot recalls being led like a prisoner by Olga and Gunter to the plane and a film project that was useful for her jealous hubby, but which meant little to her. Over and over she had found happiness, then lost it. She certainly did not like the modern hotel in Spain, nor English-speaking technicians she couldn't understand, working on this movie, as well as two others being shot nearby. Bardot had trouble speaking English, and Connery's burry Scottish brogue was doubly incomprehensible to her. His real life baldness was also disappointing, though he seemed a nice man and definitely professional. She soon became teary and suicidally nervous here. Staying a day or two longer than planned to see her through, both Olga and Gunter soon decamped, the latter choosing to distract himself with a trip to St. Moritz for winter sports and perhaps other activities. Meanwhile, their pigeon was stuck, unable even to reach Serge by phone.

Up at six a.m. for work each day and home at eight in the evening, Brigitte was too tired, dusty, and dirty even to contemplate nocturnal revenge on her spouse. Instead, a leisurely bath, champagne, and yaks with Gloria and Monique till as late as two a.m. somewhat soothed her. The nearest she came to any male consolation was with Stephen Boyd on the set, becoming a kind of hugging buddy. Pictures, however, hit the press, and again Gunter called for divorce—in actuality, she didn't come close to an affair here, unable to understand swaths of Boyd's English. Life was certainly ironic, for her friend Monique was busy at the time having an *unpublicized*, real affair with Andrew Birkin on a neighboring set! When Birkin's 18-year-old sister Jane, a willowy young lady with an illegitimate baby, arrived, and brother and sister then flew back to Paris, little did Brigitte realize that this Jane would meet Serge, and that she and he would later make "Je t'aime..." a hit. The ironies came thick and fast.

Gunter then wanted Brigitte to take a few days off from *Shalako* to come up to St. Moritz, which she did, flying from Marbella to Geneva; but she found that his motivation included showing her off to the Shah of Iran and his wife, whose astrological signs happened to be the same as Gunter's and Brigitte's. All day long Gunter skied with gorgeous blonds in the near vicinity, and Brigitte left a day early, happy to get back to her work-family in Spain. She was not enamored of movie scenes where she had to mount horses, but it went with the territory.

An aside on this era of making a western in Spain with the likes of Connery and Bardot seems in order, especially given the imminent vogue for Italian "spaghetti westerns." America of the late '60s was getting appropriated abroad, rather as late Rome became more diffused as it declined. Simultaneously, the vogue of westerns in the States itself was pretty well used up—it had been a much more alive phenomenon in the '50s. Instead, the U.S. was now having a massive *crise de conscience*, trying to join "intellectual" Europe. American hippies and/or university types were questioning pretty well everything about their country, beginning a great loosening of traditions that would persist to the present. Bardot and Connery were thus interpreting an American mythology and outlook that had all but vanished.

Back to Paris after the wrap for Guapa's licking, rollicking greeting, and thence to Bazoches to cavort with her menagerie, Bardot was clearly dimmed by yet another love loss. Gunter was still trying to make the great film, and wanting to con her into doing things she didn't wish to do. Sorely desiring some French relaxation, she instead found herself flying with her husband to Beirut. The atmosphere of Lebanon didn't entrance her, and a cruise on board the *Vadura* was even worse. Overwhelmed by waves, the ship and its occupants had to be rescued on the high seas and taken back to Beirut. She really didn't enjoy this supposedly romantic trip, and was happy to get back home.

It was the spring–summer of 1968, a year of serious campus revolts both in America and at home in Paris, where the Sorbonne would be shut down by huge protests. Everything seemed to be changing radically about her. The Catholic Church, surging into modernity, lost the power that had for so long kept people in check and given them something to grapple with; French was vanquishing Latin, priests were seen in casual garb. It all seemed excessive for Bardot, whose own excesses had always been balanced by rooted ballast she never fully discarded.[8]

Gunter and wife next spent time in Rome, but unable to sit still, he took off for the Canary Islands with Samir, leaving Monique and Brigitte guarded by his chambermaid Margaret. A vengeful Brigitte hung out a bit with a producer, though without much feeling. One morning she found Margaret spying from behind a door as she left her and Gunter's bedroom. The chambermaid mumbled something about checking her master's clothes, but Bardot's anger flared up, particularly given that her husband hadn't telephoned and was probably enjoying himself more than she was! The room was henceforth off limits to the maid. Gunter sent a sharp letter reprimanding his wife, telling her that until she and Monique left, he wasn't coming back. She looked at her wedding rings adding up to red, white, and blue, finding them utterly devoid of meaning.

She, Sveeva, Carole, and Monique then packed bags for a move to a little island near Ostia. Here there were no cars, except for a taxi, and the absence of electricity or running water threw her back to another century. Brigitte, however, found accommodations too crowded for four women, and with two of their male companions on hand as well, so she took off alone in a peasant's cart to rent a room from a widow in the middle of the island.

Back in Paris once again, she felt plainly rootless. In summer it was down to Saint-Tropez with the *amazones* in her white Rolls, and on July 7, 1968, she threw a big party full of psychedelic lights and rivers of champagne, and she and girlfriends dressed in provocative outfits. Jicky and Anne came as gypsies, as did the French record producer Eddie Barclay. Hollywood's Darryl Zanuck was there, along with reporters—for once they were welcome, as Brigitte wanted Gunter to hear about her good times. A bunch of playboys from another summer villa were recruited to court her women friends—Italians who gave a different flavor to the place than would the Teutonic Sachs. One became Bardot's escort for the rest of the summer, a man nicknamed Gigi.

On July 14 Bardot and her *amazones* did what Frankie Ford had advised in a '50s hit—they took a sea cruise, with the magnate Gianni Agnelli escorting them to the island of Sardinia. Back at La Madrague August dragged, and Alain Delon, recently separated from his wife Nathalie, came to crash for a while in a separate cabin on the beach, while Bardot continued keeping company with Gigi. By September, however, Gigi was gone, as were most of her gal-pals. Brigitte and Sveeva, the latter recently separated from her husband, cried together at night. Something about the whole era was winding down for the actress—akin to a tape recorder going backward. Over and over her life seemed to be hitting a cul de sac of "been there, done that," and she was now being bypassed, scooped in so many ways by a cultural mainstream moving from one exciting social phenomenon to the next, kicking over the traces, ideals, and norms of an old civilization found wanting!

5

Playing Out the String

GUNTER AND BRIGITTE REMAINED APART as she promoted *Shalako*, a commercial bust in the making, at a variety of European locales. And this time the German playboy really meant it about divorce, though it wouldn't be finalized until the fall of 1969.

Oddly, *Shalako* is another of those films that plays better in the 21st century than many more celebrated offerings of its era. Who knows what will last? For example, try watching the once thrilling *American Graffiti* (early '70s) today, when nostalgic oldies have been so overplayed. By contrast, *Shalako* (based on a Louis L'Amour novel) can interest any contemporary viewer who isn't too cynical. Starring Connery in buckskins as Shalako Carlin (an Apache first name), it is a western that persuades, and no "send-up" à la *Blazing Saddles* of the next decade.

European and British aristocrats, of whom Bardot plays one of the former, are on a hunting safari in late 19th-century New Mexico, promoted by a blackguard (Bosky Fulton), played by Stephen Boyd. A fine musical score throbs danger when the Apaches are angered by violation of their sacred grounds. Warned by Shalako that one couldn't break treaties with impunity, and that the Apaches would attack, the aristocrats nonchalantly vote to remain, and soon come the cut guard dog's throat, war cries, the flit of nocturnal arrows into backs, and a number of deaths.

Shalako returns to rescue Countess Irina (Bardot), the Baron von Hallstatt (Peter Van Eyck), who wants to marry her, and a few others. They make it away, climbing a mountain, with the Baron's rope technique from his Jungfrau days a plus. The blackguard Fulton also leaves on a stagecoach with a British India veteran's young wife, Julia; but the coach is attacked, and while Fulton slips away, Julia plays dead, until an Apache puts sand in her mouth as a test. Then she is passed around in a circle, clothes begin to be ripped off, and when she tries to buy freedom with diamonds, she is thrown to the ground and fed her jewelry, which kills her.

In a scene from *Shalako*, Sean Connery as Shalako Carlin shows the ropes in the Wild West to the European Countess Irina, played by Bardot. (Kingston Films, Dimitri de Grunwald Productions, 1968)

The score shifts back to romantic, as Connery, Bardot, and the Baron make it to the top of their mountain, emphatically no Jungfrau! While the Baron guards against the imminent nocturnal arrival of pursuing Apaches, the countess and Shalako embrace, and more seems a possibility for these two lone wolves from different civilizations. Then the Indians attack, and the climactic scene has buckskinned Connery in a one-on-one fair fight with the heir to the Apache throne. When he has the upper hand and is about to kill, he is called off by the old chieftain-father, asking for all bloodshed to cease. He obeys, he and the remnant of the European hunting party ride away, and at the film's last moment one sees Countess Irina on her white Arabian turn off with Shalako—old and new worlds melding.

All sorts of mythology here, to be sure; but again, a fine tribute to America, particularly by the British studio people, screenplay writers, and not least, an accomplished director, Edward Dmytryk. A Canadian of Ukrainian background, Dmytryk had had a meteoric rise in Hollywood in the late '40s, then was hauled off to Congressional committees for alleged Communist sympathies, and given a six-month sentence in federal prison. His comeback films included *The Caine Mutiny* (1954) and *Raintree County* (1957), and his tasteful direction here helps make *Shalako* a more enduring film and Bardot vehicle than generally thought.[1]

In her real life of the time—far messier than another of her unaffected performances on screen—Brigitte had meanwhile met a couple of men to help fill the Gunter slack. One was her sailing instructor Eric Tabarly, who had sailed across the Atlantic four years earlier. She truly enjoyed the time she spent at Tabarly's sailing school in Saint-Raphaël on the Riviera, learning to tack, etc.[2]

A more serious male companion at first didn't seem prepossessing at all. Patrick Gilles was a 23-year-old student and sometime actor whom Bardot met in September 1968, when her friend, Florence Grinda, asked if she could put him up along with a buddy at La Madrague. At first Sveeva and Brigitte simply had young pals on their hands, and nothing more. The *copains* accompanied Bardot to a world premiere of *Shalako* occurring on her birthday, September 28, 1968, in Hamburg. Along with them came Phi-Phi d'Exea, Florence, and her German boyfriend. They then attended a big party at the von Bismarck family castle, but Bardot slept alone and cried, while Gilles roamed around till dawn, mainly to have a gander at whores of the seaport city, displayed, as in Amsterdam, through department store–type windows.

Back in Paris Bardot gave this unardent Patrick walking papers, but he surprised her by tardily coming to his senses and falling for her. For a whole week the couple stayed in bed at Paul Doumer, letting the rest of the world take care of business; and for the next two years Brigitte would go on another wild, passionate rollercoaster ride, a very physical love in this case. In one picture of the era she is the older Cher type clad in leather and matching her young beau's own leather garb. The two lovers attended the Paris opening of *Shalako*, but eluded gossip-meisters and the beginning of colder autumn weather by flying off to the Bahamas.

There they passed their time in an idyllic bungalow by the pellucid sea on something appropriately called Naked Island. And indeed, Brigitte and Patrick went natural virtually all day long, a vogue that would sweep European beaches in the coming decade. Young Gilles also initiated her into his favorite sport, golf, still almost unknown in France. Phi-Phi, Jicky, Gloria, et al., added to a jolly atmosphere, grilling lobsters (later taboo to Bardot), and Philippe got a little motorboat, so she and her bronzed god might explore the area. However, at one point they were stuck in a bad storm, the motor killed, it was raining cats and dogs, and Phi-Phi had to send out a rescue crew. One result was Bardot's bronchial cough necessitating flown-in antibiotics, and the next day she took a Cessna ride to Nassau, where the doctor gave her an injection.

She went on to see another doctor in New York, and this time got to walk the Big Apple with Patrick in relative anonymity; her days of being mobbed were finally done. Looking up at skyscrapers, the two lovers toured the Bowery and Wall Street, but Brigitte still found Manhattan anything but her dish. Invited to the Plaza, she was ejected for wearing pants! The couple finally flew back to Paris.

Bardot of course found aspects of Patrick young and immature, and perhaps predictably, Gunter had himself moved on to a Scandinavian woman 15 years *his* junior. On December 11, 1968, Brigitte publicly announced the end of her marriage, though it was not ended in court until almost a year later. That Christmas of 1968 Patrick wanted to spend time in the Alps, so reluctantly she went off with him and some friends to the French ski resort of Avoriaz. Crunching the slopes all day, and at night, surer and surer of himself in the clubs, Patrick certainly appealed to the bunnies, and Bardot felt sick with jealousy. As 1969 dawned, that jealousy began boiling over, and at one point there was a fight with punches thrown and black eyes the result. Brigitte again gave Patrick walking papers, then spent several days stuck by the telephone, hoping he would call her. And one day he did come back, rose in hand, swearing to be good, and the love, or whatever it needed to be called, came back as well.

Both in the South of France and in Paris the couple went out a lot, and Patrick always wanted Bardot to dress in a provocative manner. At the Chateau of Verrières they met the Gaullist Minister of Culture André Malraux, once an important French intellectual, but by this time a drugged disappointment to them. There were also weekend excursions in the Sologne, though Brigitte loathed the hunting for which that region was renowned. The couple restricted themselves to walking in the forests.

Then, in the tranquil surroundings of Bazoches Bardot read scripts for her next two films, *Les Femmes* and *L'Ours et la poupée* (*The Bear and the Doll*). Bazoches was actually no paradise, for there was still a congeries here of animals, urine odors galore, shredded chairs; and the dead countryside began to repel a stir-crazy Patrick. Fleas made him scratch continually, and those that jumped on his white jeans left marks when splatted. He also kept bumping his head on the low ceilings. And the place's current *gardien* was in turn scandalized by this young man and took off.

One Monday morning back at Doumer in Paris Brigitte found Pat himself gone with most of his clothes and *her* Austin! He had also tried unsuccessfully to obtain spending money from her banker. Over and over she had set the table for men, who then took advantage. Her gal-pals were now widely dispersed, some because of amorous involvements. Sveeva had a new baby, Monique was in Rome with one Mario, and most weren't available to accompany Brigitte to the Méribel chalet she had rented for Patrick. Angry, she emptied the cupboards of his remaining things, sending them to his parents, and decided to inform the police about his theft of her automobile. Some young, would-be composers got in touch with Bardot, but none was a Gainsbourg. Fledgling movie producers also asked her out—a dinner here, a lunch there, which she used to fill time separated from Gilles. Some kid drove her to the Alps in a Ferrari, but en route her tears flowed plentifully for Patrick.

Pure-aired Méribel, however, cheered her, with Jicky and Anne on hand—friends who still represented her most dependable human currency. Jilted in love, Carole also arrived, stuffing herself with food, and Madame Renée provided good soup. At a Courchevel party with Carole—taking place at the Club Saint-Nicolas run by her friend Jacqueline Veyssière—Bardot heard of a young man named Patrick tooling about the area in an Austin, and skiing at Val d'Isère. With no less an alpine eminence than Jean-Claude Killy accompanying her, Brigitte went off to check out the story—and indeed, found Patrick devouring the slopes, accompanied by tanned *skieuses*.

Somehow Bardot pried him away from that scene, and she and Gilles eventually made their way back to Paris in the Austin, though at one point diligent police stopped them—for "stolen car" plates. In Paris Patrick got his things from his parents and moved back in to Doumer, as though nothing had occurred. But he still wasn't crazy about the place, nor about Madame Renée, Guapa, and others there. As for Toty, she considered him a gigolo pure and simple, and even Jicky and Anne, normally tolerant, could not bring themselves to like him, either.

Patrick next pushed Brigitte into a North African–Saharan trip, to which she acceded, but which didn't really please her. Mama Olga meanwhile was beating the drums for more movies, worried about her star's declining ability to bring in francs. Bardot was heartily sick of the work involved in film-making, but in March 1969 began shooting *Les Femmes*, with Patrick gaining a small part as Bardot's fiancé dropped for a more fascinating writer. During long work days she still had fears that he would cheat on her, and indeed, he pulled yet another disappearing act. On returning, he triumphantly played on Brigitte's masochism by announcing that he had slept out on her and if things didn't improve, why, he would do so again! A fight followed, again including fisticuffs, until Brigitte was able to call Jicky, who arrived to continue punching at an unclad Patrick! Her concierge ended up calling the police, and when they arrived, she rustled up a top and pants for the young man. Her friends told the 34-year-old Bardot that she was making herself a fool over this truculent pup.

The year 1969 was a bumpy one for Brigitte. She didn't like *Les Femmes*, and with good reason: this Jean Aurel film features a writer (Maurice Ronet) whose sole subject is the women he has known, and who hires Bardot as his secretary on a train to Rome. She elicits and types his turbulent memories (cum flashbacks)—of keeping women from the altar and hurting both himself and them; but this beautiful steno predictably becomes another entanglement, and in the end, a new one allows him to please his publisher and deliver his book, including the story of his breakup with Bardot's Clara.

Her actual amorous existence was in similar chaos. But she did vote for de Gaulle, a throwback to a vanished France, in a post–May Events referendum he narrowly lost; and France's last monarchial figure then announced his dramatic departure from the political scene. Meanwhile, the latest *gardiens* at animal-filled Bazoches quit! Trying to find appropriate replacements would be an exhausting process for years to come. Bardot also went on a TV show with her former lovers and famous singers Distel and Bécaud, but both seemed into themselves, as did the groupies surrounding them.

Patrick and Brigitte were again separated, but scuttlebutt had it that he was lonely in Saint-Germain and afraid to call her. Maria Schneider, the illegitimate daughter of Daniel Gélin, whom Bardot put up at Doumer, urged her to get in touch with him. The three of them (Bardot, Schneider, and Patrick) then ended up doing the jerk at Paris nightclubs.

The Bear and the Doll (shot through that Woodstock summer of 1969) was a welcome cinematic shift of gears, a farcical comedy pairing Brigitte with Jean-Pierre Cassel for a few days' shooting in Paris, then the lion's share in Normandy countryside. Bardot got on well with everyone in a new film family, Patrick was by her side, and had another small role; and just as it all appeared to be drawing to a close—i.e., her movie star existence—she seemed to be finding herself. For once Bardot hated to wrap, but she did make long-term friendships among the film's cast and crew.

This is *not*, however, a picture that bears watching today! At the outset the supposed comedy made by Michel Deville and Nina Companeez features Rossini's overture to *Barber of Seville*, a scampering flute announcing classical lightheartedness, later to be alternated in the film with dated rock. Cassel's Gaspard is a nerd with thick glasses living in a farmhouse and playing cello in a Paris orchestra, while Bardot's Felicia is a spoiled, rich, multi-divorced model in the go-go capital. They bump into each other via a car accident, and then comes a night of stubborn one-upmanship, marked by stomped

Jean-Pierre Cassel as the cellist Gaspard and Bardot as the wealthy, spoiled Felicia, during a night of screen one-upmanship in *L'Ours et la poupée* (*The Bear and the Doll*). (Parc Films, Marianne Productions, 1970)

eyeglasses, spilled inkwells, thrown-away keys, smashed vases, logs dropped on feet, more smashed car fenders, and flip lines that bring nary a laugh. Finally, on a pretty morning the couple runs to a field, sings and dances, and embraces; and the movie blessedly ends! All this feels ultra-stale, though Brigitte, wearing both elegant and *echte* '60s attire, looks suitably beautiful here.

Returning to Paris after the wrap, and to Bazoches for a check of her menagerie, she then drove with Patrick down to Saint-Tropez. It took her a while to get Normandy's sweetness out of her system—its apple trees, and especially, that family feeling on the set. On the Riviera Papa Louis, no longer the grim Paris bourgeois, was tooling around the coast on a sailboat. In Normandy Patrick had been on the straight and narrow, but here in the sun he quickly located another young female and pulled another disappearing act. Again, Brigitte was devastated. Another young man tried to take over, but waterskiing in too shallow water, the would-be suitor smashed himself up, losing teeth in the process.

In autumn 1969 it was back to Doumer, and a returned Patrick was now grousing that a larger, classier apartment would bring the couple more happiness. A more up-to-date Rolls would help too, he felt. Gilles also joined the Saint-Nom-la-Bretèche golf club, extremely recherché. Bardot won a prize for her latest film, but the Tout Paris round rapidly tired her.

At Christmas she and Master Gilles went to the ski area of his choice—Avoriaz—

and she met Papillon (Henri Charrière) there, whose best-seller she esteemed. However, the death of a friend, Lina Brasseur (from viral hepatitis), then of Mamie in January 1970 depressed her again. In Paris Toty and Brigitte emptied Mamie's apartment and Brigitte cried, seeing all the old photos, etc. They were helped out by Tapompon and Dada, the latter also not long for the world. Bardot was starting to see her own mortality on the horizon.

To bring up her spirits Phi-Phi d'Exea accompanied her and Patrick back to the Bahamas, but there, she became deathly ill with fever—doubtless owing to hepatitis she had probably caught from Lina Brasseur over Christmas. Was *she* now going to leave this mortal coil? Bardot was groggy the entire plane flight back to Luxembourg, then on the next one to Paris; and at Paul Doumer she felt death approaching, while her mother and a doctor attended to her. She lost a lot of weight, got the mumps as well, but somehow pulled through. A long, tough recovery ensued, and the aging film star didn't really emerge from her cocoon until appearing on a TV show of April 17, 1970.

Though *Les Femmes* hadn't made it at the box office, *The Bear and the Doll* did well—at least in France; but Mama Olga remained concerned. At the outset of the Me Decade Bardot was now handed a script for a comedy with Annie Girardot, and by the end of May 1970 began work on *Les Novices*. The scriptwriter Guy Casaril had seen a group of nuns in habit running to the sea and changing into swim suits, and had gotten the idea for a movie involving a runaway nun, who slips away from the others while swimming. This movie has a peaceful, easy feeling (as the Eagles would soon sing); and it's also unique in Bardot's film career for a variety of reasons. Most centrally, it is a female buddy film (Bardot co-stars here with Girardot, and not once does she have to neck with some heavy or drop all her clothes). If one wants to be picky, Bardot as the runaway Sister Agnès, filching perfectly fitting togs from a *cabane* by the Breton ocean, taking off on a motorbike, and leaving black-clad "penguins" frantically looking for her at the beach, seems a little beautiful for a nun! Once in Paris she finds herself over her head, getting into an accident with her bike, but nurtured by both a stray dog and a fast-talking whore let out at the police station where they are discussing the accident report. Girardot as the tough but good-hearted Paris hooker putting up Agnès at her place works perfectly with a more serene but klutzy Bardot. In the first half Bardot has few lines, yet her acting is marvelously funny as her character attempts a variety of trades. One involves a side-splitting coaching job from Girardot, teaching in an oddly Catholic, military manner how to walk, talk, twiddle the purse in boots, and get clients as a prostitute. But Agnès scares them off by her clumsiness, all but a kindly old man she couldn't think of having for her first time; and a sadistic American who nearly beats her up in a hotel room, until her savvy dog brings back her mentor to save her. Then comes comical ambulance-driving for Agnès, and the use of that ambulance for Girardot's *métier*; and with money gained, acquisition of a newer one. When the cops get on the scent, the pair take off for the provinces, and at one point are waved over by more police, but only to use the ambulance in order to spirit a pregnant woman to a hospital. Naturally she bears her child right there in the whored-up interior! On to Brittany, and from the title, viewers guess where the pair will finally get refuge, and who will become the next novice. This time indeed it's Bardot coaching Girardot in crossing herself, and François de Roubaix' fine music takes the picture to its close. Bardot loved working with Girardot, but found the movie's shooting atmosphere more difficult than it appears to a viewer. The director finally had to be changed midstream—Claude Chabrol taking over from Casaril—yet somehow, this one works.

Having as usual made her acting look easy, Brigitte *was* tired winding up the film, while Patrick took good care of himself playing tennis and swimming at expensive clubs. The death of Guapa at Bazoches coincided with the movie's wrap, and for Bardot represented a real loss. And Patrick took off for a while once again. Brigitte found Doumer a downer now, and finally decided on modernizing another apartment with a gorgeous view on the Boulevard Lannes. Money poured out in a steady stream as she changed architect a couple of times; then when she descended to La Madrague for some sun before starting her next film, Patrick pushed for redecoration there, too. La Madrague obviously needed a pool (though Bardot had always found the Mediterranean sufficient for her needs); it also required central heating, though to that point she had never roosted there in winter. Plus it needed bigger and better bathrooms and dressing rooms. Reluctantly, she committed herself to the transformation, and would see it all done by March 1971, permitting her in the long run to stay there virtually year-round.

Her new film-in-the-making, *Boulevard du rhum*, set in the Prohibition era, starred Bardot as Linda Larue, a 1920s movie star courted by a rum runner. In the movie she played opposite a French heavy, Lino Ventura, whom she found difficult to figure out, and shooting began from mid–September 1970 in Mexico and British Honduras, with Patrick not bothering to show up until November. (Brigitte was starting to miss him less and less anyway.) A coup de grâce came when he informed her with cynical smile of de Gaulle's passing on November 9, 1970, as though it were an event of no more importance than a tennis match. For Brigitte this was the death of family—and more, the death of a France now turning toward pornography, drugs, and other things that outdid her own revolt against tradition.

Still skinny from her illness, Bardot shot parts of *Boulevard* back in Paris studios, before a return to Mexico. At Christmas Patrick left her alone again, enjoying himself on the slopes of Chamonix, so she spent time with her family, before departing to Mexico. She was getting sick of all this travel, but Patrick flew over with her and they toured the country again. Back to the Paris of early 1971 and once more, Patrick was quickly off to the Alps to ski, leaving Brigitte with grim money realities in the capital. Though recently selected as the model for the new bust of Marianne, France's female symbol, this Marianne had to take care of much business. The Boulevard Lannes apartment was costing plenty, and there were numerous checks to sign for La Madrague, and she now remembered her father's agony getting his monthly nut during the war. Bazoches also cost her refurbishing cash. Trying to forget both these financial woes and her ever-vanishing Gilles, Bardot hit some Paris night spots, and had a brief reunion fling with the visiting American actor Warren Beatty. (They had met earlier in the decade, and surprised Jane Fonda by not needing her fix-up attempt of 1967.)[3] Brigitte checked out some other fellows, but nothing really clicked. She was certainly tired of poker nights with Jicky and Madame Renée.

So it was now off to the Alps herself, not so much to chase down Patrick, but simply to change venue. Bardot went to the ski area she liked, Méribel, then visited the Club Saint-Nicolas in Courchevel, where Jacqueline Veyssière had a handsome Alsatian for a barman, Christian Kalt, also a sometime ski instructor. At the club Bardot asked Kalt for what the French call "un slow," but employers had warned him that working and dancing didn't mix. However, a couple nights later he asked Jacqueline if he might indeed dance with Bardot and this time received the green light. In the daytime as well they continued seeing each other, and he came over to Méribel. He too was ten years Bardot's junior, but a bit deeper, she felt, than Patrick. Or was that simpler? She wasn't quite sure.

Either way she spent nights with him at his studio apartment, but was put off by the presence of his assistant barman. Christian finally resigned his job and came to Paul Doumer in Paris, replacing Patrick's expensive togs with his own more ordinary and fewer ones. When Gilles came back with bouquet in hand, Brigitte coolly informed him that his spot was taken.

For Easter of 1971 Christian wanted to travel to Saint-Tropez and introduce Brigitte to his beloved mother and father at Cannes. Her old Rolls was sold, and the new one Patrick had her buy from Charles Aznavour was in the garage, so they took a train ride, and her Morgan followed on another train. La Madrague was still getting final touches, impelling the couple to stay for a while with Jean and Simone Bouquin. They then checked out her property, where the dogs were crazy to see her, including a limping one nicknamed Talleyrand after the club-footed priest-politician.

More than Patrick, Christian fit in well with all these animals, and a simpler version of life. Tired of the nightclub scene, he didn't need much more for entertainment than his sport magazines and televised matches. And Bardot tried to accommodate, feigning interest in statistics, in games won and lost. When she tried to talk culture, however, it fell on dead ears. "You can't have it all," as she notes, and it would make another good title for her life's story.[4]

As La Madrague's remodeling neared completion, the couple made do with inconveniences, but Christian certainly enjoyed the new pool. Returning to Paris for last touches on *Boulevard...*, Bardot also drove work on the Lannes penthouse to its finish, growing to love what she saw, including a canopied bed worthy of Old Regime royalty, a large circular bath, and a fine view of the Bois de Boulogne. It wasn't quite ready, and oddly, Christian would have been well satisfied with Doumer. The couple spent long spring weekends at Bazoches to see the lilacs or apple trees flower, and friends visited, and she recalls a feeling of contentment.

Again, she had no interest in going off to Spain to shoot her next flick, *Les Pétroleuses* (*The Legend of Frenchie King*), with a co-star some called Italy's Bardot, Claudia Cardinale. Here was another western, supposed to be set in an originally French town in Texas of the late 19th century called Bougival Junction. Bardot and Kalt, along with Sveeva, took the Aznavour Rolls down to Spain for the shoot, and met the film's producer there, Francis Cosne. Working in hot Sierra country near Madrid during this summer of 1971, Bardot grew to like Cardinale very much. But news of the death of Dada on July 10, her second mother, knocked her for another loop, and film or no film, she felt she had to fly home to bury her at Bazoches.

Returning to movie-making was a jolt, and Bardot still hated obligatory riding scenes, some on a bucker obviously benefiting from stunt help. Christian then developed terrible stomach pains, and she held his hand till past midnight in a clinic, where he underwent an emergency operation for peritonitis. He wanted to go back to his mother in France and Brigitte began to see patterns here—how she chose men who required pampering, but who could never dependably support her in return. The film, too, became more difficult, with a realistic fight between her and Cardinale leading to actual shiners and split lips. By the end Bardot had a feeling of true admiration for Cardinale, though she wouldn't see her again until the '90s.

Back on the Riviera Brigitte found Christian recovering, showing her his huge scar; then the couple went up to Paris, ready to move into the Boulevard Lannes place—and Bardot simply couldn't do it! A true creature of habit, she slept a last night on a mattress at Doumer. Her mother helped with the final, wrenching move, while Christian sat on a couch reading his sports publication, *L'Equipe*. Bardot finally waved good-bye forever to 71, Avénue Paul Doumer.

Human prices to be paid revealed themselves once again. A valuable and stable Madame Renée found that the move to Lannes was too much for her to bear, so she resigned. Frantic, Brigitte promised her gobs of potential cash, but Renée's Norman stubbornness prevailed.

Poring over domestics' resumés (as in Maugham's classic story "The Treasure") yielded no treasure at all; and selling Doumer was difficult, because La Big, still anchored there and refusing to leave, abused prospective buyers. Brigitte's bank accounts were dwindling, and in a long succession, Christian was no earner. Finally, Brigitte put La Big in a clinic for a two-day checkup, and she and another woman moved all her things, plus her cat Félix, into Dada's old digs.

But with the indispensable Madame Renée gone, and Christian riveted to the sports page or to a TV showing sporting events, Bardot found herself crying again. She finally located a *maître d'hôtel* to try and fill Renée's shoes, one who loved to ogle Christian! Tiring of all these changes, Christian eventually went back to his bar in the Alps, and Brigitte let the fussy *maître d'hôtel* set a new tone in the place.

Traveling to Méribel for Christmas to spend some time with Christian and ring in 1972, Bardot found yet again that her males were slippery commodities to hug, for Christian tended bar in Courchevel from about five p.m. and didn't leave until as late as four in the morning. If the weather was bad, he simply stayed at the old studio apartment he had occupied with his friend, rather than drive over to Méribel. If he did make it, he found his schedule out of sync—for Brigitte and especially Jicky's kids were reliably up by nine a.m., and Christian would try to sleep in amid growing noise.

One of her sub-patterns with men, she says, was now starting to be seen in Christian; though he had gone back to working for Jacqueline Veyssière, he was suddenly putting on airs. She says that her beaus would eventually take themselves for Bardots, and of course despite influences that accrue in any relationship, they were anything but. At least she had Christian to herself during the entire New Year's Eve celebration, for Jacqueline fired him!

Professionally, things were coming to an end for Bardot in this era, though *Boulevard du rhum* did well and helped thereby with the marketing of *Pétroleuses*. The latter is one of those films that again feels dated—directed by Christian-Jaque, born in 1904 and the man who had made a pack of historical dramas with Martine Carol. The film, however, is musty because of its *echte* '70s atmosphere.[5] Michael J. Pollard is the Keatonesque marshal of Bougival Junction, trying to keep peace between Bardot's and Cardinale's characters, both after property bearing oil. He is a true Marshal Putz, bumbling and stumbling the entire film, losing his gun, horse, and, it seems, his mind! Other men in the film, preeminently four brothers dominated by a bossy sister and *madre*-figure (Cardinale), are hirsute simps.

In this *Legend of Frenchie King* a tone of frantic lightheartedness aims to produce laughs, but in the tradition of bad French comedies, fails utterly to do so. Bardot plays Frenchie, a bank and train robber extraordinaire, aided by her four half-sisters (same father, different mothers). In their first on-screen robbery they come upon a deed to the Little P. ranch. It is the same spread coveted by Cardinale, and the two go at each other via competitive shooting, riding, and ultimately, that drawn-out pugilistic contest; while the four brothers and four sisters held down too long lurch toward love and marriage. In the end they all amalgamate as a presumably stronger Frenchie King gang, going back out on horseback for more exhilarating stickups.

Little wonder that Bardot was beginning to value people who were emphatically not connected to the movie world. At the Boulevard Lannes she let her *maître d'hôtel* orchestrate dinners in style, with eminent musicians, artists, or intellectuals around the table. On weekends at Bazoches things were more informal, with Brigitte's pals including six goats, over ten cats (they were wild and it was hard to count), a rabbit, 20 ducks or so, the ass Cornichon, and some sheep pried from the maw of a slaughterhouse. When she wasn't keeping her *gardiens* in line there, she was reading like mad—taking on authors like Durrell, Rilke, or Fitzgerald. Placing her culture beside that of today's J. Lo's or Paltrow's is proverbial night and day.

Was the press corps finished with her? Not quite. One day Brigitte went to visit her friend Sveeva in a clinic, clad in kerchief and dark glasses, and next morning on the radio heard a man named Edgar Schneider talk about her clandestine face-lift, supposedly occurring the day before. The lie made her sick, but spread like wildfire through a variety of Parisian newspapers. She promptly dialed up her lawyer, Jean-Pierre Le Mée, to initiate a suit. Bardot was starting to hate the human race, including a non-supportive Christian, "this stupid primate," who barely looked up from his sports page during her most recent travail.[6]

Her first love, Vadim, now wanted to make a movie with Brigitte based on the new sexual equality of women—a female Don Juan saga. Reluctantly, she acceded, starting to shoot in late July, 1972. The film was called *Don Juan (or if Don Juan Were a Woman)*, and begins with a weird funeral accompanied by Mozart's *Requiem*, which becomes the basis for Michel Magne's satanic-sounding score. Bardot in her Kalt period and garbed by Givenchy never looked more beautiful. There had been a number of Bardots physically—from the pert pre–*And God...* cutie through the siren era, then a thinnish, sadder Brigitte of the early '60s; and now here she was at perhaps her most stunning. Actually this film isn't as bad as one might expect. After the funeral Bardot's Jeanne comes to get advice from her cousin, a handsome young priest exhorted into listening to confessions at her pad, including what she believes was a murder. What she really confesses to (with long flashbacks) is ruining a number of men. The first is played by Maurice Ronet, a pompous bigwig in the political world who admits to having cheated intermittently on his wife. Jeanne entices this Pierre to a vacation in Sweden and to a

Bardot as Louise King in *Les Pétroleuses* (*The Legend of Frenchie King*), flanked by two of her sisters (unidentified) in cowgirl crime. This western also starred Italy's Claudia Cardinale as Maria Sarrazin, after the same oil-rich property as Bardot's Louise. (Francos Films, Paris, Copercines, Madrid, Vidès Films, Rome, Hendale Group, U.K., 1971)

strange scene where a passed-out nude woman finds herself being helped by Pierre; both are then snapped by a photographer. The lucrative pics make French papers, blowing his career, as well as family life with wife and daughter; and he ends up a seedy drunk bent on revenge against Jeanne, now gone on to Robert Hossein's Louis. This cigar-smoking, middle-aged businessman is in a third marriage with a younger *anglaise*, played by willowy Jane Birkin, and toward whom he acts sadistically. How does Jeanne take him down a peg? Via a lesbian situation with Birkin's character en route to London, wrecking *their* marriage, such as it had been! Then comes the ruin of a third man, a guitarist at a club smitten by Jeanne, who is seduced, then opens his veins. In flashback it turns out that she did call the ambulance and did not murder him, though he died. Blaspheming all traditions was the era's mode, and Vadim's pièce de résistance late in the movie is Jeanne's amorous scene with priest and cousin, listening to her confessions. But she becomes oddly purified by a feeling of real love, and goes to apologize to the seedy Pierre, who lures her to an oil-laced structure he then lights up. In the end she nobly saves him from the flames, but herself succumbs in what is supposed to resemble the fires of hell. Despite its weirdness, the film shows at least some of the taste Bardot would later remember in Vadim and Malle, the latter himself busy overturning norms with an incestuous swath in his *Murmur of the Heart*.[7]

In real life Bardot's sojourn in Sweden for part of the shoot coincided with Christian's abrupt departure, and for good. One problem for the Alsatian was apparently a frustrated desire to marry her and put down roots. Whatever the exact series of reasons, he was yet another lover gone.

The end of this relationship sent Brigitte on a lonely, bereft drinking rampage, where she would down up to two bottles of champagne or three liters of red wine in a day! She also dabbled in pills. Her doctor sent her to a psychiatrist, but the actress wouldn't cooperate. One coup at least occurred when Madame Renée reluctantly came back into service.

Bardot was now doing her film work with almost total repugnance, and the Vadim one felt like her last. Some of those pictures of the past few years had been, as noted, commercial failures—*A Coeur joie*, *Histoires extraordinaires* (despite her part being directed by Malle), *Shalako*, and so on.[8] Even *The Bear and the Doll*, which she liked and which made money in France, caught no mainstream attention in a changed U.S.A. Bardot was in any event indifferent to these box office returns.

At the end of the '60s Brigitte had also joined a growingly popular Gallic television world, and gotten more into singing, shaped by French bandleader Claude Bolling. Eddie Barclay—the record producer who had worked with such as Aznavour—said Bardot talked songs more than she sang them; but just as in cinema, she had a special something here which grabbed people. However, discussions about forming a Barclay-Bardot record label fell through—Bardot simply hadn't the time for it. There was also some love between Bardot and Barclay, and even a brief thought of marriage; but the two ended up instead as good friends.

It was ironic that in the summer of 1972, at the end of a career, she was back cinematically where she had started, working with "Vava." And in *Don Juan...* he also launched a handsome young man named Laurent Vergez, yet another whom Brigitte would go for in her usual headlong fashion, trying to replace Kalt.

While this *should* have been Bardot's swan song on screen, it turned out there was one more film to follow—*L'Histoire très bonne et très joyeuse de Colinot trousse-chemise* (*Colinot—the Petticoat Lifter*). Set in the Middle Ages, it again featured Bardot as a seductress. Screenwriter Nina Companeez truly had to push her into the project, but didn't demand much shooting time of the aging star. Vergez came along for the ride, and Brigitte became more and more possessive of him. When he was not around, she would sleep with one of his sweaters.

On June 7, 1973, she announced her retirement to the press, having made 48 films in only 21 years. And unlike many cynics, Vadim felt she would really make her exit stick this time. For her 40th birthday Bardot attended a beach party with friends, and the group later called the Gypsy Kings serenaded her with guitar music, while she danced flamenco. Vergez was now her constant companion, and in conjunction with that milestone birthday, persuaded Brigitte to pose nude for photos he took and sent to *Playboy*.

But the routinization of the erotic in the '70s more and more disgusted her, even if she had helped blaze the trail. The normality of going topless, the banality of affairs and divorces—it all helped move Bardot in a more serious direction. Some would look askance at all this, holding roughly with La Rochefoucauld that there is no true altruism. But if so many species were threatened in a growingly technologized world, going extinct at a rate higher than ever in history; and if so many animals simply suffered horrendously and needlessly, shouldn't people have noticed? The French star ending a celebrated film career certainly did.

6

Goodbye Movies, Hello Animals

BARDOT'S HISTORY OF SENSITIVITY TO animals went back at least to the early '60s, when ahead of her time, she had begun to attack French modes of slaughter. Her clout and sincerity finally pushed the government into legislating employment of quicker electric-shock pistols in abattoirs, known as the "BB Law." Zoos too would feel her wrath—four had to close, others went on parole, while improvements were instituted. Once a fur-wearer, Bardot turned anti-fur, again ahead of the pack, and in the case of some wounded animals who had been left to die, she sported the costs of their slow recuperation.

Bardot would henceforth become known as the "Madonna of the Strays."[1] Her own menagerie had of course grown like Topsy at Bazoches, and to a lesser degree, at La Madrague. She wanted her animals to have happiness, knowing that they could feel pain and contentment the way humans did. At one point on her farm at Bazoches, she told her housekeeper there: "Our hens seem bored. They need a cock!" So she went out to the market and bought the biggest rooster available.[2] She also kept adopting, including a successor to Guapa, a mongrel named Pichnou. But if she were to help beleaguered animals in a more significant way, Bardot needed to raise money, and gone was the movie life that had once provided her a steady income.

In her Boulevard Lannes apartment circa 1974 Brigitte grew a little panicky with-out contracted projects on the horizon. And 25-year-old Laurent was beginning to get on her nerves, another in a line of gorgeous spoiled men she had known. His chief pre-occupation around the apartment seemed to be telling Madame Renée how to improve her sauces! Bardot was waiting to make her life matter, but as far as animals went, here she was sopping up canine urinations with Kleenex and Perrier on her fine floor, or walking pets in the Bois de Boulogne. At Bazoches she worked in grungies, inhaling country air and watching kittens spill out all over the place. Problems with *gardiens* were far from done with there; the latest were drug users driving a red convertible, and had

Brigitte rowing setters in the mid–'70s. The protection of animals was becoming her central preoccupation.

to be forcibly evicted by her friend Jean Bouquin, who brought an actor dressed appropriately to do the deed. (Bouquin also obtained new employees for her.)

Both a need for cash and a love of France made Bardot accede in 1974 to the French Tourist Authority, asking her to sell nothing less than the country itself to potential visitors! She duly made a commercial in a Paris studio, as well as outside—on France's regions, its gustatory delights, and so on, which led to more work in the realm of publicity.

Executives at Goya Perfumes now asked her to help launch their new mens' cologne, *Zendiq*. For this job she had to smell numerous fragrances, leaving the labs each day feeling slightly tipsy. The commercial she made for them ended up costing a bundle, because she was going to make even the smallest things she did special. Bardot brought along her own makeup artist, hairdresser, and clothes, and for 12 hours straight worked like a maniac. She also had a hand in putting together ingredients for the fragrance and designing the bottle. Her fee was substantial, but she was well worth the price. The advertisement went through the roof in Britain and in a variety of European countries.

While she was down at La Madrague and taking a summer breather from her relationship, Laurent was meanwhile showing off peacock-style, bringing lovers back to the Boulevard Lannes in Paris! Again, Brigitte was living and dying by the erotic sword. The couple got back together near the end of summer, but at Lannes hammerers and reconstructors drove her crazy, and she acquired a smaller, secondary pied à terre in the capital. And Mama Olga still pestered her to make films, including one with the now broadening Brando; but Bardot wouldn't go back into the same river twice.

She hadn't yet thrown herself completely into a life of animal protection, but certainly she gave to people. She fell briefly in love with an older journalist named Philippe G., but he was then nearly killed in a car accident, languishing in a coma in Brittany. Fabricating a story about the death of a cousin that Laurent didn't quite accept, Bardot went out with her secretary Michèle to the hospital near Quimper—and was stunned to witness something like a mummy, tethered to machines. She stayed several days by his bedside.

Her first Christmas–New Year's spent at La Madrague felt dysfunctional, compounded by poor French heating still prevalent then, making her entourage burn log after log. One reason for her presence here was that her father living nearby on the Riviera might be seeing his last Christmas. Friends had also rented a chateau in the region for a New Year's bash. There was champagne aplenty, yet the open-hearted Bardot also took time out at midnight to call her journalist friend, now in a Paris hospital bed.

She and Laurent then went to ski in Méribel, and a strained atmosphere prevailed between them. Finally, Laurent was persuaded to go back to Paris. Her friend Jicky, feeling her becalmed boredom, now phoned to recommend a sculptor and sometime actor at Méribel named Miroslav Brozek. Apparently this Czech was dying to meet Bardot. Brigitte duly went to see what turned out to be a blond dream of a man, and fell immediately.

Like so many men Miroslav enjoyed seeing the woman in her domestic scene, and apparently Bardot's eggs hastily cooked for him in her Méribel cabin did the trick. She had only rented the chalet for the month of January and had to be back in Paris for a February 6, 1975, TV program. "Mirko"? He was naturally loathe to leave the ski slopes and his sculpting workshop for a Paris apartment where Laurent might still be lurking. But he decided to make the trip.

Madame Renée gave Brigitte some meaningful looks as her latest lover silently unpacked his things in unfamiliar surroundings. He had his sensitivities, and needed a guest bed with no trace of Laurent in it. Meanwhile, Bardot's TV gig was to be her first really to address significant issues—in this case, the horrid life of zoo animals. With several other participants on the panel to debate her, she felt she needed support, but Miroslav was busy traveling between rooms at night and wanting to leave, then not leave, and Madame Renée was basically not speaking! So the "opposition" on the show overpowered a depressed Bardot. Dejected, she came back to Lannes, and a bevy of roses from Mirko. In return she decided to break her usual routine in this season and return to Méribel with him, and to his art that for a week untouched had roiled in his innards.

But M. l'Artiste wouldn't travel in a memory-soiled Porsche either, so the great spoiler of men ceded on that, too. They rented a new Cherokee-Chief with lots of room. Back in Méribel Brigitte and Mirko had to make do with a tiny bedroom in a chalet belonging to friends, where the children woke too early and kept others up. By day Miroslav went to his *atelier* or skied with Brigitte's friend Christiane Ganivet, while the star was stuck home knitting sweaters. Trying to do some skiing herself, she also had to work at keeping her faithful dogs at the bottom of the slope, rather than on her heels. When she fell heavily, her leg blew up, and while convalescing, she began composition of her memoirs on childhood—having seen so much inaccuracy about her life, she thought she would start setting the record straight.

But there were constant interruptions to cook for Mirko or take care of animals, and bouts of sheer boredom when he was gone all day. For the umpteenth time she was paying a price for love. Even back in Paris she was rattled by his profusion of sculptures, turning her handsome apartment into a "souk."[3] All his dirty instruments of creation were unpacked as well, and again she put up with idiosyncrasies that came with the territory, while inside, her animal protection obsession quietly simmered.

Even Bazoches with its profusion of animals became doubly chaotic, as Mirko asked to do alterations there with his two brothers so that he could produce another workshop. A profusion of dust, cement, and plaster bits combined with other problems that had been endemic here—preeminently, that of *gardiens*, who in Bardot's absences got used to doing little. When she returned, they seemed to dislike becoming industrious again.

To remedy the situation Mirko traveled to Burgundy where he had a farm, and where he hoped to find new *gardiens* for Bazoches. Alone after dinner one night at Bazoches, Brigitte was watching television, and the male *gardien* asked whether she might look at some photographs he had taken of her animals. With no real interest she said yes, and at first she saw animals, then suddenly a picture of the man's wife in the midst of an obvious orgy spilled out.

The *gardien* tried to show her more, and as she got nauseously off the couch, he whispered lewdly that she could join them at their meeting place. She yelled, the dogs barked, and somehow she reached the phone and dialed a nearby friend, Christian Brincourt, screaming for help, while the *gardien* grabbed at her wrist, exhaling tainted breath and telling her that he had locked the gate! Brincourt nonetheless made it inside, with a few photos still on the floor, and at dawn the couple was ushered out. Then Bardot and Brincourt made their way into the *gardiens'* cottage that Brigitte had decorated, now a disgusting mess. Summoned to return, Mirko also came back at the double, and unlike some Bardot men, was a handyman who could unplug a toilet, while she scrubbed away and cried. Her secretary Michèle found new help for the place. Returning to Paris, and still shaken, she nonetheless did a TV show there on animal protection. When she and Mirko regained Bazoches the next weekend, they found more surprises—the dogs were hungry, the cats angry, and the new *gardien* couple of 20 and 18 had been doing a poor job. Even their baby was shrieking. Bardot tried to teach the two their tasks, but they remained virtually worthless. Finally after a lot of looking, she got it right with an older couple that would blessedly stay for seven and a half years. Life for Bardot remained a series of islands in a frequently stormy sea.

As usual she had a man who understood little of financial realities and was being artistically scintillating, while Brigitte worried about how to pay the huge rent in Paris, the *gardiens* at Bazoches, the secretary, insurance, etc. Mirko himself cost her. One night they went to a restaurant with friends in Paris, and she slipped him 3,000 francs in advance, knowing that as the celebrity she would be stuck with the bill. The bill came, and Mirko was supposed to produce the money he had put in his sock, but nothing was there! In an era before credit cards were standard, Brigitte had to write out an IOU.

Another time he was supposed to fill the gas tank, and used a kind of gas-oil that wasn't right for her car—the vehicle sputtered, and was almost ruined. And of course there remained a need for reliable sources of income to pay for all these things. To raise money she did some advertising in July for a Paris clothing company. The couple then went to Saint-Tropez, which Mirko loved, but where his tools clattering on the floors and his need to move furniture around to accommodate them grated on her nerves. To get away, she ran over to visit Papa and Mama, and was sad to see her father's rapid decline to cancer.

Back at La Madrague her life slipped into a certain conjugal solitude. Continually focused on his art, Mirko would sit before the sea, planning his next moves, while Brigitte would often finish meals alone, wondering why she could never land a normal fellow! She kept busy swimming, gardening, and learning from her Provençal housekeeper how to cook southern style. And the marvelous sculptures that would remain at La Madrague certainly enhanced the decor there.

At the beginning of October she was back in Paris, but again, often alone (which also helped in the composition of her memoirs), while Mirko, crazy about his sculpture, would stay at Bazoches to work in the country air. When her mother went to visit friends, Brigitte at least got to spend several nights alone beside Pilou, a blessed occurrence to her. From his impending death she felt her own ephemerality—and the necessity of humility. Louis Bardot passed away on November 5, 1975, at age 79, to be buried in the sailors' cemetery at the foot of the citadel dominating the Bay of Saint-Tropez. Trying wanly to console a mother who had so hurt her in early life, Brigitte could not muster a familiar use of "tu," but only the more formal "vous" she had used since childhood.

In Paris, Anne-Marie Bardot soon located the sort of apartment she wanted. She was a great demander, desiring a telephone installed in her elevator and linked up to the nearest police station—and she got it. She had to leave many things behind, and Brigitte took what she could to Lannes, some of it necessary research material (Pilou's notebooks, etc.). And her mother quickly landed on her feet; a man secretly in love with her ("How long has this been going on?" in the old Gershwin tune) moved in on the first floor, with Toty on the fifth. Brigitte was a bit envious of the quality of man her mother was able to find.

She was still in this period of 1973–76 or so in a kind of hiatus—an interregnum. One can always make one's troubles into obstacles, and Bardot was certainly having trouble getting where she wanted to go. It was the high noon of the sex revolution in the west, and Bardot's next *gardien* problem at La Madrague involved a man using her Citroën *deux chevaux* to pick up Marseille prostitutes and get them into *her* bedroom. Police pictures corroborating the charges sickened her, and it came out that "Pigeonnot" had also been consuming her pigeons! When she and Michèle arrived at La Madrague, Bardot tearfully found hungry dogs, chickens in the kitchen, and the house a freezing pigsty.

Out of bad at times comes good, and for La Madrague Bardot now got a fine *gardienne* of 60 or so, Madeleine, a long-term prize. But as New Year's passed, she still had given too little to what she cared about most—or so she felt. Personal problems kept on intruding. Caring maternally for helpless animals, Brigitte now had to deal with her own possible maternality—not yet impossible; and indeed, she suddenly found herself pregnant with Mirko's baby. It happened just when she had watched a TV program showing the horrifying slaughter of baby seals, and become galvanized by it!

Here was a cruel dilemma: baby, or serious help for thousands of doomed, helpless animals? For soon after seeing the program, she conceived the idea of linking up with

The Citadel of Saint-Tropez. Louis Bardot was buried in the cemetery at the foot of it in November 1975. Brigitte's mother was later buried there.

Franz Weber, a Swiss environmentalist, and going to Canada for the beginning of the annual "cull"—the killing of thousands of baby seals on the ice floes off Newfoundland. But meanwhile her gynecologist confirmed her pregnancy of two months or so. It was now or never for an abortion, and with heavy heart, she procured one, and was truly in a bad state for her departure at the beginning of March 1976. No direct flight was available from Paris. After barely making the first flight to London, she found herself bleeding terribly, then fainted on exiting the aircraft. An English doctor told her curtly that in view of her hemorrhaging she ought to go home. Her Paris gynecologist seconded that view. Meanwhile, Weber was waiting for her, the baby seals were going to be slaughtered, and Bardot was losing blood. She made a pact with herself that henceforth there would be no turning back, *except* this one time. Predictably, the newspapers played low speculative cards—that she had quarreled with Miroslav, that she lacked courage, and so forth.

On April 2 Bardot participated in a demonstration in front of the Norwegian embassy in Paris, a key country for seal culling (and still permitted latitude on whaling as well). Hordes of autograph hounds came out not for an environmental activist, but for the former pinup symbol. However, Brigitte started receiving more mail on animal cruelty generally, and on seals in particular. Frenchmen who had been fishing off Newfoundland sent her a telegram—to the effect that they had found a baby seal abandoned on a bit of ice, and that the animal had become the boat's mascot they wanted Bardot to adopt. They advised her of their arrival date in Fécamp on the English Channel, and thither she went with Philippe Letellier, a photographer friend from *Match*, Christian Brincourt, whom she knew from Bazoches and the TV world, and Mirko.

With families nervously awaiting the boat's arrival, Bardot waited too, then lights came into view, and here was this seal who had now sprouted adult gray fur. As was often the case, the adventurous, generous Bardot had little idea of what she was getting into here! The animal needed to be fed with bottles of mineral water, as well as baby bottles mixed with strained fish, water, and cod liver oil. It had bad teeth, and hadn't learned how to swallow fish from its mother. When they stopped at a gas station, she thought the pumper would faint at the contents of her cage—"Chouchou," as she dubbed the latest addition to her menagerie. Brigitte's maternality was on display ... and yet she killed babies? Again, the best and deepest are often paradoxical.

She then left this flapping, honking creature with the *gardien* at Bazoches, and drove to Paris. At least the seal would endure longer than most of her strays, lasting into the late '90s in its final abode of Marineland at Antibes, but long retired from having to work for the crowds. Not that Bardot's other animals stopped demanding attention! For example, she watched transfixed as a favorite dog, Nini, delivered eight packets of plastic-like stuff, then licked at the babies, wanting Brigitte to watch her at work, and Brigitte indeed hugged her approvingly. She kept five of the offspring all their lives, and gave away the other three.

Bardot now wanted ardently to create a foundation for animal protection; but there were of course many administrative hurdles to overcome. Philippe Cottereau, administrator of the Fondation Paul-Emile Victor, offered the Saint-Cloud premises where his organization was lodged. The idea was that Cottereau would run both foundations—Paul-Emile Victor, named for a French polar explorer, and the first, but short-lived, Fondation Brigitte Bardot. The latter's board would include her lawyer, Gilles Dreyfus, Philippe Letellier, her secretary Michèle, Cottereau, and Anne-Marie Bardot. Jacques Cousteau also lent his support.

Very quickly Bardot learned that to get anything accomplished one needed to emulate the little red hen and do it oneself. As usual, she had gotten into something that became rapidly more complex than anticipated, especially the byzantine detours of administration.

Down at Saint-Tropez for sun and sea, she got some respite from such things, enjoying Nini's offspring of two females, as well as three males, Matcho, Moulin, and Moustique, as she named them. But the latest problem at La Madrague was a Camus-like plague of rats, and Bardot had to call in exterminators who assured her their poison wouldn't hurt cats and dogs. Sure enough, after their departure her pets started copiously vomiting, and Brigitte threatened a suit against the company.

Mirko's mother then came to La Madrague, obsessed only with making soup and doing for her son, who was still fixated on his sculptures. Bardot bought her an item of clothing for her birthday, and instead, she wanted the money so she could make one of her own.

Returning to Paris for work on the foundation, Bardot found contributions pouring into its coffers; but she had to use a significant chunk of her own income as well, especially from her La Madrague clothing line. At press conferences she wept openly about the plight of animals, and people still thronged her for the old, and to her, the wrong reasons. On to Bazoches and attempts at feeding Chouchou normally, but though much bigger, he was still on the bottle. She got him a pile of sardines, but he spit them back at her face and clapped at the joke.

As fall came into view, Brigitte approached age 42 with some optimism; contributions to the foundation were going well. But applecarts in her life were always being upset, and the latest such incident occurred when she learned to her surprise that some 100,000 francs had been siphoned off to pay debts of Cottereau's other association—accrued for telephone bills, rent, employee benefits, and the like. He had even used foundation funds to pay for sculptures he had bought! She yelled at Cottereau and then impulsively busted up her organization that September of 1976, scribbling check after check to pay everyone off.

Bardot now had to work harder on commercials for a variety of products from aftershaves to wines, and on promoting her La Madrague line of clothes. In this same era of the Me Decade she was moved by the deaths of two French giants from a truly bygone time—Malraux and her old screen partner, Jean Gabin. And she finally gave up on keeping Chouchou occupied, taking him to Marineland in Antibes, and realizing he would be better off there. Then came sickening news that the last three of her *chiennes* at Bazoches had gone scampering into the fields and been killed by hunters.

She now met a missionary-priest who had lived 30 years in an igloo at the North Pole. Both he and Bardot remained horrified by the slaughter of baby seals for fur, and, freshly inspired, she revowed herself in a vestigially Catholic way to the cause.[4]

In January 1977 she took a last-minute rental in Méribel, then back in Paris found herself pushed again by Weber and others to go help the seals. Secretly, Bardot gave Weber the then hefty sum of 200,000 francs to get world journalists to the massacre scene for a firsthand report. She also made a deal with Agence Sygma. They would take her to Canada in a private jet, and would have exclusive photo rights.

The annual "cull"—a true euphemism—was slated to begin March 15, and a day earlier Bardot's group took off in their chartered plane, hoping to get as near as possible to the ice floes where the baby seals awaited their fate. For a person who disliked flying, Bardot's trip itself was courageous. They took off from Le Bourget in a Corvette outfitted by the Franz Weber Foundation, in a group including Weber, a small TV crew, and Mirko. The plane was small and cluttered, and everyone felt cramped. Stops included a first one on the Hebrides Islands northwest of Scotland. Bardot found it a desolate landscape. Each new takeoff and landing terrified her, the only woman on board. The second was at Reykjavik, Iceland, and colder yet. Next came an American military base on a fjord in Greenland. Again, it was freezing out, and there was barely time for a washup and coffee.

And thence to Labrador for fuel—a part of the world dependent on profits provided by sealskins. It was midnight Brigitte's time when they arrived at the deserted airport in another deep freeze, and with a display of sealskin toys arrayed there. Then another takeoff and arrival at Sept-Iles at 2:30 a.m. her time, and after 14 hours of flying, Brigitte was certainly glad to hit the hotel!

On March 15 she was up early and wanting badly to reach Blanc Sablon, the quarry of a number of helicopters, and site of the ice field. But the Canadian government made things difficult for the Weber group, even though they had paid in advance for seven choppers. They now had to pay up to triple for the lone one still available. Half the journalists summoned had already gotten there the day before; the rest were stuck on Sept-Iles. The original charter jet wasn't equipped to land on such a short strip (some 800 kilometers away), but went off to reconnoitre anyway.

So Bardot remained stuck in her hotel room. Calling Paris, she heard that President Giscard d'Estaing had forbidden importation of sealskins into France! Hurriedly, she discussed the news with journalists. She also kept telephoning the Canadian prime minister's office for help, but received no return call.

Meanwhile, a press conference composed of Bardot, Weber and journalists was supposed to take place on Blanc Sablon near the site of the massacre. Instead? Bardot spoke to media people also stuck here and removed from the scene, provoking their derision. She then made an offer to locals: if the massacres ceased, she and the Weber Foundation would fund a factory to make synthetic furs, creating new jobs. She would also use her clothes line, La Madrague, to help former hunters. Still snickered at, and making more fruitless calls to Ottawa, Bardot would at this point have taken a boat or any conveyance to get closer to Blanc Sablon—but nothing worked.

On March 16 the phone jangled her awake at 6 a.m. *France Inter* wanted an interview, and so did *Radio-Canada*, among others. A Frenchman from another station called, telling her he had two helicopters available on Saint-Anthony, Newfoundland. But journalists thronged her arrival there. Knights of the keyboard from Canada, Denmark, Norway, even France hit out at Bardot for eating meat, and for wearing a parka that supposedly itself had sealskin in it. She replied with statistics: in 1900 there had been some 10,000,000 seals and now, hardly 800,000. They were en route to possible extinction. And still the journalists at the airport laughed. She decided now to get away to the one motel there—and a little sanity. Arriving back at the airport, she then learned that her helicopters had just taken off!

Flown back to her old hotel by her pilot, a disgruntled Bardot found herself hassled again by journalists and seal hunters. People were laughing and yelling, and Bardot had to yell over them, fighting for what remained of the baby seals. There was the usual "harvesting" canard afloat—the more seals killed, the more came back (one is reminded of Newfoundland's once flourishing cod "industry," or Oregon's old-growth timber). People flashed her with Kodaks, then somebody slopped in a dead baby seal wrapped in plastic—at which Brigitte cried and became nauseous, witnessing the still warm body.

The next day (March 17) she was woken up by another blizzard of calls—from the media in Paris, London, and New York; but still no call from Canada's government authorities. When she went out for air, a real blizzard swirled snow up to her waist. Then two lumbering fellows from Greenpeace appeared, telling her they could obtain two choppers for her group by next morning. They were now at Belle-Isle halfway between Blanc Sablon and the bloody ice field. There they had a camp in primitive conditions, leaving each morning to try and impede icebreakers and baby seal hunters.

Finally on March 18 salvation seemed in the offing. But the Greenpeace camp was flogged by horrid, stormy conditions, and Bardot saw these shivering impeders as utopian throwbacks to another age. They offered her a hot chocolate made on their camping stove, and she says she never enjoyed one more. That night the ex-star froze in 40° below weather, drinking rum from a passed bottle. Here were Greenpeace men and women of their early era who would lie on baby seals to save them, and Bardot was filled with admiration; Left, Center, or Right politics meant nothing to her here. The weather kept them stuck in, and the only chance was a precarious flight to Blanc Sablon, but not right onto the floes.

Once she arrived there, a bellicose French journalist promptly lit into Bardot as an ersatz actress and easy moralizer, and she cursed him back. But on the plus side petitions were sprouting all over Canada, especially among university students. Finally, on Saturday, March 19, one helicopter got her to a piece of ice in the sea near the scene of the slaughter—but too late. Nearby were two baby seal survivors, sweet and trusting. However, the ice began giving way, and Brigitte's leg plunged into glacial waters. She yelled and was pulled out in the nick of time. Mirko then brought her one of the surviving babies, and she cried, holding onto it tightly. At the present rate of slaughter all such creatures on Canadian territory would be gone in less than a decade! Bardot saw the mother seal and with heavy heart, apologized to her for these plentiful murders.[5]

Back in Paris, an exhausted Brigitte felt herself a different person now. But there was Brincourt and a TV crew to meet the beleaguered celebrity by her elevator! She was dead tired, wanting only to rest, but he got her to thunder tearfully against Norway and Canada, which in turn helped spawn more petitions and demonstrations. The usual carpers were, however, near at hand. Even Madame Renée left critical articles on Bardot, calling her a publicity hound and adding that "we aren't proud of you in the apartment building."[6] The animal protectress cried yet another set of tears, but at least she had gotten the world's attention on a significant problem, making another vow never to give up on it.

On April 29, 1977, Brigitte gave a dog birthday party complete with cake and candles. She also recalls burying the dog of a friend at Bazoches, and by the '90s would count 70 such burial places for dogs and cats there. She would cry over their graves, and sometimes place candles by them, as she did for dear departed humans, like Dada or her grandparents.

Speaking of humans, before hitting Saint-Tropez, she felt she must visit her beloved great-aunt Tapompon at Cordon. But she and Mirko stayed in a hotel where the proprietors were mean to her *chiennes!* Not only did they make them unwelcome, but the dogs then got loose in the countryside, and Mirko had to whistle over hill and dale, finally succeeding in bringing them all back.

They arrived at La Madrague, but a finely strung superego pushed Brigitte to go off right away and see Chouchou at Marineland in Antibes. And the seal seemed to recognize her by its enthusiastic sounds. Watching how it did routines for its supper gave Bardot a foretaste of her later struggle against what the French call delphinariums. On the spot she retired Chouchou—no longer did he have to work to eat.

In Saint-Tropez the chic now called her "B.B. phoque," and would whisper that she stank of seal or fish, or crack that her fur had gone white. Avoiding high society, she enjoyed the relative peace of card games, wonderful food, and good company at La Madrague.

In the same era when the openly homosexual phase of the sex revolution was in high gear she made a friend she nicknamed La Perruque, because he had a boutique of wigs. Together they discovered a wild part of the coast near Saint-Tropez, slated to be built up and ruined. She found out that the owner of this swath of land where her animals loved to play was keeping developers at bay; but then he died, and Bardot, who wanted to save it all, now had multiple heirs to deal with.

There were also continuing problems with her *gardiens*. Madeleine couldn't handle another winter at La Madrague, so Brigitte got an Arab fellow and a gardener, Bernard Poulain, to stay there, the latter remaining a longtime friend. She also made another good friend in this era, Yvonne Cassan de Valry, a very "16th," high-class, bridge-playing type. Yvonne and her husband, Louis, grew close to her. But friends were only friends, and her significant other, Mirko, was becoming less and less significant, owing to his all-consuming artistic endeavors.

Mirko's sponsor for an upcoming exposition of his work in Paris now wanted Bardot to appear, or no exposition. So she found herself again part of the media hype she had fled, realizing that yet another man of hers was hitching his wagon to *her* star. She knew that without her name Mirko would remain largely unknown, and it began to upset her.

In January 1978 came a chance for Bardot to make a difference on the baby seal issue at an upcoming meeting of the Council of Europe. So she and Mirko took off in a rickety little plane from Courchevel in the French Alps to Strasbourg, where she was well received. Over dinner she learned where officials from different countries stood on the slaughter of seals. She and Mirko refused the proffered foie gras, which became one of her gustatory no-no's. The next morning she tried her best to be rational and sane, pleading her case in front of these bureaucratic types; then came a press conference, and without knowing what effect she had had, she and Mirko took off again on their plane, buffeted, however, by wind and rain, including a stretch where their baggage fell on them in the dead of night, as they hurtled over mountains and who knew what landscape below. Brigitte started screaming, and Mirko and the pilot turned pale as well. She thought of her dogs and mother, before an emergency landing at Chambéry saved them. The pilot later admitted how close they had come to disaster.

In the airport Bardot consumed a half bottle of champagne, before a happy taxi ride to Méribel. There she was overjoyed to be back with her "petites," Madame Renée, etc. And the next day the papers gave feature coverage to her pleas at Strasbourg. Journalists phoned her, and one young man staying nearby and working for the newspaper *Rhône Alpes* (Lyon) managed to see her in person. This Jean-Louis Remilleux was dressed formally for a ski area, but would become another long-term friend. He took notes seriously, and via Bardot and his own verve, eventually made it big in the media, and would produce her future TV programs on animal protection. In the short run, Dutch authorities immediately banned all imports of baby seal skins into their country, while Danish and Norwegian politicians remained predictably recalcitrant on the issue. The Canadian government also defended their methods of killing as humane. But the fact that seal fur would eventually be banned in many countries constituted Bardot's first great "différence."[7]

Sending her mother 66 roses for her 66th birthday at the beginning of February, Brigitte was finally making peace on that front. But she remained in a permanent state of war for suffering animals. One night at dinner with friends, the host declared that Nini's son Matcho, whom he and his wife had adopted, was a bad dog, unfit for hunting, fearful of gunfire, and slated for the S.P.A. Brigitte yelled out for her "baby," learning that Matcho was stuck with other hunting dogs in an icy kennel on their property in the Sologne. The next day she and Mirko left with the *petites*, heading for Saint-Tropez with a planned stopover in the Sologne. The roads were slick, and it was very cold in the region, and finally with flashlights they found several cocker spaniels shivering and locked up, and a paranoid Matcho, who failed even to recognize her. Brigitte had a lot of trouble prying him away, and en route to Saint-Tropez he stayed angry. The *petites* licked his nose, Bardot tried repeatedly to warm him up, and eventually in the Midi the dog started trusting, realizing he would no longer be beaten.

Checking out the Riviera property she coveted near the beach of Salins, she beheld her dogs happily cavorting, and decided then and there that she must buy this beautiful, but expensive, chunk of land. She thought of putting up a rustic cabin there, and Mirko instantly worried about where his workshop would be located. And Brigitte, starting to tear off the love-bandages, found this self-centered quality of his hard to take. Leaving her to look over the terrain, he stayed back at La Madrague with all his clanking sculptures. She would have to keep feet on the ground for both of them.

Going up to Paris, she tried to face an economic problem: if she bought "La Garrigue" near Saint-Tropez, she would have to divest herself of her Boulevard Lannes apartment, now that she had a smaller pied à terre on the nearby Rue de la Tour in the capital. Totally in his sculptor's world, Mirko could care less about such financial realities. In Paris Bardot let real estate agents show "Lannes," then Corinne Dessange, part of the couple with the hunting place in the Sologne, came forward, saying she wanted an apartment that reeked of her friend Brigitte; and her husband wished to please her by acquiring it. Finally, the deal was closed, but having to move so many precious things to other abodes without enough room and selling off some of her beloved furniture made Bardot's heart sink.

Once ensconced in wobbly fashion at the tinier Rue de la Tour flat, she gave her dogs their first bathroom break in a little garden outside, and was curtly informed that dogs were forbidden here! She swore back, then for a week went into a horrible downspin. One decision loomed: to live at Bazoches with the dogs outside Paris, where she had never been much more than a weekender.

It was a difficult adjustment, though Mirko was happy to have her in what to him was a muddy paradise where he enjoyed working.[8] Her mother meanwhile wasn't able to digest food, and Brigitte had to face the reality of another cancer. Tests confirmed that the disease had indeed infested Toty's colon and part of the intestine, too.

The night before her mother's operation in Paris, July 31, 1978, Brigitte stayed on a mattress beside her—washing her feet, then watching a TV movie with her on the French Revolution. After the operation Brigitte returned to Bazoches, hopeful there was now a chance for her mother's survival; but the surgeon on the phone said her mother was littered inside—the disease had gained her liver and entire digestive system. It was a definitive death sentence.

Rushing back to the hospital, Brigitte tearfully begged Mirko to marry her and be her family when and if Mama Bardot died. She also found herself reciting a good 50 Hail Marys. At the hospital Philippe Lebraud, Anne-Marie's new man, was crying too, having probably had an easier life with her than Pilou did. Death to Toty Bardot came at the beginning of August 1978, and beside her immobile body the mourning Brigitte spent an entire night. She was told that just before her mother's passing, Nini, her setter, had howled outside for two hours.

Back at Bazoches Brigitte had nightmares and cuddled her dogs tightly. Michèle, her secretary, was down at La Madrague, which she was using, and Bardot told her to get it ready for a crowd. Brigitte would pay for plane or train fare to take all who wanted to come for the final burial in Saint-Tropez. Unfortunately their arrival would coincide with the great tourist invasion of August, and with the heat at its worst as well.

In Saint-Tropez some bystanders yelled out vulgarities at the actress in shades, and the funeral had to run early to stem the tide of tourists and photo-snappers. In attendance were people like Mama Olga, but also fishermen or small merchants from the area. Philippe Lebraud was stricken, and would sadly go the same way a few months later.

A garden party then followed at La Madrague, where Nicolas and Camille splashed in the pool, and people drank up and knocked off a cold buffet. Deeper than her sister, Brigitte was subsequently heart-torn in her mother's Paris apartment with its affecting odors—which family rings, baby cups, etc., to keep and which to sell off being the problem, sprouting emotions seen in Arthur Miller's play *The Price*. She sold her mother's property in the South for not much money; then, as if providentially, heard at the same time from her real estate agent that some Germans were now interested in La Garrigue. Bardot knew this was her moment of truth, and decided then and there to buy, before worrying about financial realities that kept leaving the men in her life indifferent! To relieve herself of such worries she would go and cry on the tombs of her dear departed, finding it hard to keep fighting alone on these various fronts.

For her birthday Bardot went reluctantly with Mirko, Phi-Phi d'Exea and his lady, Chantal Bolloré, to *La Cage aux folles*, and ended up laughing and enjoying it. At Bazoches Louis and Yvonne Cassan de Valry became real rudders for her, and in that era they all played bridge voraciously. One night the de Valrys wanted to lift Brigitte's spirits by taking her to a celebrated restaurant nearby. Reluctantly again, Brigitte allowed herself to be dragged out on a snobbish three-star outing. Starting with champagne, she became uneasy, perusing a menu of foie gras, ortolans, frogs' legs, then entrees of steaks, duck, hare, etc. She finally ordered an artichoke salad. To make conversation, Brigitte told Nelly Guerlain how much she enjoyed Guerlain perfumes, then Nelly complained to Yvonne and Louis about their last hunt—why they had had to chase the damned deer into a pond and knife it repeatedly, before their dogs finished it off, ripping the recalcitrant animal to shreds! And *she* had caught a cold in that water!

Hearing these words, Bardot wanted to scream her displeasure, but for the sake of her friends simply asked Madame Guerlain to refrain from such subjects; otherwise she would have to leave. The table went cool, and Yvonne started talking about the fashion world, before Nelly got back to discussing the large number of pheasants they had recently shot, so many that they ended up leaving some for the dogs, who were glad to eat them cum feathers and beaks!

As in a famous 1890s cartoon of a lunch group trying to avoid speaking of the Dreyfus Affair, this was the boil-over point. A furious Bardot stomped out into the rain, and Mirko followed. At home, cold in her soaked clothes, she finally let herself sob freely.

The winter of 1978–79 was a sad one; few came out to visit Bazoches in that season, preferring the glitter of Parisian lights. But at least Bardot used her gray loneliness positively, getting back to writing her first volume of memoirs, while Mirko sculpted round the clock. Sheep bleating, dogs barking, various animal smells—none of it bothered either of them. Every so often Mirko would emerge from his *atelier*, asking her to read page after page of her work in progress.

The year also saw Bardot publish a fine children's book called *Noonah: Le petit phoque blanc*, beautifully illustrated. The story is a sweet one of seals cavorting with their young, until hunters arrive with clubs, hooks, and knives on the ice floes, and start massacring the babies for their white fur. Noonah is a baby seal saved by a crying Eskimo boy, Irkou, who paddles the pup away in his kayak to an igloo, then sees the seal turn into a gray adult. Noonah's hope is that the world's women in big cities will no longer wear these blood-ridden furs.[i]

Everything froze solid that Christmas season of 1978, and the ducks and cats were slipsliding comically on the ice. It was also the first Christmas without her mother, so Brigitte invited Camille and Mijanjou, Nicolas and Jacques Charrier for a festive meal. However, it did not work out very well.

She then got the flu, receiving visitors in bed, while everything remained frozen outside. It wasn't much of a New Year's for her. But others had troubles to which she could still relate. Odette, her old makeup artist, had been ejected from the Porte de Saint-Cloud apartment in Paris that she had occupied for 30 years. Her husband had also abandoned her for a proverbial younger woman, her two sons were with their own families, and here she was at age 60 in the street! In tears she phoned Bardot, and Brigitte went to work on finding and buying her a suitable apartment, which she would enjoy for over a decade.

Bardot had also been corresponding with a woman in the Massif Central region, and there had been mutual support during each others' funks. Now the lady had organized a demonstration for baby seals in her town of Chamalières, complete with reality films and press coverage. The well-known TV producer and, later, much published and consulted animal protector Allain Bougrain-Dubourg phoned Brigitte, telling her that she ought to be there. And she duly appeared, speaking with all the horrifying images behind her. It was a success, though the lady died a few months later, and there were the usual debunkers who said Bardot did everything for publicity.

To bring in that necessary commodity called money, Bardot went back to work when Réal brought out its spring–summer 1979 collection, *La Madrague*. She was photographed wearing some dresses she didn't like, and some she did. She considered the fashion world a bit like the political realm, but at least it brought her needed cash.

While in Paris, she also went to see Tapompon, who was dying in a hospital. Brigitte spent hours and days at her side, with Tapompon bitter about having to leave her grandchildren and daughter-in-law anything. They especially wanted her diamond engagement ring (which Tapompon had received from her husband, who later died from the effects of a World War I gas attack). One day in that spring of 1979 she simply slipped it onto Brigitte's finger. Brigitte came often, and Nicolas at the time was nearby, so she often took him with her as well, a pleasant experience.

One day en route to the hospital Bardot found herself at a red light beside a little

S.P.A. truck. She was gestured to stop at the next intersection. The driver had just picked up and was taking to a probable fate of euthanasia a young orange and white *chienne*, and another dog with German shepherd in him. Impulsively, Bardot forked over 500 francs to the driver and brought the dogs illegally to Tapompon at the hospital. And the dying lady was overjoyed, giving them sugar and biscuits, and hugging them. One Dr. Bouvier arrived, laughing, then everyone else lightened up, too; and "Pîqure" (Needle) was adopted by a young nurse, while the German shepherd went with an assistant doctor.

When Tapompon fell into a semi-coma, Brigitte hardly left the place, eating meals there, and lying in an armchair for the night. She would hold "Pompon's" hand, trying again to give her her strength. Finally, the sick lady emitted a last sigh, and with hands still entwined in Bardot's, passed away.

"Tap" had always said she feared the cold of the tomb, so Brigitte placed socks on her feet and a shawl around her shoulders for the final journey. The church was full of people who had loved this woman, including 19-year-old Nicolas. Then came the great sell-off and giveaway of material things, and the apartment too was put up for sale.

Freaked by the horror of being enclosed in a coffin, Brigitte was happy to fly away to Saint-Tropez. La Madrague that spring–summer of 1979 was hot and beautiful, and she enjoyed watching the sun set on the bay. But something was missing here, too. She had lived for four and a half years with the talented Mirko, yet felt increasingly alone. Having emptied the most beautiful room of its furniture to make a place for his tools and sculptures, she no longer felt loved, and La Perruque advised her to consult a medium he knew. The medium looked at Brigitte's hands and said it was all negative there. From the tarot cards she said the ex-actress was entering her "Carré de Pluton" ("Pluto's Square") phase, a prolonged period of crisis. She had lived a number of other lives, including as queen of France, but would now have to make it through this Pluto's curse. And Miroslav was about to drop her and go off to the U.S.!

Having paid 200 francs for the reading, Bardot returned home very skeptical. As if Mirko, her only real family, would leave—it seemed preposterous. But arguments between them worsened, and one night he hit her over the head with one of his steel sculptures. Another time a suitcase slung into her belly made her fall on the steps and she sprained an ankle. He also tried to kill *himself* by banging big cement stones on his head! All he received was bumps. Nothing daunted, he ran into the kitchen another day at La Madrague, with a carving knife aimed at his gut. Even the dogs went around scared, often diving under the furniture.

Faithful, as she says, to that point, a fed-up Bardot finally took a young Brazilian guitar-player as a lover. A jealous Mirko then followed her around, blood coursing inside, and tried to spy. The couple's violent scenes spilled right onto the thronged August streets of Saint-Tropez, and artists one meets in certain galleries there today remember these public blowups.

For a while Bardot stayed there, while Miroslav went up to Paris to work on a jewelry collection with an acquaintance named Fred, and she felt lonely again. His latest obsession was jewels. The pair's idea was to use Bardot's still important name to attract the press to a cocktail party for an opening of their collection. At the same time she realized that Mirko no longer even liked her! On the eve of the Paris event, having given her tentative assent, Bardot decided to pack and go to Bazoches.

Allain Bougrain-Dubourg and a radiant Brigitte Bardot, at a press conference in the late '70s for animal welfare and protection of animal rights. (SIPA/News-Com)

Regaining healthier obsessions, she then had to travel to Marseille for the December 4, 1979, trial of one Professor Sarles, a vivisectioner extraordinaire. Here she was forced to think of millions of animal victims killed each year in laboratories—hung in machines getting pancreas drained, unable even to lie down or scratch until death, etc. Not to mention having vocal chords cut so they wouldn't bother neighbors!

By happenstance she found herself seated beside Dr. Death himself, Professor Sarles. There she was forced to contemplate a man who looked deceptively gentle on the surface, but was obviously tough enough to hurt animals for his own advancement and perhaps pleasure, too.

Photos from the lab kept revolting her, including of a German shepherd on whom they had grafted the head of a Pomeranian, creating a two-headed monster. Here was a monkey stuck in an iron collar or helmet, body parts in tubes, slowly turned to various positions in order to check circulation of the blood to various parts of the body. A cat was stuck in a similar contraption, with a steel gismo keeping its mouth open, while they shoved electrodes into his head. A dog in a cage was slowly starved for over 50 days, but forced to watch other dogs eat! To prove what? That humans are sadistic? Bardot remembers it all as worthy of the Middle Ages, while other observers might be reminded of Khmer Rouge or Nazi tortures.

Quite a few doctors and professors came out for Sarles. Giving Bardot strength on the other side was Bougrain-Dubourg from television's *Antenne 2*, pushing her to speak for these martyrs who couldn't. There was also Joël Le Tac, a deputy who had introduced a law into France's National Assembly to regulate vivisection, and some distinguished scientists (though fewer on that side of the spectrum). There were also representatives from the Ligue française contre la vivisection.

The judge forced the opposition into another hall, where the press crowded in on Bardot, and 20 cops were on hand to protect her and the others. The prefect of the department supported Sarles, and the judge then threw out the case, advising a different court venue. Making a difference in such a realm would demand patience, and induce much heartbreak.

In mid–December Mirko suddenly made the medium's prophecy come true by flying with Fred to that great city of migrants, Los Angeles. Bardot found herself all alone at freezing, mournful Bazoches. On December 18 she had a TV program in the offing on animal protection, but it was the season when solitude hurt worst. She wanted to beg off the show, but Bougrain-Dubourg pushed her into it.

Going to Paris and staying at her Rue de la Tour apartment, she tried to read a book by an ex-trafficker of wild animals, 90% of whom perished in voyages. It was too depressing for Brigitte in her present state. In Paris Bougrain-Dubourg started taking her hand and becoming a support. The TV show she had to tape included Joy Adamson of *Born Free* fame (dying a mysterious, gruesome death soon after), zoo directors, etc. Bardot was passionate in defense of trapped animals, but one Alexander Bouglione took out an old picture of her in a movie wearing fur.

Allain now started coming out to Bazoches during the holiday season. There was no Christmas tree, but she and her fellow activist were happy simply to have an omelet by the fire. However, she also missed Mirko. To liven things up, Allain brought over some friends on Christmas day, but Brigitte wasn't crazy about these media stars from a former life. They drank, smoked, and nibbled, while she served and emptied ashtrays.

Allain was another younger man with earnest ideas. He would even bring her a ring to make things more marital at the Rue de la Tour. Then at Bazoches as 1980 was dawning, they had a lovely kind of celebratory dinner. But somehow an old ghost, Mirko, having jumped the fence (the gate was locked), burst into the kitchen. Bardot easily made up her mind, and her most significant other of the Me Decade was ushered out for good.

7

Allain and the Animals
in the '80s

AS A NEW DECADE CAME INTO VIEW, Bardot kept on trying despite personal problems to do right for animals. In *Match* she saw photos of monkeys in a lab used to study the effect of car accidents. On seats with rollers they would be zoomed at different speeds against a wall, body parts smashed, brains splatted for humanity, while the other monkeys waited in terror, knowing they were next. Thousands received this treatment, but Allain said that nothing could be done about it. Bardot, however, was obsessed, deciding to call up President Giscard d'Estaing himself. And the president promptly gave orders to his appropriate cabinet minister to get these experiments cancelled!

Bardot also became aware in early 1980 of horses transported for butchery in awful circumstances. The picture was a depressing one: days and days with nothing to drink or eat, broken bones, mothers and colts crushed by others' falls, and these horses already so sensitive and easy to scare. Bardot wanted nothing less than to end the consumption of horsemeat in France. She met the president of a group on "Martyred Horses," Roger Macchia, an old soldier who had started up the group, and who provided graphic inside detail. Macchia had actually taken trips with horses from Poland, observing their manic terror and deaths from cold and hunger, and tears came into his eyes as he related the experience to her.

She and Macchia then went on *Antenne 2* to make their plea together. But her TV appearance and press interviews did not move the Minister of Agriculture, though there *was* a sudden drop in French horsemeat consumption.

Back at Bazoches her *gardien* told her that a contingent of irate horse butchers had come with knives in hands and bloodied aprons to put the fear of God in the former star; so she called up friends to come and protect her. A couple of days later she heard

126

of a mare who had worked at some fair for 24 years, sustained an injury, and was about to be butchered. For 6,200 francs Bardot bought off "Duchesse," who lived another 17 years, becoming another fixture in her flock!

By spring Brigitte couldn't wait for a hit of Saint-Tropez sun. But Allain's normal work week meant a weekend migration there, which she had always avoided, due to the traffic. Allain said he would take her and her brood in her Range Rover on Good Friday, 1980; but the idea of a clogged freeway didn't enchant her. Surprisingly, he allowed Brigitte to ring up Mirko, residing again in France, to ask if he would take her during the week. Mirko said yes, drove Bardot and her flock, and went to bed at La Madrague in a guest room. He also packed up the last of his *atelier* bric-à-brac and left with it all.

A new routine of weeks alone started getting Brigitte down again (but helped keep her memoir-writing on track). She remembers cheese sandwiches and bottles of red in front of the TV at night, and even when he was there on weekends, Allain brought work along. She meanwhile had found old card-playing friends slipping away, wanting to allow her rare conjugal moments in peace. The latest *gardien* once under Mirko's thumb was also slipping from her grasp. Bardot saw that though she paid well, a woman alone hadn't enough power with this kind of person.

The female cats were also having babies, and Bardot had to make multiple trips to the vet. And there was marketing and cooking—a house lady curved by arthritis and smoking heavily wasn't much help. Then there was a daily country walk with all the barking mutts and the fear each time of losing at least one.

On Friday nights Brigitte would pull herself together and force smiles for Allain's arrival from Paris. To compound her preoccupations, she had just bought La Garrigue, four wild hectares by the sea across the bay from La Madrague; and building a place there would bring many snafus and delays.

When on a Saturday she brought Allain over to comment on future walls and such, he would chainsmoke Gitanes and look at his watch. A one o'clock TV program back at La Madrague made such expeditions shortened ones. She would have loved to stroll the beach with him, but instead was forced to call back her dogs, so that he could watch a television which then remained on all day, while he scribbled for new programs. Even after his evening whisky and dinner Allain watched more TV, ignoring beauties outside.

An alarm clock then sounded Monday mornings at five, and Brigitte made Allain coffee, before he drove a spindly road to catch the seven o'clock flight for Paris at Hyères. He was a man of quite unvarying routines, and predictably, the two started fighting. Sometimes in the middle of the night Allain left to take a hotel room, demanding *her* Range Rover for his escape! If she felt overly angry, Brigitte forced him to take a taxi.

After such post-altercation departures, she rather enjoyed being with her kitties and dogs. But the next day loneliness and guilt would assail her. She would wait by the telephone, but Allain was stubborn, and these waits felt long. Usually she was the one to crawl, and in the throes of fragile reconciliation, she would then have to put aside La Garrigue and its construction problems, coaching *gardiens*, shopping for food, the works.[1]

It was during this era that Bardot met a nice human shipwreck, her seaside neighbor, Christine Von Opel, one of Gunter's cousins. Emphatically no Cartesian, this foil for Allain was full of problems. Her parents were dead, and though young and pretty, she had been involved with a man using her for his drug trade. When Bardot got to know her, Christine was on a kind of pre-prison parole. Bardot would take her to La Garrigue to look at work in progress, but police would follow. Christine had a daughter by the dealer, and her own childhood nanny to provide dependable care. Von Opel had herself tried his product, and when the man wouldn't supply her, she drank bottles of vodka.

Bardot grew to love Christine and got Jicky to come out and visit, figuring these two human strays might help each other and perhaps fall in love. In fact Jicky did fall, but Christine was still stuck on her dealer, and drunk all day long. That November she would be given ten years in prison, leaving child and nanny behind.

Robert Badinter, who was Christine's lawyer, and once Bardot's before a financial squabble, naturally came to ask the ex-star for help. The idea was to reach Giscard himself. So Bardot went to see the president of the Republic, but thinking she was lonely and between men, he apparently made a pass. She explained that she had come for Christine and he was taken aback, pleading his utter lack of ability to sway the Justice Ministry.

Badinter had to pull strings just to arrange a pre–Christmas visit to Christine in prison. Brigitte and Jicky flew together to Marseille, and entering, Brigitte was searched carefully. When she saw Christine all pale and thin, she cried profusely, and there was no privacy for the ten minutes they had together. Bardot never saw her again, but the story had a happy ending. When François Mitterrand took over as France's president, Badinter became Keeper of the Seals, and Christine was released in 1981. And apparently, she led a happy life after that experience.

In summer at Bazoches, obviously much nearer to Paris than Saint-Tropez, Brigitte too found more happiness in her relationship with Allain. There he helped by cutting dead trees, and giving the *gardien* an agenda. Then in September he drove her and her animals back to the Riviera, and to celebrate her 46th birthday later that month, took her to dinner in a quiet, deserted restaurant. He still, however, had things to learn in the realm of flowers or perfume.

And he was also put off by the human shipwrecks Brigitte collected, especially around Christmas-time—an old Chilean friend Gloria, in France to divorce Gérard Klein; Germaine Aziz, author of a memoir on being forced into prostitution at 16, which Bardot had read, initiating a friendship; Jicky, divorced and bitter; and "La Perruque" together around a table.

In the spring of 1981 Allain got permission to film a female boxer in an experiment to replace heart, lungs, and circulation system. On the phone Brigitte asked for Allain's help to save the dog, but he demurred—it was already a big enough deal for doctors even to let him in to make this documentary.

She promptly went and lit a religious candle for the dog. The animal was in a coma and the doctors were trying to revive her, working two days to see if they could get her out. (The experiment was to aid in a procedure that might eventually be used on children.) When she came to, Allain was too busy to get the dog, so Brigitte went, and found a messed-up animal with a huge scar.

For a week the former pampered actress spent her time teaching the poor animal to urinate and caressing her, while Allain gave daily antibiotic injections. She then left the dog with the house lady at Bazoches, and went back to regain the rest of her animal brood at La Madrague. A few days later, she says, a young girl was saved by a machine for which this "Amélie" had nearly died. On April 7 Bardot was appropriately back in Paris going one on one against Professor Jean Bernard in a TV special on vivisection. She found the man inhuman, hiding behind his putative love of children, but worried that the program accomplished nothing.

In Saint-Tropez Prosper, an old dog she had found with a string around it at her gate 14 years earlier, died, La Perruque cooked up a storm, and Michèle and the rest ate heartily and couldn't feel Bardot's pain. And the *gardien* merry-go-round continued apace. That year Bardot had 17 in week-long trials at La Madrague between May and October. Usually, they took off after only a few days. She got drug addicts, artists, and a bevy of candidates who generally considered themselves too good for such a job.

It was not a period that pleased her—the sex revolution still going strong, not to mention a drug scene that had taken its time arriving in France, but was now fully established. Plus louder and worse music, it seemed. (A la Woody Allen, Bardot preferred older, more enduring fare, like New Orleans jazz.) She had also had it with a polluted and, for her, garish Paris, living mostly in the South. Like the late General de Gaulle, she worried a lot about France's decline. In that year of 1981 she supported the presidential candidacy of Giscard d'Estaing, partly since she knew him, and mostly because he seemed friendly to her causes, though regrettably enjoying hunting safaris! Otherwise she would call herself apolitical; politicians only mattered if they could aid her animals.[2]

When Mitterrand took office, it meant a loss of protective friends in high places. Bardot, however, looked forward to July, and uninterrupted time at Bazoches with Allain. But he made a surprising announcement—he had decided to spend his annual vacation this year in Kenya!

Reluctantly, she stayed down at La Madrague, despite invasive hordes, and life continued, with the 14th *gardien* candidate found dead drunk, and given the boot. Michèle, occupying a nearby rented house with her husband, looked pampered and pretty, while Brigitte felt dowdy and alone, making do with the enjoyment of sunsets, kitties purring, dogs saved and grateful. La Garrigue was now completed, too, which meant moving furniture on numerous trips over to her new spread.

Allain's routine resumed—he would arrive on weekends, sailing and grilling fish, and with dirty laundry on hand for Madeleine. Bardot kept putting ads in the papers, and finally located a couple of fellows who ended up loving La Garrigue, and would cook, iron, and clean reliably. For La Madrague these same *gardiens* found suitable people, too.

But the more animals Bardot adopted, the more problems ensued. One dog she had found thin and lost on a beach in Saint-Tropez was dubbed "Voyou" (hoodlum); however, this pet who enjoyed both love and independence had terrible stomach problems, vomiting uncontrollably. Bardot went through more hell to keep him alive. The only vet around then in the Saint-Tropez area was in the small town of Cogolin, and there he and his assistant operated on Voyou for some intestinal occlusion he later said was the wrong diagnosis! He sewed up the dog, and Bardot passed the night there, and learned how to attend to yet another dog's functions.

The recuperating mutt then slept gratefully by her bed at La Madrague. When she woke up, however, there was blood all over, and the vet had to come and put the bottle she had been manipulating in the correct place. Finally the dog started eating, then a week or so later his stomach seemed to be hanging down, his sutures had ripped, and he had to be sewn up again! Most would at that point have put the animal down. And indeed, Brigitte was exhausted by the process, calling Michèle to come and help her. The latter arrived all Paris-elegant, not Provence-casual. Voyou had to be operated on yet again! He managed to live, but Bardot eventually started a lawsuit against the vet, who had also killed a cat with a bad sterilization. But she got nothing from it.

She was never done with these quixotic mini-crusades on behalf of animals. In the fall of 1981 she learned that a florist in Saint-Tropez had beaten her cat to death. Neighbors had heard the mother and son finishing off the pet, and the next day Brigitte confronted the cat-killer, who told her to mind her own business. Bardot called her a bitch, people gathered around to enjoy the spat, and the florist would later institute a suit for defamation of character, one that would drag on for a year.

Bardot's mail piled up, particularly after TV shows she did on animals, signaling abuses among those supposedly sheltered in refuges, burned, and worse. This support impelled her to keep using her celebrity positively and to telephone or write politicians, or mobilize lawyers. Yet by her lights not enough was being obtained.

At Bazoches Voyou and Matcho, Nini's son, were now fighting constantly. The obvious problem was that Bardot picked up these wounded creatures with chips on their shoulders, and it finally drove Allain nuts, leading to an ultimatum like the one Zagury had given her about the chick in bed. *He* wanted to come first.

But even her human menagerie took away Bardot's attention. A grandmother figure without family named Suzon was ailing in hospital, someone Bardot had already helped a good deal. Back in 1961 at the height of her fame, the star had received a letter, then visited and brought presents to this unknown suffering from throat cancer at the Hôpital Lariboisière. Then she helped put things in her place, such as a television, which over protestations, she later replaced with one in color. Each year around December 15 Brigitte and Suzon would lunch together—routines that were almost a religion. Now in late November 1981 Suzon was lying in a hospital bed, unable to eat, and clearly dying. She nibbled at strawberries Brigitte tried to feed her, and passed away in mid–December.

Another of the human animals Bardot took care of was Dany, her old double on films, who had survived cancer of the intestine, then followed her husband to Canada, a man who didn't care much about his wife's pain. Dany couldn't adapt there, and returned to France, broke and without abode. Brigitte promptly called up Odette to ask if a flat was available in her building, and fortunately one was. She bought it for Dany and Dany was now near Dédette, and despite worsening health, would have a good life for quite a number of years.

But animals remained Bardot's chief, unremitting concern. In her mail, among many other items, she heard about the abominable state of a shelter at Long-Prés-les-Amiens. The letter described a dog dying horribly where cold and hunger were prevalent, and where weak dogs were at the mercy of stronger ones. Bardot rang up Liliane Sujansky, director of the Paris S.P.A., read her the letter, and Sujansky cried. It was

December 23, a time of year when people normally burrow in for festivities. Instead, Liliane put together a "commando" group for the next day, including herself and her husband, Brigitte, and Allain, who had to be talked into it.

The operation was slated for Christmas Eve, when most people would be *en famille*. Allain and Brigitte left in cold and fog, and driving on icy roads, met the rest of the group at the outskirts of Amiens. There were several trucks to take away hopefully rescuable animals, and a vet on hand for medical problems.

Arriving at the kennel, they cut their way in with what the English call burglars' jemmies. The dogs cried out, and unable at first to see them, their liberators found themselves getting jumped on and bitten. Once lamps were lit the horror came clear: dogs dead from the cold were being eaten by ravenous live ones, and drinking water was frozen solid! Bodies were decomposing around them on the floor.

Each volunteer had to take a few prisoners, but toward the back of the building Bardot found an even worse lockup. Anorexic dogs in tiny cages where they couldn't even turn were busy yelling! She opened them all, and some moribund ones were unable to emerge. A nauseating, powerful smell assaulted her nostrils, but she persisted, still trying to open one stuck cage encasing a little *chienne*. The others warned that the cops would soon arrive, but finally she used a bar on the ground as a lever and opened up. The *chienne* bounded out and licked at her liberator. Then came the feline part of the refuge, where some 50 were suffocating to death from cat hay fever (*coryza*). The group took all they could, and now had to make a run for it.

In a skein of cars and trucks, these French crusaders somehow eluded police, avoiding the autoroute for fear of being stopped at a tollbooth. At five a.m., dead tired, they reached the warm S.P.A. of Gennevilliers, getting their suffering animals lodged and fed there.

After all *that*, Bardot then had an emotional Christmas with her *human* wounded on hand, admittedly much better off than those dying, incarcerated animals. Here were Nicolas, Odette, Dany, Allain, Phi-Phi d'Exea and his 80-year-old mother, and her *gardiens*. At night Brigitte went to see Noëlle, the *chienne* she had liberated from the stuck cage. The dog licked her hand and ate chicken, and Brigitte caressed her a lot; but she had also contracted a bronchial cough from that cold night. Outside the trees were beautifully iced up. On New Year's day the vet phoned her to say that this Noëlle whom he had examined was now dead, and the news brought more tears to a bounteous heart. In her superstitious way Bardot thought this would surely be a bad year.

Allain was in one of his cut-off phases, but Michèle, though snobbish, was a good friend to have. Just as she was recovering from her bronchitis, however, Bardot was informed by the doctor that she was now in danger of a heart attack! Above all, she needed calm in her life. Having just left her, Allain (in a yo-yo–type relationship) heard this, and came back.

At the same time a perennial problem came back, too—that of the *gardiens* of La Madrague, telephoning to say they were leaving. Brigitte's heart beat dangerously, but they were luckily replaced.

In her mail she got another moving letter from one Nicole, originally taken by the TV program on vivisection. Nicole had a bad cancer and was alone, loved animals, and wanted to do something useful in what time remained. Bardot telephoned to ask if she would help out at La Garrigue, which the latest two *gardiens* there had just vacated. Nicole had two dogs and two cats, and was happy to move to such a place.

In February 1982 came Operation "Open Door" to adopt the dogs of Amiens and others at Gennevilliers. Otherwise, it would be the grim reaper of euthanasia for too many. Newly made a producer, Allain set up a TV program to help create awareness on these issues. Bardot would have loved to take all 600 dogs from Gennevilliers, but Allain said the nine at Bazoches were quite enough for him! She too was involved in the TV show, and her impact helped get 500 dogs adopted in one day, and another 100 over the rest of the week.

On a Saturday in late February Brigitte was alone and Allain in London on business. As she did each day, she drove her dog menagerie in the Range Rover for a run in the countryside. Suddenly she heard the yelping of a terrible fight between Matcho, lying on the ground now, and Voyou and Amélie, who were murderously set for the kill. Voyou had his teeth in Matcho's neck and throat, while Amélie was busy biting him all over. Bardot yelled, but there was no one around to help. She tried to pry open Voyou's jaw and get him off Matcho's neck; but instead, his furious mouth just clamped onto her left hand, he bit down, and one of her bloodied fingers was dangling! There was still no one to hear her cries, and Brigitte felt like she was going to faint. Staggering into the Range Rover, she hit the horn to bring what dogs she could together, and saw Voyou and Amélie running behind the vehicle, having left Matcho prostrate. Once most of the dogs were safely inside, she went back out, where Matcho was lying in a heap, neck bloodied, sides bruised. He was heavy to lift, but severed finger and all, she somehow got him into the passenger seat. The car was red from blood as she drove to the vet at Montfortl'Amaury, who confirmed Matcho's severe injuries. He also gave Bardot's wayward finger a makeshift bandage, then she went back to the fields for her remaining dogs.

At home in Bazoches she drank whisky from the bottle and cried, feeling alone, and scared about losing her finger, along with beloved hobbies like guitar-playing. She wanted to be given a "there, there"; instead, a cussing *gardien* took her to the hospital in Rambouillet, where she waited in Emergency, hearing snide remarks on how inelegant she had become. She then fainted! A doctor tried to push the bone in place, but a revived Brigitte saw stars from the pain.

For six weeks she had an iron gismo tethered to her finger, the doctor hoping to "fuse" it back. Meanwhile, Matcho went through a tough operation with another Paris specialist, crazily luxurious perhaps to the cynics, or even realists. And Allain returned to help, exiling Voyou and Amélie to La Madrague, so that the wounded dog could convalesce in peace. For a month and a half, Bougrain-Dubourg considerately brushed Brigitte's hair, and helped her wash and dress.

It was still raining letters on animal abuses everyone wanted Bardot to hear about. From one she learned that the Greeks had an old law stipulating that only horses no longer fit for battle could leave the country. So they sent these old horses to France for slaughter and consumption, having first punctured their eyes and broken their legs! Stuck in cargo holds with no water or food, many arrived dead in Marseille. Brigitte and Allain visited a number of ministries to discuss the matter, but nothing resulted. One night in the tub with candles providing light, she told Allain how depressed she was about it all. The difficulty of getting such policies altered was making her think again of suicide.

But Bardot was also hoping to reveal her latest, truest self to the public, overcoming stereotypes that still clung to her. Allain and a colleague then decided to do it up as a documentary movie for Antenne 2. She really started opening up about her chaotic past, and Allain carefully, lovingly took notes.

However, as the date for the beginning of shooting at La Madrague approached, Brigitte became anxious. She wanted almost no crew, not even a lighting expert: shooting in the sun would do fine. Yet on the day before the cameras were to roll, she grew so anguished that Allain said she could cancel, if she wished. She now felt hesitant about revealing so much publicly. However, the old actress in her knew the show must go on, and nervously, she kept herself on track.

The first day of shooting brought back mostly bad memories of her old trade. To get away and relax, she took her dogs in her Mini-Moke for a walk at restorative La Garrigue. There she recovered some equilibrium, and returned to La Madrague, where the dogs gamboling around would become part of the documentary.

Correspondence she received in abundance kept revealing things that outbid her own current troubles and fears. One kindred spirit Bardot met through letters was a barefooted French lady devoting her life to saving mistreated and beaten animals in the Third World. This Edith Lesprit showed Brigitte that there was virtually no limit to human sadism. The lady's most recent letter came during the movie shoot, direly informing Bardot that she would have to leave Thailand, where she was being tossed out by the government. And she had quite a bunch of dogs and cats, some traumatically injured, to take along. A worried Allain tried bringing the quixotic Brigitte to earth—there were quite enough problems in France, and with her own menagerie! So Bardot canvassed friends to adopt, and of course everyone pleaded a full plate.

Meanwhile, Michèle was busy calling up airlines for prices—i.e., to bring Edith and her brood to France. Finally, Brigitte sent tickets to Bangkok. In addition to resolving that problem, there were the usual ones to deal with concerning *gardiens*. She found the help at La Madrague hardly the best, and soon to leave anyway; then a trip to Bazoches, where shooting continued, revealed a pigsty there as well! The thatch above the dovecot needed repair, and with difficulty she located one of the last at the trade able to do such work. But when alone, he heard derogatory things about Bardot from the current *gardiens* there—she was impossible to be with, tight with money, the lot. Brigitte thought of how she had shared her life, her festive dinners with these people! Not one to do things by halves, she promptly gave them notice.

Next day she was off to Paris to catch Michèle before her August vacation. Michèle complained to her friend that she and her husband hadn't the money to rent a house in Saint-Tropez at the height of its season; so Brigitte offered her new, unlived-in place at La Garrigue. Machiavelli might have warned her about being overly generous to friends and acquaintances, but while down in Saint-Tropez, Michèle promised to look for a couple who might suit there, while Brigitte would do the same for Bazoches. At La Madrague Michèle did indeed locate *gardiens*, who stubbornly insisted on their own couch to replace Bardot's in the little furnished house on the premises. Michèle sketched out care and feeding problems of the animals they would find there, then skipped off to La Garrigue for her vacation.

Bardot, however, had no such respite, with more *Telle quelle* segments to shoot, Matcho requiring an operation on his tail (part amputated), Edith and *her* brood soon to arrive, and new *gardiens* requiring instructions at Bazoches. Edith's arrival with her animals then sent Bardot's cats under the beds for at least a couple days! Over and over it was the old Spanish proverb on parade—take what you want and pay! Only in Bardot's case it was also *give* what you want, then pay. Among other dogs, her heart went out immediately to Edith's Radjak, bitten by a poisonous snake and left for dead, and Sambo, beaten repeatedly by a stick-wielding sadistic master, and now limping gamely on his front two paws only. Edith herself was quite the specimen, having bunked down outside in dirt for almost a year, but at least not given to dependent personality traits.

August vacations were sacred even for new *gardiens*, so here was Bardot trying to prepare for shoots at Bazoches, but also having to cook for the crew and feed numerous animals—a Harold Lloyd–type juggle. And there were constant repairs, requiring electricians, plumbers, etc. But being in such chaotic circumstances helped give *Telle quelle* its ultimate authenticity and power.

Urged on by Allain, Brigitte also recorded a song for the film, *Toutes les bêtes* (All the Animals) by Jean-Max Rivière, who had composed *La Madrague*. On the B side was his *La Chasse* (Hunting)—with half the royalties going to Greenpeace, half to the S.P.A.

The most surprising "help" blow was now about to descend on Bardot. Having taken full advantage of her generosity, Michèle returned from a pleasant August vacation on the Riviera. In September Brigitte recounted her current troubles to this friend, who looked relaxed and well. Bardot was in Paris, having obtained a short meeting with the Minister of the Environment, hoping to impress on him the cause of the French Anti-Vivisection League, and all the tortures so many animals underwent in the name of science. At a moment when she wanted to be right for this slim window of human opportunity, Michèle suddenly demanded an August salary that Bardot purportedly needed to pay her for vacation time. This request from a sister-figure to whom she had already given a lot (including many items from both her mother's and Tapompon's inheritance) simply floored her. The two had shared a good deal, but Bardot realized they were done. Her meeting with the smooth politician also came to nothing, and once back at her Rue de la Tour apartment, she scribbled out a letter, formally firing Michèle.

On receiving it the latter simply huffed off with Bardot's address book, offering no explanations or apologies! Crestfallen, Bardot thought of one Maryvonne, who had written her about being an unemployed secretary in Soissons, which had led to a trial clerical job with Allain on *Telle quelle*, where she passed the test. After 15 years of friendship, losing Michèle was a blow, but Maryvonne would now take her place—at least jobwise.

By the first day of fall—a new season compounded by another birthday—Brigitte felt more in sync. *Telle quelle* was almost wrapped, Edith's animals had settled down, and the *gardiens* at Bazoches were habituated to their new routines. The tourist hordes had mostly deserted Saint-Tropez, so Bardot went down in a more peaceful mindset to find a still strong sun there.

But after the long trip, she arrived to encounter another holy mess! The place reeked of odors like cat urine, and there was dirt and disorder everywhere. The *gardienne* there, an aged hag, and her toothless husband seemed to find it all normal. After a bad night, the ex-star was awakened in the morning by the wife's clattering in the kitchen, and her cheerful hubby raking outside her window received a yell for quiet! Brigitte soon told them to find another job. Allain had to fly back to Paris for work, and with no one to support her, she was forced to listen to the couple's arguments in favor of their retention. Why were they being fired? Because they were loathsome was what Bardot essentially responded, and a day later they received a registered letter, ratifying their dismissal. But while the bumbling husband stomped off to look for work, his wife helped herself liberally to pills and booze, and began talking incoherently about death, until Brigitte dragged her to the couch in their little, now malodorous and disheveled place on the property. Bardot then called a doctor to help this woman, who needed her stomach pumped at the hospital. The husband at her bedside there then insisted that she needed recovery time at La Madrague! A frustrated Bardot almost dialed up Michèle for help. Allain remained far away and in his own world.

It turned out that the one she had rescued now became Brigitte's rescuer. Edith telephoned the next day from Cannes, where she and a friend named Elizabeth were staying. Could she come and see her rescued pets, Cannelle and Malouk? Very quickly she intuited Bardot's disarray on the phone, proving her mettle as a new friend. Once on the spot she simply got a rental truck and filled it with the *gardiens'* belongings, all emptied out by nightfall! She then recommended a new man named Joseph, a great human gift for Brigitte's birthday of 1982, who would serve her well for five solid years.

October passed with no upsets rivaling September's, and on November 11 Allain came to enjoy a still bright Riviera sun, and to dine with Brigitte at a beachside restaurant, putting off the migration back to Bazoches. Bardot nonetheless found another animal emergency en route to her fancy dinner, seeing an exhausted dog lying on the road, paws bloodied from obviously running for miles behind a car on the highway. Stopping and hurrying over to the animal, she managed to twist her ankle, and repressing nausea, lifted it off the road. Passing friends stopped, and she asked if they would take this wounded dog; but they were afraid of sullying their upholstery. Allain nervously pulling at his cigarette, the grateful spaniel now in the car with head on Brigitte's lap, the other dogs invited for the occasion barking at this intruder, and Allain reluctantly giving consent to taking the foundling to Roger's, but *only* to leave it there: this was the latest Bardot scene in a life replete with them.

On the restaurant's terrace Brigitte ate with her aching foot in a pot of water, asking others around her to keep the dog at least till the next day, while she tried to find an owner—but none volunteered. Allain voted for the S.P.A., Roger voted to leave the mutt on the beach, while Brigitte's adoptive heart wanted to keep him—and Allain grew irritable. At home he put his foot down: either he took Bardot to Bazoches next day minus "Toutou," or she would have to find another lift! Brigitte got her own hackles up, and in the end kept Toutou, who became a leader of the pack, and also a lasting love for his savior.

On the professional level she allowed Allain to complete *Telle quelle* according to his own taste, and didn't care to review footage. How she looked now mattered less than what came from inside. In any event she was busy with much else—for example, writing an open letter to French representatives for an upcoming meeting of European ministers of the environment in Brussels. The annual March slaughter of baby seals that continued was her impassioned subject. The well-paid, yet dilatory character of French politics still disgusted her. She called up an old friend, Christine Gouze-Rénal, for help. Brigitte hated pulling connections, but Gouze-Rénal's sister was married to the president of the Republic. Crying into the telephone, she got blunt advice from her friend: write a letter to Mitterrand, and Christine would deliver it personally. Through her tears Bardot tried to make the president visualize mother seals having their babies each spring, and humans then killing such innocents so wantonly, easily, and copiously.

She also rang up Hubert Henrotte at Agence Sygma, another old friend, thinking a call to this Mitterrand supporter might help. She told him about her idea of mounting a public opinion poll in France concerning the seal slaughter. Hubert reckoned a cost of some 60,000 francs, and Bardot thought of her per month income of 45,000 francs a month tops, and got both the S.P.A. and Greenpeace on board. Four days later came the poll, based on a representative sample of 700 French people aged 15 and older. Were they for or against hunters seeking the fur of baby seals? Only 2 percent supported it, while 97 percent opposed, and 1 percent were "without opinion." Learning of the results, a happy Bardot ran to the sea, kissing her own animals, and saying prayers of thanks.

News of the poll hit the media internationally, and she received an immediate telegram of support from an official in the Ministry of the Interior in West Germany. Then came support from France's Minister Crépeau, though he would not last long in his position; but for the moment Bardot felt vindicated. She had again surmounted her chaotic life to make a difference.

That November included another high—the premiere of *Telle quelle* at the Salle de la Grande Armée in Paris, where Bardot beheld her less pulchritudinous, but real self with as much surprise as the others there. Passionate applause at the close revealed approbation of her new direction. A more mature Brigitte was being taken seriously both in France and abroad.

For Rebecca Hall's moving book of the era on animal suffering, Bardot wrote a passionate preface that Hall translated into English. Bardot's first lines leap out at the reader: "Who has given Man (a word which has tragically lost its humanity) the right to exterminate, to dismember, to cut up, to slaughter, to hunt, to chase, to trap, to lock up, to martyr, to enslave and torture the animals?... Who authorizes the genocides, the atrocities, which lead to the extinction of whole species?" Hall's book detailed many of the abuses Bardot would take on in coming years. The reader even wonders about drinking milk and eating cheese after Hall describes the terrible suffering of lactating mother cows torn from calves, they and offspring mooing for days on end, trying to find each other, while instead of staying out in nature, the cattle are often chained at the neck and stuck in factory-type situations as prisoners.[3]

Back on the Riviera of late fall came more local animal problems for Bardot to deal with—one being a mother dog found chained by her master in a pile of mud, and her two babies similarly mistreated, and Bardot and Nicole (the current *gardienne* at La Garrigue) mounting an intervention. It hit the papers that Bardot and friend had stolen a Doberman! Marketing in Saint-Tropez, Bardot then heard of another dog cooped up for eight days in an apartment, while its owners had gone to Canada. The apartment's owner was scared to enter and feed the angered beast; so Brigitte plucked up her courage, opened herself, and was received by a huge German shepherd thankfully licking her face, though dying of hunger and thirst. In tears Bardot took the animal out to her

Mini-Moke. Having shopped at a butcher's, Brigitte had two kilos of meat on hand for the starving animal. Nicole took this "Malika," along with the Doberman and its young, to live at La Garrigue.

On December 18 the first of three installments of *Telle quelle* aired on TV, starting with Brigitte's early life. An overwhelmingly favorable response of public and critics surprised her, and still available on video, the segment remains pleasing today. A second installment ran on Christmas, and Allain and Brigitte watched with neighbors at Saint-Tropez.

But police now forced her to return the Doberman mama to its negligent owners. Bardot was allowed to keep its offspring, with one finding a good home, the other remaining with Nicole, while the mother dog went home to a lack of regular feedings, ultimately impelling her to forage in garbage for mussel and snail shells that stuck in her throat and took her life.

The year also saw Bardot's quarrel with the mayor of Saint-Tropez for permitting its transformation into more and more of a French Coney Island. In 1982 Marine Minister Louis Le Pensec also went after private enclosures on the beach, personally commandeering a bulldozer to knock down one that protected a villa—until to his chagrin he discovered that its owners were French Communists! The latter declared that the Socialist minister would have done better to persecute a more celebrated neighbor, such as the conductor Herbert von Karajan, or Brigitte Bardot. Bardot retorted that if *her* protective wall came down, she would move to another country like Mexico.[4]

The superstitious Brigitte began worrying about the coming year, and what was in the cards for her. Was she due for a string of more bad tidings? At a small New Year's gathering Bardot made a place for a suicidal old friend, Pierre, down on his own luck. Here too was one Nelly, a newcomer who had just come to La Madrague with four German shepherds and a teary disposition. The keeper of both animal and human sufferers kissed Allain at midnight, then all of her dogs and cats.

On January 1 the last *Telle quelle* installment aired, this one featuring Brigitte with her animals—and she took pleasure sitting with them and pointing out their faces on TV. In response to the programs, she would receive some 10,000 letters, mainly supportive.

Her old pal Jicky was now in divorce proceedings with his wife Anne, and out of a farm they had rented for 13 years; so the ever generous Brigitte opened a joint account with him in Saint-Tropez, permitting him to build a little dream home at one end of La Garrigue. But the year indeed started badly with a terrifying *coryza* infection that quickly got to some 40 of her cats. Trips to the vet outside Saint-Tropez with her *gardien* "Jojo" became frequent. Constant cat-sneezing and spit-ups of mucous forced Joseph and the star to chase down recalcitrant felines and give them antibiotic shots, earning them many bite and scratch marks. At night Brigitte was disturbed by her cats' labored, croupy breathing, and a constant threat of suffocation. She had an "Ozotine" cage built for them, kept lugging dying kitties to the vet, and meanwhile, Allain came home on weekends and was not amused to find his loved one with so little energy left.

Each loss took a lot out of her, and Allain was also enrolled for preventive injections. As if this weren't enough, Brigitte was then dragged into court at Draguignan by the florist she had called a bitch. There she was flanked by her lawyer, Gilles Dreyfus, and when he could make it, by Allain. The opposing lawyer let fly with both barrels, calling Bardot a mainly selfish woman who had only scored in life by baring herself on screen. After a month of this, Bardot got off, but the vengeful florist planned an appeal.

Near the end of March Allain asked Brigitte if they could take the dogs for a run on the Salins Beach, which she loved, and which he hoped might get her away from her troubles. Instead, it brought new ones. She adored this stirring beach setting near La Garrigue; but somehow, with a storm approaching, they lost Nini, her beloved setter. When the rain came down in buckets, a soaked Allain, then firemen searched with no luck, and Bardot hoped against hope that Nini would find her way back to La Madrague on her own. Allain having thrown in the towel, Brigitte went back out alone into the pounding rain with Pichnou, yelling against the wind, then growing scared on the dark, deserted beach not yet in season.

The next morning Allain took the plane for Paris at seven; and meanwhile, Nini, a smart animal Brigitte loved, and mother of her setters, was still lost. A distraught Brigitte sought out a medium, who determined that the dog was stuck somewhere in water. Bardot and others tramped around and the medium proved correct—the dog was indeed found drowned in a swimming pool! Wanting to grieve, Bardot saw herself absurdly out-cried by Nicole, and was angry also at Allain's workaholic remoteness. Only her dogs consoled her, sensing her melancholy, and ceasing their customary barking and fighting.

After digging a grave, Brigitte looked hard at the earth that would eventually reclaim everyone, including her. Allain then yanked her away with a slew of animals to Bazoches—hoping to get her mind off this loss. For her grief she also consulted a priest in Paris, and left with instructions. Each morning before ten she must say prayers for the departed dog, and every evening after ten too, and for three months straight.

A rather dead Bazoches didn't seem to be cheering her, so Allain decided to take her back again to Saint-Tropez cum pets. There without Nini, and with Allain back in Paris, Bardot's great friend now became alcohol, and she could easily knock off an entire bottle of champagne in an evening. This couldn't have helped soothe pains in her stomach that Dr. Fayard in Saint-Tropez traced to an ulcer. Here was a man who had cured people around the world, and whom Bardot admired; then he too added to her string of bad luck, going off to the Alps for a three-day skiing trip, where he was found dead under a pile of snow with his skis still on. A distraught Brigitte added this Fayard to her mourning, and with her housekeeper gone, also had to do washing, shopping, cooking, and ironing, then hide her disarray from Allain whenever *he* called! On weekends she gave herself positive-thinking pep talks, trying to get herself together for his visits.

In late June 1983 her spirits revived with the warmth, and with Philippe d'Exea's marriage in Saint-Tropez, giving her almost a month of dancing and merriment. When tourist hordes became unbearable in mid–July, Allain drove her with some of her cats and dogs up to Bazoches; but his silence en route portended some sort of announcement. Finally he blurted out that back in April one of her favorite goats ("Samedi") had died. He had wished to spare her by keeping quiet about it, but she was astounded that both he and the *gardiens* could have maintained this silence all the way through July! The couple then started a predictable quarrel, Allain asserting vehemently that his tasks at work were more important than billy goats, and that he was tired of her constant crises, and that a split was advisable. Yes, he would drop her and the pets at Bazoches, but this was the end. Smoking compulsively, Bardot tried hard to mollify him, but they slept apart that night at Bazoches. And then he left, and Bardot found herself mired alone in the country. On Sainte-Brigitte Day (July 23), Allain dutifully arrived with flowers, then abruptly left again, inflicting more passive-aggressive hurt on her. After a relationship of four years Brigitte felt abandoned, and there was no one in peak-of-summer Paris to console her (*they* were mostly on the Riviera). The *gardiens* here spoke about upkeep and nothing much else, and Bardot went heavily to the red wine or champagne.

August 1 marked the fifth anniversary of her mother's death, and Brigitte suddenly wanted a substitute mom. She phoned a few people near and far, then downed a bunch of pills and liquor as well. She was found passed out in the living room, a doctor hurried over to give her a shot, and her neighbor Yvonne called Allain in the middle of the night; but he wouldn't make the commute. When she came around, Bardot began yelling at her old friends, Odette and Dany, to get out—she only wanted Allain! The doctor told her that was an unreal expectation. Allain would soon be taking some of his August vacation at the Ile de Ré to be at his parents' place there, and with a sister about to have a baby. A sad Bardot asked Odette to call Allain's mother, who stonewalled her. Then Bardot went back to the bottle, informing Odette that she was driving her nuts, whereupon the latter left for good.

Drinking during the day, Bardot staggered about alone—a part of her reputation cynics still like to hurl at visitors to the Riviera. Then Allain showed up on August 17 to find a disheveled, surprised Brigitte, who offered him a glass of red, and bread, cheese, and salad—all she had on hand. But he had only come back to announce an imminent departure to celebrate his 35th birthday at a dinner offered by his sister, and with other friends. Brigitte sent him off with a gift—a lovely wooden Buddah from Thailand.

She felt that this was indeed the end, and rang up her medium to consult stars and cards. The lady confirmed that the relationship had had the biscuit. But Brigitte's old Chilean buddy, Gloria, fortuitously filled the void with a welcome letter. The two hadn't seen each other in a few years, and now planned a reunion in Saint-Tropez. To get down there Brigitte called up Mirko, and he drove her in her Range Rover with animals—still an intermittent friend, but no romantic replacement.

The Côte was in its high, crazy season, and Bardot realized she couldn't be the nocturnal swinging single here that she might once have been. She loved the smells in the air, the change of scene, and began again to think of the world's suffering animals. Old friends showed up, including Gloria, arriving from Chile in September. Bardot heard of dog hunting and eating in Tahiti, and penned a protest letter to the island's governor. A law was finally enacted to stop the practice there.

Allain's departure still hurt, however, and Bardot had a psychiatrist from Toulon come and consult—no woolly Adler, the therapist arrived at La Madrague in a crimson Ferrari! Once there the hip shrink stayed for lunch, and the extent of his consultation was to make a play for Gloria. As her birthday of September 28, 1983, hove into view, Brigitte still had girlish hopes that Allain would somehow fly in to honor the occasion. Calls and flowers did arrive in profusion, but nothing from Bougrain-Dubourg.

That evening she drank champagne with old female pals, turning her classical music to a loud volume; but after each glass, Brigitte discreetly went to the bathroom to swallow barbiturates two at a time as well. After five glasses and ten pills, it was hard for her to recall in retrospect, but somehow Bardot slipped out the bathroom window and into the sea in clothes, swimming out in a daze. Thankfully, Gloria jumped into the water soon after, succeeded in grabbing her friend by the hair, and dragged her to shore. There was another hospital stint at a clinic in Saint-Tropez, and the press publicized the ex-star's latest suicide attempt. Descending on La Madrague, they embodied their usual *Schadenfreude*, particularly when it came to the great and famous.[5]

In shaky recovery Brigitte continued to miss Allain terribly. She tried to distract herself with a bit of nightlife, then came more terrible news—that she had a large lump on one of her breasts. In shock she visited her doctor in Saint-Tropez, who sent her to Professor Léon Schwartzenberg, a specialist in Paris. She then called Allain's secretary, and he came through, meeting Bardot at the plane and driving her over. A quick operation was called for, and she opposed it. But Marina Vlady, a friend of Schwartzenberg's, personalized matters by telling Bardot of her sister's death at the hands of this disease. Taking required steps was absolutely necessary, and on October 25, 1983, Brigitte went through with the ordeal at a clinic in Paris. And Allain stayed for the operation, though he had to leave for Austria the next day.

With two bottles stuck deep in her afflicted breast, and hooked up to two drains, and under her arm a big scar, Bardot could have little confidence in the future. The surgeon thoughtfully drove her home, sketching out her coming rounds of chemotherapy. At Rue de la Tour the atmosphere was cheerless. No victuals were there to nibble, and in the mirror Brigitte examined with horror these large black wires dangling and banging under her arms.

That night, however, Mama Olga brought her some soup, and the two ate together. Allain continued to phone now that Brigitte was completely down and out. But she wasn't one to give up easily, and even with those humiliating things tinkling under her arms, she found strength on November 5, 1983, to attend a demonstration against hunting.

The surgeon then removed the draining mechanisms, but her left arm hurt whenever she tried to raise it. She went off to convalesce in Saint-Tropez; however, it was Joseph's vacation month, and nobody there seemed to want to take the job of replacing him. Allain came on weekends—a swallow returning to a perhaps less threatening Capistrano; and Bardot gained some equilibrium by working at some of Jojo's chores. She also got a kinesiologist to aid her non-useable arm via exercise and massage.

Joseph was back in December, and Christmas with Allain, Gloria, and the usual motley crew of human loose ends was a pleasant one. Jicky had now moved into his new home at La Garrigue, but at age 69, arthritis, growing deafness, and the impact of divorce had altered his once sunny disposition.

The *va et vient* with Allain was at least in a more stable phase, even if only as weak, post–Vesuvius aftershocks. With 1984 in its infancy Bardot's patterns, however, continued, this time with the latest *gardiens* at Bazoches, to whom she had been generous, but who defected after a year and a half there. They simply left 15 cats and other assorted creatures out in the cold. When Bardot and Gloria arrived, they found a goat dead, sheep shivering half to death, and much work to do. It snowed, Brigitte was by no means out of the woods with her aching breast, the vets were kept busy by the Bazoches menagerie, and she also had to commute intermittently for disagreeable radiation treatments at the Necker Hospital in Paris, generally squired by Bougrain-Dubourg.

A southern princess, Gloria was out of her element toiling in this cold and muck, and finally, they got a couple with daughter to take on Bazoches. Gloria wanted to stay and work in France, but at something interesting; and generous Bardot, always running for an ultimate fall, had the idea of starting a boutique in Saint-Tropez that "Glo" would then run. And so they spawned "La Madrague," daunting to mount, but eventually filled with Bardot memorabilia for sale—posters, records, books written on her, etc. For a while the place became a hit, mobbed in season by tourists and by journalists, too.

With spring the warmth returned to France, but so did quarrels with Allain. They had a good row at the end of April in the confines of La Madrague, and to avoid a deeper rift, Bardot slunk off with a favored dog to spend the night at La Garrigue, where a young couple had replaced Nicole as the latest *gardiens*. She got up next day, and Gloria arrived to tell her that Allain had himself left during the night.

For Brigitte, May 1 had always symbolized spring, love, and hope, and now seemed empty and desolate. She watched happy couples around her, the odd old friend came over to lunch, but nothing helped. Alcohol rebounded as her main source of solace. Like a character in *Days of Wine and Roses*, Brigitte started emptying bottles again, trying to get rid of them discreetly. She wanted constantly to call Allain, but was afraid to do so.

Of course there was always the animal campaign, and Bardot took in an abused English setter she called "Douce," feeding it up, and reforming a personality that became an eventual replacement for wise Nini. Finally she got up the courage to call Bougrain-Dubourg at work, and he told her flatly that she really needed to change for there to be *any* chance of a reunion. She had to be less tough as majordomo of her various abodes; she must complain less—and to each of these demands Brigitte cooed her assent. They began to talk more regularly, and with the latest patch on a leaky relationship tire, were again wobbling in the right direction. Bardot's weekends became more cheerful ones.

With this problem tentatively fixed, Bardot could really thrust herself back into the cauldron of animal suffering—and did. A mare imported from Poland and about to be slaughtered in an abattoir up the coast at Nice had just given birth. The only reason she was still alive was a law stipulating that no mare could be killed when on the point of having an offspring. Bardot used her still numinous name to press the department's prefect, as well as Michel Rocard, Minister of Agriculture, to help save this equine mother's life. Political-bureaucratic inertia being what it was, however, she, Allain, and her *gardien* Joseph decided to hatch an operation of preemptive action. Having linked a van to the Range Rover, they nearly succeeded, but were then nabbed. Allain was put in jail, but Bardot finally reached Rocard on the line in Brittany, where he was enjoying a fishing trip. She threatened flatly to throw her famed body in the way of the mare's executioners, and rather than endure such publicity, Rocard gave in to her demands. "Polka" and offspring were freed, and so was Allain.

Just that one story, that "difference" showed what influence celebrity could wield—and in so many possible directions. If only Bardot's personal sea had remained calm, but of course it didn't, couldn't. New storms were bound to arise, and the next occurred on a fine day in early July, when she received a blistering call from Allain. One of the journalists she had received during her lonely period apart from him had just brought out an article in *Paris-Match*, describing her solitary life. Surrounded by her animalian courtiers, including at one count seven dogs and some 60 cats at La Madrague, she had complained to this *Match* interviewer of how tired she was of being alone, of crying at night, of having given a lot in life and gotten too little. She spoke of her multiple disappointments at the hands of men. Simultaneously, she said she had basically given up hope of a Prince Charming ever appearing again.[6]

Reading all this, Allain was plainly steamed. Who was *she* to bare the soul of their relationship in public? he thundered. He was *far* too good for her. Brigitte tried to reply that the interview had occurred in May, when they had been broken up; but Allain remained irate, saying this was finally "it," the limit, no backtracking this time, as in the past. Down went the peremptory phone.

Bardot's private life had again hit bottom, especially when a couple days later she received a call from Maryvonne (in theory her secretary, as well as Allain's), and the latter read out a letter from her Paris boss. It put more clearly and coolly what he had blurted on the phone, and Brigitte was monumentally hurt.

For Gloria's birthday she tried getting away from her blues, dining at Chez Roger on the beach. One of the young journalists she had met, Jean-Louis Remilleux, was on hand, and so was another handsome young man. Bardot had Allain inside, but as in the old pattern, she now began to think of infidelity. She also knew that she was no longer in the first flush of youth, and that it wouldn't be easy living such a life now.

Going up to Paris she got back to business, meeting with Huguette Bouchardeau, the current Minister of the Environment, to whom she had written an open newspaper letter on the use of jaw traps. In her published diatribe she had averred that Huguette had dropped drawers for some 2,000,000 French hunters! Yet in their meeting, the politically savvy woman was unexpectedly cordial! Bardot then went and saw Professor Schwartzenberg for blood work and other necessary upkeep of her health problem.

Back in Saint-Tropez Bardot also tried to busy away the hurt, signing interminable photos or record albums for Gloria's shop, which was doing brisk business. At night Gloria was a party girl right out of a Fitzgerald novel, but Brigitte now found such an existence vapid. She preferred to stay home with her animals and look out at a bay she had made famous. She would watch Gloria and/or La Perruque go out, dressed to the nines, and remain behind, feeling a bit like Cinderella. Letters still poured in, bearing all the horrors of cruelty to animals that fans and acolytes saw fit to jar her with—horses tortured on trips from Eastern Europe, whales still prey to Japanese or Russian hunts, elephants still slaughtered for ivory on which so many cultured had tinkled sonatas, birds exhausted by their migration from Africa, then finished off by French hunters when they came home to roost in the Médoc, cats and dogs badly mistreated, and on it went. It all drove her to tears, and to drink. Everyone somehow assumed that *she* could handle such matters!

With a stable love life all this might have become slightly easier to deal with, but Bardot didn't have that, and what could one do? She decided impulsively to write President Mitterrand about her animals and hopefully see him. Might as well go to the top and try to do something useful. Yet her deracinated loneliness persisted, until near the end of July 1984, when the phone rang at La Madrague, and Gloria answered to Allain Bougrain-Dubourg.

Breaking his protracted silence with a flood of emotion, Allain declared that he was unhappy, that he couldn't live without Brigitte—and yes, that he would even marry her. He said that he would come immediately, that he would call en route, and that he would be there at four in the morning. Bardot began crying, but for once out of happiness.

At the end of the month she decided to pamper this returned loved one with a weekend yacht trip to less thronged Corsica, which Allain had never visited. Just the two of them, and a crew of three to run things, while the animals would be taken care of at home. Allain agreed, and they enjoyed the tonic sea air, watching dolphins jump, and arriving on Napoleon's island to dine at a fine restaurant, beside a lovely little beach that seemed all their own. Unfortunately, even at that late date, the odd photographer flashed, so they returned to the yacht, and thence to La Baie de Girolata, where they found an even more sublime restaurant and setting.

Here, however, the unspoiled surroundings also meant a plethora of animals milling about, some clearly malnourished. One dog in particular began obsessing Brigitte. Though she was feeding all she could from the restaurant table, that one dog wouldn't eat. He was clearly ill, and a now fidgeting Allain could see what was coming. Bardot couldn't hold her tongue for long—yes, she wanted to help this ailing creature, take it on the yacht, and Allain balked. What had happened to their romantic getaway, their vaunted reunion trip?

They agreed to sail next day and find the only vet in northern Corsica, but Allain went to bed coolly angry. After a bad night he skulked out early the next morning to fish, and on returning, seemed refreshed. The dog full of ticks on his fur, as well as pus-filled boils, was carried lovingly to the boat. They set a course for Ile-Rousse, with France's female icon flicking bloody ticks into the sea! Corsica was broiling, and a taxi driver also had his temperature rise to find la Bardot as his passenger, but they made their way to find one Dr. Voisin.

At Voisin's office they had to wait, until the vet also realized he was dealing with Bardot, and then offered red-carpet treatment for the feverish, dying animal. The doctor gave the dog antibiotics, and carefully cut out its pustular spots, and didn't demand any fees.

Back in Saint-Tropez this "Gringo" then had a luxurious shampoo and fur brushing treatment! Picking over rough patches in its fur broke combs and scissors, but the eventual result was a transformed, handsome, and quite loving pet.

Besides animals, Bardot still had her humans to worry about, and was particularly anguished over Nicole's terrible cancer at 53. She knew that Nicole was all alone to face an operation in early August, and too proud to ask for help. The afflicted lady had beautified La Garrigue and made it livable; she had babysat Bardot's dogs and cats, and always put shoulder to the grindstone for the cause of animals.

In the press Bardot's upcoming 50th birthday was already an item. But belated news of Nicole's horrible nine-hour operation, removing much of her stomach, seemed more important. Why had Nicole kept this operation from her? It took much research to find the lady's number—she obviously wanted to remain self-reliant and aloof.

The only real worry the ailing Nicole evinced was for her cats and dogs, and Brigitte, always giving, decided to award her Bazoches to that end. But she was also a *fragile* giver, and a letter of September 18, 1984, from a lawyer for her son, Nicolas, hit her hard. They were planning a suit for phrases used in that *Match* article of July! Bardot still felt Nicolas to be an important part of her inside, and the letter made her cry. Now in love with a Norwegian woman, he had been absent from the apartment Brigitte had gotten him for his 20th birthday.

For the evening of September 28, 1984, she and Allain went to dine at a small restaurant in La Garde-Freinet, and Gloria and Yvonne came, too. Vulnerable to superstitions, Bardot found even the poor service an omen. Was Pluto about to inflict more damage?

In early October she heard of a hunting party chasing a wild boar into the garden of one Cosimo Lipartiti, whose gate bore the inscription "HERE BEGINS RESPECT FOR LIFE AND THE LOVE OF NATURE," and who wanted to protect the frightened animal. One of the incensed hunters managed to murder this Cosimo, and even members of hunters' organizations were shocked. So too was Bardot. She took it on herself to visit Lipartiti's widow, vowing to mention the event in her upcoming visit to President Mitterrand.

With Allain she prepared on October 16 for that appointment, but there were last-minute problems in Paris. Even this late in the century female visitors were not allowed to wear pants, so Brigitte had to get a skirt. Nor were unmarried couples permitted such a rendezvous, so they promised Christine—their go-between—that they would have a marriage license by January!

And they duly got to meet with Mitterrand, though for him it was mostly a photo-op session. He gave them a tour of the Elysée Palace, and also crowed about the Louvre's new Pyramide. But in an office far from labs or pounds replete with suffering he could feel nothing. And in the aftermath Bardot also received flak from organizations she strongly supported, such as the S.P.A., which criticized her for speaking for *them*. She started to feel Pluto and the bad cards at work again.

One of her perpetual concerns was hiding all these sources of melancholy from Allain. Spending Christmas with him and with a *gardien* couple at La Garrigue, she was determined to put on a happy face. But there was no call from Nicolas, which hurt her, nor from her old friend, Jicky, though he was near at hand.

Predictably, yet another Allain crisis was in store. A homosexual couple friendly with both of them—press representatives for the S.P.A.—casually informed Bardot over dinner that half the money collected for an anti-vivisection campaign she had mounted went to their organization, and this without her knowledge or consent. Of course there was need all around, but Bardot grew angry, and Allain felt caught in between. The couple was staying in the "Microbus" at La Madrague, and on the evening of December 29 she stomped over there, where Allain was eating with them, and chased them out. Allain's betrayal saddened her most.

He took off soon after, and receiving a call from Edith, a natural carer, Brigitte cried into the phone. Edith and her friend Elizabeth came right over the next day, and though they prepared a lovely New Year's Eve dinner, Bardot was unable to eat. Instead she hit the bottle. Staring into the fire around eleven, she decided impulsively to drive out alone to La Garrigue, where she cried on the graves of Nini and a recently deceased cat she loved. She wanted once more to end this mishmash of a life, and there were pills there. At midnight she whisked down a dozen, then, using a large glass of champagne to swallow more, another dozen. She then lay down by the animal graves.

At twelve Jojo had rung up the new *gardiens* at La Garrigue to wish them a happy New Year, and the latter mentioned seeing Bardot's car, but no Brigitte. Jojo instructed them to search for her, and two hours later they found her unconscious. Again, the slender thread binding her to life was very nearly snapped. Jojo and the young male *gardien* at La Garrigue frantically piled her body into the car and sped her to La Madrague. Edith, a doctor in the blood, tried to hear Brigitte's heart, but couldn't. It was a bad time to locate requisite medical aid. They raced to a clinic, but the staff there wasn't of top quality. Edith yelled for action; Bardot's heart was still faintly going, and an intern finally pumped her stomach. Edith meanwhile whipped back to La Madrague and found Schwartzenberg's Paris phone number in Bardot's address book. She dialed and got him, asking him to call the clinic and walk them through necessary procedures. She also called Allain, waking him up, but he wished to be left alone.

From Paris Schwartzenberg stayed on the phone all night with the little clinic on the Riviera. Only in the morning did Bardot regain consciousness, and that afternoon she was driven to La Madrague. Coming around, her superstitious mentality finally brought something positive: a personal vow *never* to do this again. Every sign from Death had told her clearly that he (or she) didn't really want her yet!

Vow or no, teary, depressive mornings with piles of work to do, and having nobody she cared about at her side continued to make life after this latest suicide attempt a slog. From friends like Madeleine, another cancer survivor, she did derive a sense of comparative good fortune. And Allain began visiting again on weekends.

But he was too often gone, and yes, "a drunk, I was becoming a drunk!" she confesses.[7] Bardot's feelings of bereftness only increased when she heard in a Saint-Tropez shop that her son had been married in Norway. In the company of women she knew, she tried to go out and forget troubles, but such outings bored her. She did meet a young, married singer-composer, who phoned persistently. Meanwhile, Allain's calls remained perfunctory, even when he rang up to announce casually that Nicolas and wife had just had a baby girl, and that Brigitte was a grandmother!

But her men had been nothing if not unpredictable, and several days after that, a clearly split Bougrain-Dubourg called with an offer of two plane tickets for a little vacation in Agadir on Morocco's Atlantic coast. Did she want to go? Bardot said yes, flying from Hyères to Paris to meet Allain for what, however, became an uninspiring trip.

Their digs in Agadir were full of tourists, precluding real privacy, and no one made up the room until they finally learned who Bardot was. Then the manager of the complex took them to his private, seaside home, and even that (for someone used to Saint-Tropez) wasn't much by comparison. While dining, Bardot filched all the food she could to feed mangy animals outside, including sheep, some of whom would have throats cut during Aïd-el-Kébir. She did get the fawning boss to promise he would feed the dogs regularly here.

Arabs in turbans and a busy souk didn't cheer Bardot, nor did a landscape virtually without vegetation. As is generally the case with couples in disarray, no vacation—certainly not this one—could prevent their continued slide downward.

She then came home to more depressing news—another terrible epidemic of *coryza*, and immediately obsessed, she began pressing Kleenexes to runny noses, surveying distended tummies, and arranging for cortisone or antibiotic shots. Her cemetery at La Madrague filled up, and knowing Allain wouldn't want to talk to her in a saddened state, Brigitte instructed Jojo to answer the phone.

She meanwhile connected with other animal saviors, such as Anne d'Arcy, an aristocratic English woman living in a village near Saint-Tropez, and caring for some 150 dogs whose owners had left them. The lady was doubly heroic, given her paralysis from a case of pre–Salk polio. With admirable will and ingenuity, she had finally attached strings to some of her dogs, who managed to pull her from bed, and she painfully relearned how to walk. Bardot came to meet and value a wonderful woman, but with a disorganized interior, including plentiful rats. Bardot then produced an unsought check for 20,000 francs. Some 50 of her dogs in heat would need spaying, and she would pay the vet. She would also push the village mayor to make Anne's place a receptacle for *all* lost dogs of that area. In April Brigitte learned via journalists that she would be graced with one level of the Legion of Honor, which pleased her, but which, she says, has become devalued since. She remained at La Madrague, since Nicole was still at Bazoches, though patronized by the *gardiens* there. The ailing lady was a valuable long-distance phone friend.

One bugbear in this period was the horrible state of the S.P.A. in Lille, an industrial city of the north. Dogs in a deplorable state were dying in droves there, and Brigitte kept pressuring the mayor for change. Finally the current one informed her that they would open a new S.P.A., wanting her to attend the opening ceremony. In mid–April she and Allain went to a fancy luncheon in Lille, and then to the new shelter, with TV cameras shooting footage.

At the beginning of May Allain called her about the poaching of turtledoves in the Médoc, outlawed by French law, but a persistent problem. Driving across France and giving a press conference, Brigitte and Allain got little respect from those they wished to convert—rotten eggs were lobbed at their car windows, and certain irate hunters wanted to strip the ex-actress, then tar and feather her in the plumage of dead birds! Stopping for a bite, Bardot and Bougrain-Dubourg got no service from the waitress, either. Bardot did make Allain turn off near Carcassonne to meet one of her supporters, whom she knew only through letters. The lady's husband nearly dropped dead seeing Bardot arrive, but the stop at least provided a touch of sweetness in a fruitless, bitter campaign.

Back in Saint-Tropez the heat was bringing the sybaritic down in droves, including Gloria, back from Santiago to sell tee shirts, sunglasses, and "La Madrague" beauty items that Bardot herself used. Sometimes Bardot would go into the shop, and people quaffing a glass of champagne or whisky would be happy to meet her—some from her past, most newcomers she had no real wish to know.

Allain was yet again on the outs with Brigitte, and Gloria urged her to try out the nightlife of that era. But Bardot still found these people on the town as "stupid as brooms," and not at all to her taste.[8] However, Jean-Louis Remilleux came down and livened things up. She and the young journalist went off for Mother's Day to visit old people immured at a retirement home, something she—and they—truly enjoyed.

One day Bardot was pawing over items at an antique shop in Saint-Tropez, and went crazy for a beautiful Russian icon. This was actually no antique, but made by an eccentric named Véra de Kerpotine, who lived on the Plain of Cogolin in that region, turning one out every few months to stay solvent. Impulsive as always, Bardot went to visit the lady in a cabin lacking even running water, not to mention telephone or electricity. For the animal lover here were a bunch of cats and one guard dog, and up in years, Véra to preside, though dying of cancer.

Bardot offered to bring food for the cats, and her jewels to use for the fabrication of icons, and to take care of the kitties in the event of the lady's death—the latter's great worry. Véra in fact died soon after. And the old Catholic girl made good on her vow—with one friend taking some of the cats, and Brigitte moving a good ten to La Garrigue. Véra had painted up her wedding chest, dear to her, and before she died gave it to Brigitte as a token of gratitude and affection. In the nick of time, two hearts of gold had found each other.

Bardot kept connecting with these sensitive, and in varying degrees, lost souls. During this period she would be out driving, and repetitively noticed a young blond driving a car nearby, or crossing her path while walking. There seemed to be meaning there. One day while taking pages of her autobiography in progress to a typing service in Saint-Tropez, Bardot found this blond inside; but the girl darted away like a startled minnow. The typist, Dominique, had no idea who she was. On another day Brigitte and "Glo" were in their boutique trying to lift boxes, and Gloria called one Mylène to help. It was the enigmatic blond, and with no trouble, she lifted them into BB's car. Brigitte then invited her over for dinner. Mylène was a 20-year-old who blushed often, and who at first held her tongue. As time went on, however, she became a kind of daughter to Bardot. Mylène learned how to vaccinate animals, and also to soothe Brigitte through her down times.

In the men league the odd ex-lover came around, and there were some new ones, too, but it was all ephemeral. Bardot simply felt too old for the singles life (and of course new diseases had also become prevalent). Eating dinner one evening at Chez Roger, she met a tanned ex-tennis star and current auto racing phenom, who seemed interested. Prankish, Bardot decided to make him jealous by turning her attentions elsewhere. Finally, she broke down, inviting him to one of her outdoor Provençal lunches filled with herbs from the garden. It turned out that both she and he were on the rebound. Beside this handsome, bronzed fellow Brigitte felt rather plain, no longer able to take the sun since her cancer. He said he simply wanted to hold her and forget his wife who had taken off. But like so many he couldn't remain in Saint-Tropez, and was soon off to Paris for work, and mostly gone thereafter.

When Bardot went up to Paris and outskirts, her most nourishing visit was to her sister-figure, Nicole, another sensitive person entirely devoted to each animal at Bazoches, but clearly dying of lung cancer. Bardot then went out in noctural Paris with Jean-Louis Remilleux, the young man trying to intuit an epoch he hadn't known. He prodded her on the song Gainsbourg had cut with her, "Je t'aime moi non plus," and which Jane Birkin had made a hit. Why hadn't Bardot brought it out? She mentioned the jealousy of Gunter Sachs, and Remilleux exhorted her to find Gainsbourg and do something about it now.

Feeling hesitant to reconnect after so many years, Brigitte nonetheless located Serge, living in predictable artistic disorder. And they did indeed bring out the old record in 1986, relaunching a phone relationship as well.

Pluto, however, still seemed always to hover nearby. Bardot's loneliness in Saint-Tropez at New Year's, pet troubles, and the need to hurry back up to Bazoches, given Nicole's rapid demise—none of this seemed to augur an improvement in fortune.

Hoping against hope for Nicole, Bardot rang up Dr. Schwartzenberg, and he declared a horrible operation her one slim chance. At Bazoches Bardot and a neighbor, Yvonne, worked through Nicole's lachrymose fears, and the 54-year-old finally went to the clinic. Back at her little apartment on the Rue de la Tour, having had to taxi everywhere, and with nothing to eat there, Brigitte felt overwhelmed by all this sadness that clouded her life. Shaking herself from her torpor, she dialed her old friend working at the Agence Sygma, and he invited her out to dinner. She was too tired, so he got a pizza delivered to her, and also provided a car with chauffeur to get her around in greater Paris.

For Nicole's operation Allain joined Brigitte at the clinic, but he wouldn't speak to her, and both waited silently through the night. When Nicole finally came to, she couldn't bear the pain. Having done what she could, Brigitte was ready to fly back home to La Madrague, but not before more pain up here. At Bazoches the *gardiens* had fed rabbit to the dogs, and one Diégo, a foundling now nearly two, died, probably from choking on bones; and Bardot threw a fit. She also had to inform Nicole of this development, which gave that already suffering lady a panic attack.

In Saint-Tropez a mountain of mail greeted Bardot, providing more melancholy news of sadists neglecting, experimenting on, even scalping pets. Crying about this to Gloria, the two decided on the spot to bring back the Fondation Bardot. The decision having been made, they started with headquarters in the small shop of "La Madrague"; but the two enterprises were too different for healthy co-existence. Bardot then decided to rent a little room with telephone in the rear part of "Bureau Service," where she brought her typing. A reliable woman became the secretary there, and subscriptions began filling coffers.

In late April 1986 Bardot received a call from the *gardiens* at Bazoches. Nicole had died and Allain had organized a hasty funeral. A saddened Bardot took an early flight from Provence, and at Bazoches beheld Nicole's body being eerily combed by crawling ants, until she got her moved to the chapel. And then came the funeral, where Nicole's favored pets, held on leashes, had the front spot near the coffin. It all spawned more tears for a lady who had already cried proverbial rivers.

Bardot then faithfully distributed animals as a kind of inheritance—one of them to neighbor Yvonne, lasting right up to the latter's death in the mid-'90s. But a German shepherd named Vélo actually died of a broken heart at Bazoches. Another, Citronelle, blended in with Bardot's own brood.

At La Madrague more animal misfortune awaited her, but in May Bardot had to go up to Paris again, and at the Rue de la Tour, she fielded a call from the new prime minister and longtime mayor of Paris, Jacques Chirac—a dedicated fan. And he wanted to help her "animalian" cause. The next day she went to the Matignon Palace, taking Allain along for ballast; but in retrospect, she wondered if she had been alone, she might perhaps have lost her heart to this elegant political figure. For years to come Bardot and Chirac remained intermittent friends.

Having tasted the glamour of power, however briefly, she flew home to La Madrague—and back to animal pills and needles, and a decidedly unglamorous life. The dogs were in a manic gear, some plainly in heat, the males were fighting, and Bardot trying to affix a kind of diaper to the females was again in the midst of another slapstick comedy. At least the help situation improved with the arrival of a solid man named Raymond, whereas older friends like Gloria now disappointed. Bardot had helped her with the boutique, and now found that in a half year or so it had only brought in some 6,000 francs of revenue, versus significant expenses and taxes. Gloria was obviously doing the job in a superficial manner; however, bristling at Bardot's poor evaluation, she ran off to live with friends who she then turned against her benefactor! In addition, Noëlle, Bardot's likeable secretary of the foundation lodged at the rear of the Bureau Service, got in a row with Dominique, its owner. So Brigitte had to move the operation to the Microbus at La Madrague, putting in office equipment there.

In terror of breast cancer, which would indeed kill her in her fifties, this Noëlle soon went off to visit Dr. Schwartzenberg in Paris, vacating her position. That autumn became a low one for Bardot, but her solitude in this last, pre-clicker TV period in France at least made her an omniverous reader. She loved the classics—Balzac, Stendhal, etc.— and also historical novels, generally on peasant life circa 1900.[9] To put herself in the ambiance she lit candles, and read herself silly by the light of oil lamps.

The '80s also saw an intermittently combative Bardot strike back litigiously at those who seemed to take advantage. It had started back in the '60s with unauthorized photos or the unauthorized use of her name on certain items; but recourse to her lawyer, M. Dreyfus, now increased dramatically. In 1983 the magazine *Hara-Kiri* released a series of touched-up nude photos, purportedly of Bardot. She asked for the equivalent of $8,000 and got it. Then her lawyer went after a Spanish magazine, *Interview*, for telephoto lens photos taken of Bardot from up to a third of a mile away. This time the sum demanded was over $20,000. Other magazines felt her wrath as well, particularly those who used the hidden telephoto lens.

Other bugbears included the increasing popularity of kiss-and-tell memoirs. In 1985 she sued Sacha Distel for his autobiographical revelations, and then came "Vava" himself. Vadim's memoir of the '80s, titled in English *Bardot Deneuve Fonda*, had gone out to the exes in draft, and while it didn't bother Jane Fonda, it did bother Deneuve, and most emphatically, Bardot. In 1987 a Paris court ordered him to pay $10,000 to each of Bardot and Deneuve.[10] She even went after an old friend, Eddie Barclay, for using her voice on a video cassette, and in the late '80s, fashion designer Paco Rabanne. Not to mention the company which had made some of her automobiles, Rolls-Royce.

Financially too, her foundation was hard put to keep afloat. A plucky Bardot decided to hit the marketplace of Saint-Tropez in the cold, but authentic season of March–April 1987, operating in the mornings from seven to noon. There she sold off old dresses, beautiful silver, autographed photos—anything to raise money. The garage sale atmosphere was enjoyable, and sympathetic Tropéziens brought her coffee, food, and even flowers. Finally, Bardot found herself tapped out.

On a visit to Minister of the Interior Pasqua, she got nowhere for animals, but picked up practical information that began obsessing her. A *real* foundation, she learned, required an untouchable, income-producing minimum of 3,000,000 francs; otherwise one could face numerous legal problems. So Bardot now decided to mount a real auction—no square in Saint-Tropez during the off season, but Paris, and one run by professionals. She immediately rang up Maurice Rheims, who came to assess her finest things.

It all came together for a televised auction presided over by Maître Jacques Tajan on June 17, 1987. At this event vociferous applause brought tears to Bardot's eyes, and she made a much-quoted statement: "I gave my youth and beauty to men, today, I'm giving my experience, and the best of myself, to animals."[11] Allain was on hand, and the stuff fairly flew out to the sound of a practiced gavel—tables, furniture, lithographs bearing names like Chagall, film costumes, the wedding dress she had worn for Vadim, guitars, and even the 8.36-carat diamond Gunter Sachs had given her a decade after their divorce. Family items she had carefully kept wrenched Brigitte's heart as they departed at Tajan's live auction, or to bids fielded over the phones from around the world. Tajan ended by offering his own gavel, asking Bardot to lead the auction on it! It brought 20,000 francs. Noble, he also bought a fine little *coiffeuse* Brigitte loved, and discreetly gave it back to her after the show. And she got very near her magic number of 3,000,000 francs. She then kicked in the rest from savings, and as president of a legitimate foundation that would be based in proper Paris headquarters, had won another battle in the animal protection campaign.

Of course the road ahead for someone who took on so much would obviously reveal more potholes. La Garrigue again needed *gardiens*, and with summer season approaching, it was hard to find replacements (people worked in restaurants and so on). Once new ones were installed there, Bardot was ready for her annual trip to Bazoches cum animals. In searing heat ten mutts could at least stay cool in the Range Rover, which had just been outfitted with air conditioning. It was nonetheless a big operation, including outdoor bathroom breaks. Allain accompanied her, and Bazoches seemed blessedly well run; but he departed soon after. She had a good friend there, Yvonne Cassan de Valry, to break the loneliness, pushing her to shop in Montfort-l'Amaury or swim laps in the pool. Bardot also stayed in touch with the Foundation, overwhelmed with abandoned animals; but loneliness and nocturnal tears continued to plague her. She read like mad, did crossword puzzles, and learned that her fine new *gardiens* at Bazoches wouldn't stay the winter (being from the South).

The trip back to the Riviera with a friend named François became a comic nightmare worthy of another film. The road was chock full, and the car gave out right in the middle of the autoroute! This was before cell phones, so François went off on foot for help, leaving BB alone with her panting, barking dogs, some having to go out to relieve themselves. François got Yvonne and a new Jojo at Bazoches to come back in two cars, but it all took an hour.

The animals were then shepherded back to Bazoches, but no place specializing in Range Rovers was open for repairs. The next day Allain was located at his office, and he set up a private jet for Brigitte and her brood. It cost a lot of money, but he pushed Brigitte into spending like a star on her own needs. The dogs on this chartered plane slid back and forth, but it all worked out, and became an annual tradition.

At La Madrague the empty fridge and having to test dog urine and the like—none of that cheered her much, despite the pretty surroundings. But she kept throwing herself into the fight. There weren't only rotten shelters in small towns to visit and reform, but also in cities like Toulouse, against which she had inveighed for quite a while. Dominique Baudis, the mayor of Toulouse, kept promising and putting her off, and meanwhile, animals aplenty were dying in this cave-like, moldy atmosphere. Finally, via press threats, Bardot forced the planning of a new shelter there, scheduled for completion by the end of 1987.

She kept going to bat as well for single animals, like a paralyzed German shepherd on his last legs, who got the star's sweet loving, and a blessed year and a half with her; or an old cocker spaniel shut up in a freezing, padlocked place by a gross hunter, and yowling till neighbors complained—and who would pull this poor "Gold" out? Why, Bardot, of course. She brought Gold to La Madrague and gave him a miraculous change of life. She would even save mice from her La Madrague cats! As she put it, "I feel more animal than human...."[12]

Stability? It came and it went. To reach Toulouse in December she had to take a tiny plane that teetered in awful weather, and then arrived to flashes and journalists she bashed aside as she entered the new shelter. A practiced hand, she opened cages amid the scoldings of a tough *directrice*, grabbed dogs and paid for about ten of them, then returned in still awful Sunday weather to La Madrague.

A phone call informed her that photos of Bardot and dogs at the Toulouse shelter had made the papers and that subsequently, adoptions were brisk. On the minus side she had come back to blood all over the place from Mouche's breast tumor rupturing! She got hold of a fine vet in Sainte-Maxime, who patched up the dog, as he had once patched up soldiers in French North Africa.[13] Then on December 20 she heard of the sad death of one of her animal-protecting colleagues, Maryse Lepape, who had ironically swerved her car to miss a dog in the road, and hit a tree.

The soap opera continued at Christmastime when Mylène found a new *gardien* to work in at La Madrague, and this crazy from the Haut Var tried to rape Bardot in the middle of the night. She fought off the man, until finally help came—cops nibbled at by the dogs, and asking her all sorts of distrustful questions.

Saint-Tropez in this season became a pretty site that distracted her from such horrors, and Allain made it down on Christmas Eve with a dog she had saved from the Marseille refuge, Domina. There was a latecomer tree, champagne, dogs all swirled up with Christmas decorations, and even Domina getting into the swing of things. It was a snatch of happiness—for Allain was set to fly off Christmas day to see his parents, and the old Jojo of La Madrague was leaving for a new post before New Year's.

The *gardien* merry-go-round continued, with Bazoches finally OK, but a dumbstruck young couple at La Madrague obviously unready to fill Jojo's shoes there. Bardot received many cards wishing her a happy New Year, and a sweet call from Chirac, who told her how nice it would be to relax on Mauritius; but her life continued to be filled with dog feedings, clean-ups, etc.

By mid–January she was back in "term"—not at college, but on a mission to the awful shelter at Cabriès. Again, she came to *see* (something the chattering classes rarely do), then act. And what she saw exceeded her worst expectations.[14] Some dogs there could barely emit a sound for help. In tears Bardot sent off an associate to buy food, and procured a vet at several times the normal rate; and he made his selection of those dogs and cats that might still be salvageable. The shivering kitties all had *coryza*, but wolfed down their food, TV people were mobilized, and Bardot made a difference on yet another day of her life—with some 50 lucky animals adopted. She got home that night stinking and hungry, and her helpmate at the refuge, Lesly, had to whip up a regenerating meal of salad, omelet, and camembert cum red wine.

The next morning they all went off to shut down Cabriès for good, emptying it of its animals (the untaken slated for other shelters, some far afield, and moved at Foundation expense). Bardot found herself in the thick of rats, excrement, and cleaning solution, while journalists, including from the U.S., watched. And still her heart went out to the disinherited—including one dog simply lost in the fuss, and whom she learned was blind. That one she piled into her Range Rover.

The ex-actress with a heart of gold came home to food that was this time prepared, and with five new kitties from cages, awestruck at their new happiness. But the next day municipal authorities at Cabriès overtrumped her work, reopening the place, and immediately she called higher bureaucrats in the department of Bouches-du-Rhône, emphasizing how this town had ignored all the rules for shelters. She also thought of taking them to court.

More animal deaths claimed her emotions at home. At La Garrigue a caterpillar infestation killed her mare Duchesse, who was buried by her bedroom window there. Brigitte was worried about which animal would next eat something with a poisonous caterpillar on it. Then came the death of maternal, 15-year-old Pichnou, one of her favorite dogs, and on it went.

In spring 1988 the presidential contest pitted Mitterrand, not her preferred fighter for animals, against Chirac, who seemed more committed to such causes, but lost. It was also the time for a new director of her foundation, Liliane Sujansky, to find old but costly headquarters near the Trocadéro in Paris (Rue Franklin). With quite a number of administrative headaches, everything had to be moved from Saint-Tropez to the capital.

The couple who had only wanted to work at Bazoches in the warm season now gave way to downright thieves! Gone were some of Bardot's records, her guitar, and **In public demonstrations or at home, Brigitte placed the defense of animals at the top of her list of priorities.** things of greater value. The authorities took the matter under dilatory advisement.

Back to Saint-Tropez in one of the

smaller aircraft that terrified her in bad weather, and watching Foundation bric-à-brac leave the Riviera, Bardot prepared herself to leave with a friend, Roland Coutas, on November 30, 1988, for an infamous zoo at Vendeuil. Here were more animals living a hell on earth, trapped behind bars in icy cages and swimming in excrement, and she again had to *see*. On arrival she beheld a bear who had plainly gone insane, and catatonic monkeys in their cages, and a zoo director who couldn't keep up, and was prepared to sell all for 80,000 francs. Impulsive always when it came to animal protection, Bardot's heart said yes, while her reason wondered where she could place these poor creatures.

Liliane Sujansky, however, knew a man in the West of France who could care for such animals in semi-wild surroundings; and Brigitte regained her Paris apartment, feeling only slightly better. She kept wondering why people had to trap, cage, and ruin the lives of all these defenseless creatures in the first place.[15]

Before returning to La Madrague, she had dinner with Remilleux and Coutas, and both urged her to get back into the media floodlights for animals. Their idea was a series of TV programs on various protection issues—four a year to be aired, and with some 100,000 francs of pay to aid the Foundation, which would also have a hand in the production. Bardot was worried about going back into the old arena, and as a female icon past her prime physically; but she said yes, and the first shoot on the decimation of elephants and the ivory trade was slated for early 1989.

Christmas was a thin one back at La Madrague, especially from a human point of view. And there were the usual problems with her extensive brood, particularly sheep and goats at La Garrigue, dying more frequently now due to the lack of a dependable vet. Mylène presented new songs to Bardot, hoping to hit Paris for auditions with a demo tape; but none of that allayed Brigette's problems at this point in her life. All she had was a pile of mail showing her the most disgusting sides of animal suffering.

Her radiant preface to a book published that year by a distinguished animal rights crusader, Roland Gillet, helped focus people on such issues. A longtime deputy and senator in the Belgian parliament, Gillet's book is an intellectual paean to a world where animals might be treated kindly. Especially ghastly are his pages on vivisection—distinguished professors at Yale or Brown getting vast sums of grant money to drown animals in icy water, shock them, make them vomit, inject them with nicotine, or to note how many liters of water are needed to fill up a horse's lungs and make him/her die. Not to mention sewing up the eyelids of cats, starving other animals for a week on end, and of course ripping out vocal chords to prevent any aural evidence of such sufferings.[16]

At New Year's 1989 Brigitte received calls from Liliane, Yvonne, and a few others, and her current flaky *gardien*, wearing a flimsy bathing suit in all seasons, gave her a peck. But in terms of animal abuse there was no break at all. The era saw her protracted fight with the "Dog Connection" of Agen—a racket involving animals taken from refuges, really stolen for another vivisectioner in academe. This Dog Connection had become bolder and bolder, with brisk sales to labs of dogs filched from their owners, to the point where no one wanted to let their animals out alone. Some even had leashes cut. Or trucks would drive by with a dog in heat to attract males, who would then become guinea pigs. The police didn't know how to handle all this—especially one unsavory "F.," who cut off identification tattoos on dog's ears. This F. had his own shelter, and

Bardot applauded the courage of raiders who found captive dogs there, doped them to prevent a commotion, then pirated out about 100 to safer shelters. Even then, F. had the gall to contact authorities, wanting to recover dogs he had himself stolen!

Bardot's blood was up for the combat, and on January 16, 1989, she, Liliane, and Roland went to the biggest S.P.A. near Paris to defend their saved ones against an imminent incursion by F. Police were there too, but F. didn't show. The stink of urine and feces, and the cold, got to Bardot, but nothing deterred, she herself took one of the dogs slated for execution, and emboldened others to do the same. (This "Kiwi" would make it five years, until run over by a car at Bazoches.)

For her televised *S.O.S. Animals* series the one-time national symbol of beauty prepared herself with new clothes and a haircut, and got back on the cover of various French magazines. This period also saw the 20th anniversary of her Marianne bust, of which there were now some 8,000 in town halls around the country. There was a bigger anniversary coming as well, the 200th of the French Revolution's outbreak.

In April came the taping of her first program devoted to elephant poaching and the ivory trade, and Bardot first had to stomach documentary footage showing the hunting of these poor, waddling, helpless creatures. Her emotions couldn't be disguised as she begged viewers and the government to fight against ivory importation. After dining in a *brasserie*, she still saw the elephants being killed as she went to bed at the Rue de la Tour.

The next day she hit the Senate for the first time, awed by the surroundings, but less than thrilled by political foot-dragging on a law for animal protection. She also used her time in Paris to watch the Foundation grow into a more up-to-date organization in its new digs. A co-worker, Frank, was a computer buff, and began to make the wheels run more smoothly here. She also got to visit Chirac, who as Mayor of Paris co-sponsored an adoption weekend slated for the Vincennes racetrack, and honoring St. Francis of Assisi.

Back on the Côte d'Azur Bardot didn't rest on her laurels. There were still bad shelters galore to publicize, and to alter. Starting with a big one in Toulon, she and Liliane participated in the cleanup—dodging rats, smelling the usual awful smells, seeing new dogs assaulted by more hardened ones, and cats coughing continually from *coryza*.

The next stop was the shelter of Brignoles in the rain, and again there was a "concert of barking" here,[17] dogs forced to live in their own detritus, rat bones all over the place. Right in her home department of the Var, Bardot saw plenty of abuses—from these poor shelters to poachers to sanguinary, if legal hunters.

At La Madrague she nervously prepared to watch her *S.O.S. Eléphants* program with Roland and Mylène; and it was a success, garnering many viewers and racking up over 20,000 phone calls during the program itself. Several days after it was aired, Brice Lalonde, Minister of the Environment, told Bardot that France would cease importing ivory, and then it snowballed to the European Union, and in theory at least, to some 100 countries!

Bardot then taped her next *S.O.S.*, this time on animal experimentation, which had so taxed her the past year; and on June 23 at 10:15 p.m., *S.O.S. Expérimentation animale* ran. She had to watch awful TV footage of dogs cooked alive in ovens to test anti-burn products, or others left without food for up to a month to fuel yet another report on the effects of starvation! The army was a part of all this, testing napalm, for example, by turning dogs into howling balls of flames Bardot couldn't forget. And again, the response was positive—almost 20,000 calls received, but producing no immediate changes on the political landscape.

Animals in need abounded everywhere, including at the overwhelmed Foundation headquarters in Paris. And the *gardien* problem never abated for long. The exhibitionist of La Madrague left, and Bardot found out that he had killed a few of her trees, injecting them with gas to prevent dropped leaves from ruining his car. In a panic she called Mirko for help, and he and Madeleine unearthed a new gem of a *gardien* named Adrien, a long-term one at La Madrague, as it turned out. And to replace a toothless fellow at Bazoches, who never learned to drive, this Adrien found a couple who wanted to be near Paris, and Bardot gave them a tryout. The husband soon got work elsewhere, but his wife, Bernadette, loved animals and became a mainstay there.

The mayor of Saint-Tropez, Alain Spada, had meanwhile started a campaign to keep dogs off the beaches, and Bardot threatened again to leave. Dozens of villages around France begged for her residency—sending her flyers, gifts, etc. Finally Spada relented, and kept the police from bothering her.

She continued fighting—at this juncture for 29 monkeys stolen by a raid of May 20 in Lyon, and whom she wanted the Foundation to buy. She had real empathy for the courage and organizational skills of commandos from the Greystoke organization, and when it came time to defend them in court, paid for adept lawyers.

Jean-Louis and Roland then had her watch the movie *Gorillas in the Mist*, and she was both moved and depressed by the great fight of Dian Fossey put to screen, and the near extinction of magnificent creatures whom the murdered oddball had protected. When Bardot shot her next TV program in September in Paris, *S.O.S. Hunting*, she used this depression and inner turmoil to excoriate men she wished animals could shoot back! Meanwhile, sardonic hunters continued blasting away, even at Bazoches, where some took playful potshots in Bardot's direction![18]

On October 1 and 2 came the annual adoption weekend co-sponsored by her foundation and the town hall of Paris, with Chirac in attendance at Vincennes' hippodrome, but Bardot weakened by a bronchial cold. Dragged to the mike, she could barely speak, but the crowd applauded her anyway, and some 500 cats and dogs found new homes.

Still fighting bronchitis at Bazoches, Bardot was now obsessed by the need to take her foundation to the next level—i.e., considered by the State to be of "public utility." With enough money to place it on that footing, she could avoid a heavy tax burden, and the organization could also launch civil suits against vivisectionists and other foes. But it was harder to do than she imagined.

A visit from Serge Gainsbourg, recovering from an operation, constituted an interesting diversion. Dining at Bazoches, he downed an entire bottle of 1970 champagne, and was clearly in disarray; but he also took out his checkbook and impulsively gave the Foundation 200,000 francs. Bardot felt very close to him, and to their memories—one of her band of sacred, wounded human animals in the twilight of a life.

On October 30 *S.O.S. la chasse* aired on TV, garnering a record-breaking 100,000 telephone calls! La passionara of animals had made her impact, and over 10,000 letters vigorously supporting her anti-hunting stance also arrived. But the political arena was harder to sway. In the name of sport millions of animals would continue to be killed or wounded each year in France.

Bardot was also moved at a special Paris showing of what she considered her finest picture, La Vérité. When those in the audience applauded vigorously, she cried profusely, knowing that despite her denigrators, she had also touched a lot of lives in her first vocation. She would of course get the same old question Artie Shaw received many times after quitting bandleading: why *had* she given up movies?[19]

Having answered by rote, she could now teeter back to the Riviera on a little plane full of animals and with Roland at her side; but on landing, no Mylène to meet her with the Range Rover! It turned out that the young lady had been frying on the beach, and lacking a watch, simply forgot the rendezvous, creating a nutty scene of Roland and Brigitte calling and chasing dogs all over the tarmac!

The next day was November 5, 1989, and Brigitte went to the cemetery below the Saint-Tropez citadel that had once guarded this coastline. It was the 14th anniversary of her father's death, and she placed a rose there in his honor. On her way back home came the sudden idea of donating La Madrague for the Foundation to obtain the money needed to give it more clout. Bardot signed the first set of papers on Saint Nicolas Day (December 6), honoring her son; but the state required a big cut, and the two notaries she needed to work with in Saint-Tropez and Paris would require another two and a half years to complete the transaction bureaucratically.[20]

Bardot was happy on the Riviera that December of 1989; but a necessary flight back to Paris would jar her short-lived routines—a shoot slated for Christmastime on S.O.S. Butchered Animals. The flight was again draining, but not nearly as much as documentary footage she was then forced to imbibe—abattoirs she knew well, including ones exempt from the 1962 law requiring that animals be unconscious before being drained of blood. Both kosher butchers and Muslim ones permitted up to 15 minutes of torment, keeping animals conscious until entirely bloodless. Not that that was the only kind of slaughter impelling Bardot into vegetarianism. She thought often as well of the millions of geese and ducks made into foie gras for the delectation of the rich—force feedings of these creatures until they were simply stuffed, bursting livers and dying awful deaths. Bardot was nothing less than the French Upton Sinclair of that period!

8

Battles of the '90s

AFTER BEING GINNED UP for her latest TV shoot, Brigitte went to see Serge Gainsbourg again—mainly so that he could help Mylène get the go-ahead for a recording of his song, "Harley Davidson." But she found the old French-Jewish composer a drunken wreck en route to a death he seemed powerless to avoid.

Back in Saint-Tropez she and Madeleine watched the S.O.S. program on slaughtering a few days after New Year's 1990; and again, Bardot grew teary, hoping that the millions who went that way each year to end up on plates might gain something concrete. Then came January trips with Liliane to more shelters of the Var, and the Dog Connection of Agen was also brought to trial, implicating a number of top professors, a trial Bardot attended in the middle of the month. However, the wheels of justice required their usual laborious oiling, and for now, nothing was decided. And star-struck Mylène offered no solace, constantly asking Brigitte for feedback on her songs. When solitude became unbearable, especially in the wee hours, Brigitte found herself plugging away again at what became *Initiales B.B.* Sometimes she worked till five a.m., distracting herself with bittersweet memories of another life.

And then there was Spain—almost an "issue-country" in itself, with festivals in various towns where people used animal suffering for catharsis! Bashing asses to death; throwing goats off church tops, while the priest said prayers and the crowd let itself be splattered with blood; beating hens and roosters to death in one town; men on horses chasing a bull and the first to cut off its testicles receiving a prize in another; in May the slow strangulation of bulls in one place; in June arrows blinding bulls in another, and again, castration following; in August a greased pig chased and strangled; in August also, dwarfs mutilating bulls to the laughter of children—and there was much more.[1]

Then came pleasant news from Paris that meant added media attention for the Foundation. A company that cruised boats down the Seine wanted to name one of them

157

the *Brigitte Bardot*. And they wanted Bardot herself on board for the first voyage. With some misgivings she and Mylène arrived, and on the cruise heard a band play some of her old songs, including "La Madrague," which she impulsively sang at the mike. Then she and Mylène rocked together on "Harley Davidson," and the place erupted—one of those rare respites that soothed her soul.

While in Paris, Bardot also felt she should do business—including a press conference denouncing government inaction on animal protection. What if you lose the battle? asked a journalist. "I'll blow up the government," replied BB.[2] Of course she didn't mean it, but the quote headlined in *France-Soir* the next day. She also shot her latest program, *S.O.S. Animal Trafficking*, and visited the Foundation, reeking more and more of foundling urine.

On returning to Saint-Tropez at the end of April 1990, she got her usual passionate reception from her pets, ripping happily at her clothes. In early May Bardot watched *S.O.S. Trafic d'animaux*—on creatures plucked from jungles or forests, and trapped interminably in warehouses or zoo cages; but familiarity was apparently breeding contempt, and France wasn't responding as much as before.[3]

Spring also meant the onslaught of slit sheep throats during the annual Aïd-el-Kébir festival—these animals bled to death in car trunks and bathtubs, or in meadows that Arabs paid to use. It would grow more widespread through the decade.

The heat came early this year, and brought tourists early as well; so Bardot was glad to pack up with her brood for an early summer trip to Bazoches. That meant her Noah's Ark plane ride, and then Bazoches too was burning under the heat. But here were Yvonne, as good a friend as she had, and Bernadette, a wonderful *gardienne*, to provide companionship, while Bardot watered and watered, or drank sangria at night. An Italian cook made treats to go with the drinks, and her pasta or ratatouille racked up pounds, which Brigitte didn't mind—no man in view to impress. Yvonne's chain-smoking also had an osmotic effect, and Bardot began smoking more herself.

In early July pressure from Brigitte and her foundation, along with other environmental groups, forced South Africa's government to announce the temporary suspension of a Taiwanese business deal involving the clubbing, stabbing, then bleeding to death of 25,000 seal cubs and 5,000 adults. The main purpose was to export carcasses for the manufacture of pet food, and from the genitals of adult male seals, to produce aphrodisiacs for the oriental market. Bardot offered some $22,000 as compensation to South Africa's government, which stood to make eight cents from each slaughtered seal. But the whole matter infuriated and sickened her, making her hate the era even more.[4]

A call from Jacques Chirac provided a momentary lift; but then the roof on her existence was about to fall in again, as so often it had done. At the end of July Bardot received a "questionnaire" on Aïd-el-Kébir (or Aïd-el-Adha)—from *Présent*, a French Catholic daily she was warned was on the Right. Bardot noted that she would have given her response to the Communist newspaper, *L'Humanité*, had *they* called. Forthright as always, Bardot proffered her opinions, and a press brouhaha came fast and furious, lodging her in a Rightist, xenophobic box that was an absolute distortion, but would continue to plague her through the coming decade.[5]

In early August she went to bat for a chimpanzee and orangutan mired in a Japanese underground laboratory. They were imports from France, and Bardot met with a bowing, tea- and saki-offering, but ultimately stonewalling Japanese ambassador in Paris. One of the animals died, and Bardot demanded that Japan immediately return the mistreated chimpanzee (Chloé), stuck in freezing conditions at Kyoto's Primate Research Institute, whom they had gotten in return for ten monkeys. Bardot made this Chloé in a basement without space, sunlight, or affection real to at least some people; but then the animal passed away of heartbreak several days later—bringing more heartbreak to Bardot as well.[6]

Her next S.O.S. program was announced on TV one night in August, when she hadn't even shot it yet! She returned to Paris to excoriate what authorities she could find in that dead season, and got a contract to tape in early September, and for a larger potential audience.

August, however, stayed scorching at Bazoches, and at Cahors too, where she went to see dogs panting and dying of dehydration in the cages of a poor shelter. She fought to adopt, tried paying off euthanizers who made good money, and finally denounced them to the town's mayor, threatening a media blitz there. She ended up saving dozens of the condemned, and having made a difference yet again, flew home exhausted, and with a new dog in tow, Lune.

All the while, the ex-star who fought so hard for animals was intermittently and unjustly critiqued for not extending that fight to humans. However, she did find time that summer to lobby for Romanian orphans stuck in cells, working with a journalist from *Paris-Match* on a campaign to free them, and again unfurling her checkbook to the tune of 50,000 francs.

In early September she finally recorded S.O.S. *Sea Mammals* and once more had to contemplate things like ponderously pregnant sea turtles having eggs snatched away, and being slaughtered in the abattoirs of Mauritius (where Chirac had invited her to relax). It all affected her strongly, and her emotions came easily for the shoot. To calm her, friends like Mylène were not as dependable as they had once been. Mylène was busy shuttling between the Riviera and Paris, working on her new career, and treating Bardot rather as hired help, it felt. She even used Bardot's private line for business, as though it were her own. Thankfully, things would return to normal when Mylène didn't last as an entertainer.

In addition to her latest program, Bardot got on TV as part of a different one with a panel format. Here again she tried to denounce the slaughter of seal pups off the coast of Namibia, involving the usual clobberings and stabbings, which made cow seal mothers emit coughing sounds of mournful panic for days on end, having been separated from their doomed offspring. However, Bardot found herself overwhelmed by others on the panel, discussing issues like taxes.[7] She raced back to Bazoches to watch her S.O.S. *Mammifères marins* (September 12), and though 16,000 calls lit up the boards, people in power didn't seem once more to be watching. Who would *act* for these huge, defenseless animals?

Her 56th birthday came soon after, and all she had was a pile of flowers, champagne—but no man. Mama Olga sent her new book, *Moi, j'aime les acteurs*, but on reading it, Bardot found her agent, somewhat like Vadim, taking a bit too much Pygmalion-like credit for the former Bardot phenomenon. However, Olga certainly confirmed the horrors of the paparazzi for a once young star, and was consistently warm to her there.[8]

In early October came another annual adoption weekend in Vincennes, with Bardot and Chirac attending; but the crowd seemed too interested in getting close to a celebrity, while all Bardot cared about was moving animals out of cages and into homes. Thankfully, some 600 cats and dogs were adopted that weekend.

Early October was also the time for her annual private plane trip back to La Madrague cum dogs—never an easy one. Nor was the return; for there were always surprises in store, and more *gardien* blues, this time at La Garrigue, where everything was a mess, and the animals were in bad shape. Her help there had killed off a number of goats by giving them only broccoli to eat for a week, reminiscent of Mussolini's castor oil! Needless to say, these latest caretakers were promptly fired.

An analytical aside, however, seems à propos here. Bardot had kept bringing these people into her life to whom she lent both her discipline and largesse. There was that split in her still between the old puritan, Catholic doer and the generous, impulsive, easygoing *révoltée* and romantic. Had she been one *or* the other, perhaps these problems with help and so-called friends would not have occurred at quite the same rate. However, one takes la Bardot as is, and while she may not have made every *gardien* or friend happy, she certainly did a consistent job for many hurting creatures.

Still bothered by these goat deaths, she now raced back to Paris in mid–October to shoot another TV documentary—her schedule tighter because of summer delays. This time it was *S.O.S. Animal Combat*, and she was forced to discuss forms of cruelty that a Nero might once have showcased at the Coliseum—pit bulls decimating declawed bears, cocks fighting each other, cats or rabbits fed as bait to attack dogs, not to mention the balletic stabbings of bulls in *corridas*. She watched the depressing footage, did her shoot, returned to her lonely apartment on the Rue de la Tour, and then started becoming dizzy. Managing to find one friend on the phone, Frank, she was soon treated by a doctor, saved once again from a possible death that would have taken away an irreplaceable benefactress.

On October 17 Mylène brought out her recording of "Harley Davidson," and Bardot's program on animal fights also ran that night in Saint-Tropez; and this time the impact was huge—25,000 calls received at the station, and eventually, 4,000 letters. Subscriptions to the Foundation shot up, and journalists in other countries wanted to use the film for more reports on this worldwide form of sadistic pleasure. But governments continued on the whole to drag collective feet.

Bureaucratic torments kept assailing Bardot; legalization of the La Madrague donation was far from final, and her foundation might still need to be dissolved. She found it all a persistent headache, and resorted to booze and cigarettes with a vengeance, until finally, hitting a kind of bottom, she decided to make a pact with the Virgin Mary and go clean for six months. In return, she asked that her favorite sick dog, Douce, be allowed to live. And for six months she would keep her side of the bargain.

It was getting harder and harder to leave Provence and run up to frantic Paris; but it kept being time to tape again—still on a tightened schedule. The latest program dealt with fur-bearing animals. Again, there was more horror to imbibe visually—trappings, gassings, and cuttings up—not only of minks, but of dogs, foxes, rabbits, even cats, whose fur was in some places used to combat rheumatism. Not to mention baby seals. The show ran on December 5, and Bardot watched at La Madrague, finding that on this issue

Brigitte Bardot and Jacques Chirac at the annual pet adoption weekend in the Paris region, early October 1990. The event was sponsored by Bardot's foundation. (EPA/NewsCom)

her foundation had much international company—PETA, the Bellerive Foundation presided over by the Aga Khan, actresses like Anouk Aimée, and other people in England who showed films of bloodied furs.

The results were palpable: not only 10,000 calls to the station, but a large drop in fur sales, and women who wore them now getting paint thrown on them, or fielding insults. One can of course nuance historically—furs *had* once kept European life going in harsh winters and jobs had depended, and still did, on the industry; but as computers had replaced typewriters, so there seemed to be no reason by the '90s why synthetics could not (in most cases) become a replacement.

Again, a variety of European journalists wanted to contact Bardot on this supranational issue, including one from Holland, who phoned and made a connection with his nice voice. He asked for Bardot's private number, and against her better judgment, she somehow gave it to him. The man then wished to come and see her, and made good with a surprising visit to La Madrague in mid–December, the visit (it turned out) of a balding little Rumpelstiltskin! Who also needed to be fed at this late hour, and briefly put up with, until Bardot could get rid of him. Lonely or not, she told herself not to fall for any more phone voices.

On New Year's she and Mylène played *Trivial Pursuit*, and she kissed all her kitties and dogs, wishing them and herself a better 1991. But a new year brought no surcease to her constant campaign for animals. The Foundation learned that elephant poaching was up in former French colonies like Senegal and Mali, and they sent people down there. Then came 80 Mongolian wolves pried from certain doom in Hungary for refuge in the Parc du Gevaudan in France. The doping and transfer of these animals to pleasant surroundings was a heroic operation, taking place at the beginning of March, and one that made a splash in the media.[9]

Bardot was also pestered by journalists for interviews on the death at winter's end of a tattered Serge Gainsbourg, when she only wanted the luxury of grieving alone.[10] To soothe mind and soul, she went to see another soul brother, Jicky, living at one corner of La Garrigue, and mostly indifferent to her animal obsession. Dussart had raised a son who dialectically became anything but a reclusive artiste; rather, he was a topflight French golfer. Bardot and Jicky had very different concerns, but his poetic presence gave her sustenance—it was the intermittent, yet enduring relationship of two people who had long understood each other.

Paris then called her back for a March TV shoot on horses, and how they were transported and slaughtered for their meat. Was such slaughter really necessary now? In Europe only France, Belgium, and Italy still allowed horsemeat consumption, and even the rest of the world mostly disdained it. Why perpetuate all that needless suffering? Bardot felt that it might help to stress the already clogged arteries of a cholesterol-sated civilization.

While in Paris she also attended court proceedings being held against commandos of the Greystoke group, who had taken some 20 baboons from a laboratory in the mid–'80s. She procured a well-known lawyer, Jacques Vergès, to defend them, put her money up for bail, and again, her own reputation was on the line.[11] After all the stress involved, returning to La Madrague was very welcome, though she found it killing not to smoke or drink in honor of the dying Douce! Taking the latter to her little chapel at La Garrigue, she prayed there, Rousseau-like. But on March 16 Douce passed on—more sadness for Bardot, despite a beautiful Provençal spring.

On April 1 she watched *S.O.S. Chevaux*, and again the results were significant—a good 30% drop in horsemeat sales, and scary death threats from those in the trade via letters and even home phone calls. Playing her guitar with Mylène, Brigitte tried her best to ignore them; or else she joined Liliane Sujansky for more crusading trips to awful shelters. Her life remained anything but a placid one.

The poachers of Médoc were still shooting as well at exhausted turtledoves, arriving after their winged migration over the Sahel desert and the Mediterranean. These hunters would often leave the murdered birds on the ground, not even bothering to cook them. In 1880s America it had all seemed limitless; but anyone with a smidgen of environmental consciousness now knew the fragility of such creatures already at death's door, then having to dodge gunfire.

Impelled by Bougrain-Dubourg to publicize the issue, Bardot flew to Bordeaux and met Patrick Mahé there, an editor at *Match*. A contingent of police was also present for security. At a press conference someone dropped a still warm, but emphatically dead turtledove before her, and Bardot picked it up and waved it at the journalists, trying her best to jolt people out of their comfortable insulation.

At the end of May she switched gears, presenting a petition with over 40,000 signatures to the president of the European Commission in Brussels, hoping to end fur imports into Europe. But the Commission temporized, it couldn't be done until 1995, and even at the turn of the next century, loopholes were still being found and exploited.

In Paris she also shot *S.O.S. Dogs and Cats*, where some of the most damning footage didn't make it past censors. She had to witness attack dogs warmed up by ripping cats to shreds, and the rest of a sad litany. She also went to see Chirac, still mayor of Paris, trying to move him on the exotic animal trade (parrots, snakes, monkeys) stuck in cages around the city; but finally she "got it" that he was first and foremost a politician, which meant keeping meaningful changes mostly on hold. Issues like the disgusting Chinese trade in bear paws weren't *his* central concern.

June was beginning, and La Garrigue stirred Brigitte's soul; but even by the beach of Salins, there were problems—one of her cats missing, then found dead, and a few more to follow. The culprits? Soon after, Bardot read in *Nice-Matin* of three roving dogs of an as yet anonymous owner, terrorizing and killing cats and presumably smaller dogs around Saint-Tropez. It made for a fearful June, given that her kitties loved to wander the beautiful outdoors down here.

Then there was the persistent issue of Muslim sheep slaughter in France, which would eventually land her in deep trouble. A precipitous rise in the number of the animals killed at Aïd-el-Kébir (almost doubling through the decade) impelled Bardot to ring up the new Minister of the Interior, ending with the activist slamming down her phone in disgust. Yvonne's arrival at Saint-Tropez made her spirits rise, however, and with Mylène in attendance, they watched *S.O.S. Chiens et chats* on June 17 at the hardly prime-time hour of 10:40 p.m. Yvonne cried, Mylène became angry, but would there be real changes made?

Especially vexing to Bardot during that nascent summer season was the usual rise in pets left behind by owners seeking fun in the sun. Bardot was harder on women here, who, she says, were usually the ones to drop animals at an S.P.A. or the Foundation. Their tearful explanations cut no ice with a person of high standards in this domain.[12]

The Foundation was truly becoming inundated, so it began transferring more and more of these pets to "La Mare Auzou," the retreat in Normandy, where sheep, horses, and other animals could gambol in peace. But right in Bardot's own backyard of Saint-Tropez, there was the usual summer heat wave that fried vehicles left there all day (at monstrous parking prices). Dogs were too often locked inside, while owners strolled the town, checked out galleries, had leisurely meals, or took sea cruises. Many of these animals would then succumb to the airless heat, with slow, horrible deaths resulting. Even here, where she liked to relax, Bardot had to make a difference, and at considerable time and expense, she started up a free dog-sitting service during summer day hours—a cool, nicely furnished place. Unfortunately, it would fold after only a couple of years for lack of personnel (unemployment benefits a big competitor to jobs).

Bardot herself was sick of that summer heat, which did her body (after breast cancer) little good; but on migrating to Bazoches, she found everything burned out there as well. Chain-smoking Yvonne, informed by a specialist that she had throat cancer, but unwilling to quit, worried her too. She loved Yvonne, but was finding her suicidal stubbornness hard to bear.

In mid–September Bardot got back to business, giving a press conference in Paris on jaw traps, soon to be made illegal by nations of the European Union, save for her own France! But the happiness provided by progress on that front was dimmed for her by news of Yvonne's upcoming operation, slated for late October.

Bardot then attended a third annual adoption weekend at Vincennes, with Chirac again on hand, but the crowds scaring her. Another 500 animals were taken, and Bardot herself adopted a kitty no one had chosen. There were also smaller "adoptoramas" to attend, such as at a shelter near Valenciennes, where too many cages had too many abandoned animals inside them. Brigitte was saddened to see the little ones go faster than big Labradors or German shepherds, sadly stuck inside their metal boxes and hoping for another day.

There were now numerous trips to the hospital to comfort Yvonne, including to hold her hand when the operation was about to begin. Afterward her friend was much weakened and a candidate for chemotherapy; but Brigitte still saluted the job done at the Hôpital Américain. With this ailing friend in her thoughts, Bardot then shot her next program in Paris—S.O.S. *grands singes* (Big Simians). She thought of Yvonne, but also of Dian Fossey, paying with her life in the mountains of the former Congo; and of all the poor chimps or orangutans stuck in prison at labs or zoos.[13] She thought too of threatened, intelligent gorillas tracked and killed so their hands might be dried and sent off to make knick-knacks like ashtrays! Or their heads becoming wall adornments in too many countries.

The program moved *her*, but the western world was drifting out of an environmentally conscious phase into a more frantic, and simultaneously, more indifferent era (the "low dishonest decade" of the '90s, to rework W.H. Auden). Bardot wanted to regain La Madrague, but Yvonne begged her to stay near Paris into November. Finally it got so cold and foggy that her Noah's Ark flight to La Môle's tiny airport at the base of the Tropézien mountains became more chancy. Brigitte hated leaving Yvonne, but knew she had to do it. From La Madrague she continued to phone her ailing friend several times a day, and also stayed up on foundation fights, for example, against cosmetic brands relying on animal experimentation. (Bardot herself knew which ones to avoid.)

In December 1991 news of her donation of La Madrague to the Foundation then hit the press. But Bardot never rested on her laurels. In early January she shook herself out of a depression, traveling to a rat-filled shelter with almost 200 cats and dogs in cages, many beyond hope. Again no proverbial star, she had to *see* these rats by the hundreds, scurrying amidst kitties and canines. The Foundation went right to work on cleansing the place, and then finding a better locale to lodge these incarcerated animals.

And thence to Paris for a kind of summing-up show called S.O.S.: *Already Three Years!*; and soon after, the welcome news of the Conseil d'Etat (Council of State) *finally* recognizing her La Madrague donation, and the Foundation becoming one of "public utility," protected henceforth from crushing taxes, and able to launch suits against mistreaters of animals. Of course the old Spanish proverb about taking what you want and paying came back to haunt Bardot: the Foundation was now under three separate ministries, Interior, Environment, and Agriculture, creating much more administrative paperwork, and demands on one's time.

At Saint-Tropez there were the usual deaths of beloved animals, and on March 23, a distressing cancellation of Brigitte's recent S.O.S. show, deferred (she only learned at midnight) for another day and time. Irate, Bardot shot off an impulsive letter of resignation. She had broken off with men and with the cinema, she could cut off with this, too! (Regrets only came later...)

That spring she got another helper at La Madrague named Michèle, excellent with animals, and a good friend too. The end of March also brought news of a U.N. prize awarded to Bardot for her pro-animal activism, giving her (she hoped) more clout in her own country.

In April 1992 she went to Brussels to give a press conference, denouncing the cruelty of Spanish fiestas; and then came a Paris flight home to the little airport of La Môle, where one couldn't land after 9 p.m. To get out of the capital expeditiously, she and her associate, Frank, rented an ambulance (shades of *Les Novices*) to blow through stoplights! It was great being back home again with her animals; but then to offer support for a protest, she went down the coast to Fréjus, where tamed boars were allowed to delight tourists, but would (against her wishes) later become hunter fodder again.

Then when summer season approached, she went to see shut-in old ladies on Mother's Day at the local retirement home. Unwanted photographers' flashes confused them, and Bardot still found herself unable to master the media's omnipresent power. She also fought for a mother of six menaced with losing her children—once again, she was hardly in the corner of animals alone.

In June Yvonne came down to La Madrague, now able only to whisper; so to put her at ease, both Brigitte and Mylène whispered as well, and they had a good time—the last, as it turned out, of Brigitte as a single lady. For her life was now about to change in a very big way.

It all started with her lawyer on the Riviera, Maître Bouguereau, inviting her to his place for drinks on June 7. One of the guests would be the politician Jean-Marie Le Pen, who wanted to meet Bardot. She had encountered him once at a hospital back in 1958, where both were visiting soldiers wounded in the Algerian conflict; and now on a day when it was pouring like mad, she wanted to cancel the engagement. But Bouguereau wouldn't hear of it, nor would Yvonne. Reluctantly, Bardot attended, and she found Le Pen more interesting than the shibboleth view of him (he was a raconteur, singer, joke-teller, and was obviously well read). At the party someone suddenly took hold of her from behind—an unknown named Bernard d'Ormale. And it became another headlong romance!

In the personal realm Bardot had had seven lean years (1985–1992) basically alone, in some ways a blessing, including for the composition of her memoirs. As seen, most of her relationships had eventually sprouted hefty price tags, partially due to her public notoriety. The man she would break her fast with in the '90s, and pay with (and for), was this d'Ormale, whose name sounds like old French nobility. In fact his real name was Bernard di Chiara-Ormale, and his origins were Italian.

Born in Marseille in 1941, Chiara-Ormale, like Sachs, had had a peripatetic childhood. Perhaps Bardot, herself a kind of lost puppy, had always had a need to give a home to other lost human puppies. Di Chiara-Ormale had resided in Paris, South America, then in early adulthood, francophone Africa, where he became a businessman. From a movie on the soccer star Pele he made money, then moved fully into film production and distribution, altering his name to Bernard d'Ormale, for which some would consider him an arriviste. He did seem to have the sensitivity many Bardot men had possessed, as well as real skill at raising money. (Other sides of his personality were not immediately apparent.) From oil sheiks and other deep pockets d'Ormale had managed to wangle some $25,000,000 for a business idea to transform Nice into Europe's Hollywood. But when Mitterrand was elected French president in 1981, placing several Communists in his cabinet, Americans and other investors stampeded away. D'Ormale's business life would remain one of hits and misses. But Brigitte had rarely gone for men who hadn't to some degree been cut up by life!

The next evening there was a dinner on the beach at L'Esquinade. Bardot prettied herself up and quaffed wine, but found that Bernard was no drinker; instead he stayed with coffees, and with cigarettes by the bundle.

On June 12 Yvonne turned 63 and for her birthday celebration set up another dinner chez Roger at L'Esquinade, with Mylène and Nicole playing and singing bossa nova, and Brigitte singing and dancing too. And Bernard appeared! Obviously invited.... And bringing a bouquet of flowers for each of the women. All this made Brigitte happy, but happiness with her was always slated to be an in-and-out-of-the-clouds phenomenon.

For d'Ormale then went off to Picardy on some kind of business, while Bardot resumed her usual life of pet illnesses and the like. It then took a week, but the phone finally rang; and it was Bernard, telling Brigitte that he loved her, and that the next evening (June 20) they would dine again at L'Esquinade. And suddenly a pattern began asserting and reasserting itself—that of the disappearing man! Brigitte, Mylène, and Yvonne showed up that evening, had drinks, ate, enjoyed themselves, waited, checked out another place in the hill town of Ramatuelle (had he meant a different restaurant?), returned, and Bernard finally arrived at one a.m., without apology.

When Brigitte took him back to La Madrague around three a.m., this fastidious fellow was assaulted by her jealous dogs, and also displeased by the profusion of cat hairs that sullied his fine clothes. And the *gardien*, along with Michèle, flashed worried looks, obviously wondering about Bardot's future. To get to her bed M. d'Ormale had to jostle animals who were perfectly comfortable there, and the problems continued when the sun came up the next day. Brigitte then had to inhale odors provided by a four-pack-a-day man, whacking back multiple coffees as well, while Bernard was put off by garlic and other smells emanating from what was cooking in the kitchen. It didn't seem 100% auspicious!

One could certainly cite the fine Broadway song here, "What I Did for Love"! One thing Bardot did for love was get back on lethal cigarettes herself. She also learned to respect d'Ormale's "space," as he went off for interminable meetings. Already there were significant differences between the two, and they would only intensify.[14]

Mylène got Brigitte back to ordinary pursuits, including her first zip around the bay on a single water-ski in eons, and at age 57. There was also the prospect of renewing her contract to do more S.O.S. programs in Paris, but she just wasn't in the mood. Getting used to Bernard took too much energy—his clean-freak habits began driving her crazy, as he seemed to be interminably wiping cups, disinfecting surfaces with a cleanser, ironing his pants, or spraying at mosquitoes or flies. He also had much ill to say about whatever was on TV, unless it happened to be a political show that pleased him.

Bardot's commitment to animal protection naturally wavered, and when Foundation people called, Bernard would grumble and cut them down, his jealousy overt. Of course he got out to do his own thing, but not predictably; he hadn't a 9-to-5 routine, and that was a big part of the problem.

On July 31 he pushed Bardot into an outing aboard a yacht where Le Pen and his wife also turned up, and photos were snapped; and Bardot soon got a reputation that would dog her (and her foundation) from then on. Suddenly, as she says, she became some sort of Nazi to sectors of the public! And she hadn't even wanted to go on the blasted cruise in the first place.

There were frequent dinners as well at L'Esquinade, where Roger's wife, Edna, sang the praises of her native Norway. Both she and Bernard then started pushing Brigitte into a trip there. The idea was that she would not only see a beautiful country, but would finally meet her daughter-in-law, and her two grandchildren, little girls she hadn't yet gotten to know. An early August heat wave was pounding the Riviera; it was bound to be cooler in Scandinavia, so she acceded, and on August 12 she and Bernard left on the trip. Edna would travel there too in order to show off her Viking land.

At first Bardot loathed the summer airport crowds, but then was happy to encounter a cool and indeed beautiful northern country. Her granddaughters were darling, but spoke no French, and it was nice to see Nicolas and his wife, except that they were petrified photographers might shatter their privacy. Fjord excursions were spectacular, but Brigitte couldn't help thinking of the whales that the Norwegians harpooned, and seals they slaughtered.

The trip's apogee for Bernard and Brigitte was an improvised, private marriage ceremony, an unregistered one; and then came the post-nuptial quarrels. Bernard insisted that he could drive and find a restaurant near Oslo which Edna had recommended. The latter had offered to take them there, but no, he could manage it without her help. The French newlyweds then got good and lost, trying to speak what English they knew to people who couldn't help; and finally, they arrived very late, after blowing up at each other. The restaurant was wonderful, but almost immediately, things were ruined when Nicolas leapt from the table and almost strangled a photographer! His wife became agitated, and some 20 more photographers lurking outside were also ready to pounce. They then began flashing when Bardot ran out of the restaurant. Next day the papers had Edna and Bernard together as an item!

Still digesting all this back home at La Madrague, Bardot found the usual animal problems to confront, the vet to consult, etc. Each death or disappearance still weighed heavily on her, but worse were the continuing arguments with Bernard. A terrible one ensued on her birthday, September 28, 1992, when he went into town and locked up his downstairs "apartment," where she also had things *she* needed. By the time he returned she was irate, and a huge fight for the first time went physical—she fell, hit her head, and cried, and after the shouting was done, he barricaded himself in his room! Then he stomped off, and Brigitte went out for her birthday celebration with Mylène, who brought along one of Bardot's male admirers, making her feel a little better.

She wanted desperately to emerge from this personal muck and resume her animal crusading, but couldn't seem to do it easily. The annual adoption weekend at Vincennes October 3 and 4 went off without her this year. Finally she got up to the Paris region in mid–October, wishing to show Bernard Bazoches, and to comfort Yvonne. But again, a dinner was set up, Yvonne and Brigitte waited for him to arrive, but d'Ormale was stuck in the capital on some kind of business, and only returned at two in the morning! Men had hurt Bardot before, and here was the latest in a long line.

That October, news of their secret Norwegian marriage belatedly hit the press—with *Match* getting the best scoop cum photos.[15] In Paris Bardot put finishing legal touches on "La Mare Auzou" in Normandy, those seven hectares where saved animals could live peacefully; and then it was back to Saint-Tropez for her own. And here there was little peace—only a few days back, she ran into boar hunters at La Garrigue, brandishing guns and threatening to kill her! It would take legal time and energy to get them away from there, but eventually, La Garrigue became a haven for these boars, not to mention foxes and other hunted creatures.

Zola's great novel *L'Assommoir* kept on paralleling her life: Bernard was the strolling Lantier or Coupeau, men who went semi-idle and had views on just about everything their women did, and on everyone in her life. Bernard criticized Bardot's fine housemaid Nicole for not cleaning to his standard, and in anger, she quit, necessitating a replacement in a region replete with unemployed, who seemed satisfied to remain that way. Then came another, more recently located gem, Michèle, whom he also found lacking when it came to dirt, and who packed and left, too. This was a big loss, as Michèle had been wonderful with the animals, and a human support system for Bardot.

The relationship with Bernard was really wearing her down, and yet another suicide attempt landed her in a clinic! Then came Christmas, never an easy time for her, and certainly not in 1992. Bernard was fussing with decorations and other preparations, and even the cats felt his nervous vibes. Finally the couple exploded at each other, and Bardot had Christmas without a tree, and with no Bernard for a while, too. New Year's at the antiseptic modern home of one of his friends was little better—political talk spun out non-stop, and finally Brigitte had to interrupt at midnight, planting a kiss on her loved one.

More serious world problems intervened early in January with news of a great oil spill decimating bird life off the coast of the Shetland Islands. Frank and Liliane tried to get there, and couldn't; and Bardot felt awful for the many tarred birds condemned to agonizing deaths. But she was herself stuck, glued in a life that had changed significantly.

She soon got word that Gretchen Wyler had launched an International Brigitte Bardot Award, for the year's best film on animals. She was enjoined to fly to the U.S. for proceedings on February 28, in order to crown a film on vivisection; but of course she wouldn't make it. She did, however, appreciate this American show of support, hoping it might get her own French to take her foundation more seriously.

She continued to find time for Yvonne, giving her comfort on the phone, and holding back on her own problems. Yvonne's cancer was spreading, and she would have to go in for another operation; and Brigitte felt she had to be there for it. So she left Bernard behind—a bit queasy on how he might be with her cats and dogs, but knowing he was no fan of either Yvonne or hospitals! At Bazoches before the operation, she found everything frozen up, the silvery trees gesturing arthritically, and Yvonne quite hopeless as well. Bardot pushed food into her, made her tea, did whatever she could; and then when the operation came, she held her hand again, trying to transmit some of what remained of her own health and energy.

In early February she got back to La Madrague and on the 10th found a favored black cat dead, and then another, and she couldn't figure out the reason. She also lost another *gardien*, Odette's son, at La Garrigue, who wanted to try the big time in Paris. And nobody was good enough for Bernard! It felt nothing short of miraculous when Bardot located a fine Provençal couple, clean, organized, and good cooks too, to take over at La Garrigue.

On March 20 it was off to Marseille to demonstrate for an old priest fighting to keep a dog shelter intact there, despite a planned freeway extension. The fight would continue through the decade. Bardot also had to do a fair amount of trekking to Paris for foundation business, including putting "La Mare Auzou" on a final legal basis, with again, no less than three ministries to placate. And of course there were visits up there to Yvonne, who had lost hair and spunk.

With Jane Goodall, whom she admired for saving and feeding baby chimps whose mothers had been poached, Bardot also went to bat for one old chimpanzee, mired in an African zoo (Brazzaville) since 1948! The animal was now given more space to frolic around, another of Bardot's small but important victories.

At La Madrague there were the usual vicissitudes: a *gardienne* who didn't take care of a sick Domina, letting the dog die, was promptly fired; and Bardot begged Nicole to get over her Bernard problem and come back. Surprisingly, she accepted. Another plus of the era for Brigitte was receiving a letter from a hospitalized old aunt (on Toty's side), then going to the hospital in Cannes and cheering this Nadine and others there. Brigitte became a phone interlocutor daily for the rest of the woman's life.

When Bardot fled the tourists for Bazoches that summer, Bernard stayed behind a while to savor the Riviera—rising at midday, taking dips, working on his tan. When he finally arrived at Bazoches, he looked very well. On the telephone he had been indifferent to news of an insect bite that had paralyzed Bardot's arm, forcing her to take a heavy dosage of cortisone. But revenge of the gods occurred when he descended from his vehicle, splendidly attired, and was jumped by the dogs. Of course he went right to work on his competitors—Mylène was using Bardot on the road to fame, Yvonne was a boring old bag with cancer, and the *gardienne* here was worthless, too. When Bardot defended her intimates, an inevitable fight ensued, and Bernard took off.

On the festival of Sainte-Brigitte, an improvised July 23 bash at a nearby restaurant-gallery in Montfort l'Amaury revived her spirits. Some of Bardot's oldest friends like Phi-Phi d'Exea, plus Allain Bougrain-Dubourg, were on hand, and so was the founder of a group she had always loved, the Gypsy Kings. The music made her dance, and photographers from *Match* caught it all in pictures.

But lest Bardot lapse out of her underlying seriousness, she also allowed herself to be interviewed for that issue by Henry-Jean Servat, using the forum to sound off vividly about the decline of environmental concern in the early '90s. She admitted how much her combat for animals sapped her, but how could one retreat? She was still busy, having dispatched a letter in Russian to Boris Yeltsin, in order to help save baby seals slaughtered there; and a missive in Chinese to Deng Xiaoping in behalf of bears who got their paws cut off to make soup. And she didn't let her fellow French off the hook for abandoning thousands of cats and dogs at vacation time, some ending up euthanized in S.P.A.'s.

Bardot may have repeated herself on these issues, but she never lacked *gravitas*, nor did she bore.

However, it wasn't concern for animals, but the lighthearted pictures in *Match* of Brigitte dancing flamenco-style, and with Allain on hand, that brought an undoubtedly jealous Bernard back to her life. He then indulged in what she saw as his good side—a passion for interior decoration, framing and placing photos, and the like. Yet his sniping at her intimate friends and those who provided needed help continued apace.[16]

In the fall she met a new Minister of the Environment, who wouldn't hear of her concerns on exotic animals (scorpions, snakes, etc.) being brought into Paris and kept in apartments. Sometimes she won—*her* pressure helped get Belgium to call off an annual horse race that on a slipslidey track made nags ready for the slaughterhouse break legs.

And though this year she attended her foundation's annual adoption weekend at Vincennes in early October, Bernard rapidly disappeared from the event, more worried about sullying his shoes in the crowd than protecting Brigitte. Then another roof fell in—her trusted staff at the Foundation went on a kind of strike to get extra pay for attending that weekend event. To her consternation Bardot found Liliane and Frank in the forefront; but Frank and almost everyone else involved eventually came back to her side. The sole person who burned bridges was Liliane, and it was a big loss.

Her shoes were to be filled by a man Bernard knew, a prim consultant type making ersatz moves, and in too many directions. The Foundation really had financial troubles, but this "bow tie," as Bardot called him, wasn't the one to shape things up. Eventually she located a woman to help him, and together they worked well at their task.

On January 26, 1994, Bardot appeared on a TV show, again denouncing the butchery of horses, and receiving more death threats in the process. The show's host also received some, and backpedaled on his next show. Despite her problems with Bernard, Brigitte kept giving all she could for animals: with the S.P.A. president she spent a day, for example, at a horrible, freezing shelter where rotting carcasses littered the premises and a lynx batted its head insanely against a cage. A few changes were made, a clean-up—but would anything last? At least Bernard now came along on some of these trips, starting to be less of a bon vivant.

On issues large and small there were protracted Bardot campaigns, such as the one to save the life of an Akita on death row in the States. In behalf of the Akita, she wrote Christine Todd Whitman, New Jersey's governor, and for years lobbied for this 100-pound dog who had bitten a little girl's lip in 1990. The dog lived until the dawn of a new century.[17] It wasn't much of a battle, compared to, say, her contemporaneous fight against baby seal massacres in Russia, where some 18,000 were "culled" in spring in just one region on the White Sea. Concerning that massacre, she didn't hesitate to call the pens that held these seals gulags.[18]

There was a constant tussle in her priorities between such international concerns and local ones, such as the latest caterpillar infestation on the Riviera, killing off her animals, as Mylène raced around, frantically sawing branches and demolishing cocoons. In March 1994 Bardot was back in Paris to inspect new Foundation premises on the Rue Vineuse, near the Trocadéro subway station. She also saw Yvonne, giving her more comfort. Then back to Saint-Tropez and again, she tried to intervene with the Russians; but no more success occurred than would have been the case under Stalin.

On it went through the '90s—Brigitte more used to Bernard, and back to campaigns on all fronts. Aided by an outbreak of trichinosis, imputed by authorities to horses France imported from North America, she wasn't through with that sector, and there were more death threats received. At a Foundation press conference one man shouted at Bardot for several minutes. She continued opposing hunters of varying stripes, including those still shooting at migratory turtledoves in the Médoc.[19]

She also went after a series of mayors for pigeon killings, including the mayor of Cahors, who had supervised the netting then gassing of almost 1,000 there. Bardot called this "genocide," when the pigeons' sole crime was soiling public buildings! In another town the mayor replied to her critique of pigeon extermination by citing experts, to the effect that it was necessary to get rid of some 1,700 pigeons a year in order to prevent diseases from spreading among humans. The mayor of Bessière's call for a pigeon shoot drew a goodly supply of local hunters, and despite Bardot's protest, as many as 1,000 were eliminated there. Then came the mayor of Saint-Tropez, and again Bardot threatened to leave, due to *his* failure to cancel a hunting convention of June 1994. Near-riot conditions and a kind of civil war ensued there, and a picture of her handing over her La Madrague keys to Mayor Jean-Michel Couve made *Paris-Match*.[20] She even took on the mayor of Paris, brunt of an open letter from Bardot concerning the catfish introduced into France in the '60s, but now, according to her, a menace in the lake of the Bois de Boulogne, allegedly eating ducks, swans, turtles, even little dogs! This outburst brought down the wrath of Rhône fishermen, delighted by the "silure's" propensity to grow ever larger.[21]

While he was still alive, she also urged President Mitterrand to abolish presidential hunts, or she would return the decoration of the Legion of Honor she had received in the early '90s! She later took on Prime Minister Alain Juppé for an admission that he had consumed bunting at a get-together, a bird technically protected by French law. Bardot went on to excoriate a pack of French politicos for such gourmandise at the expense of these vulnerable creatures. In the same period her foundation went after the Minister of Agriculture, Philippe Vasseur, for allowing importation of kangaroo meat into the country. Not to mention a continuing fight against consumption of those hallowed French gastronomic items, foie gras and frogs' legs.[22]

As the '90s marched on, Bardot and her foundation kept fighting the good fight around the world. The list of targets is a long one to cite even in small part: a delphinarium off Tahiti for the death of dolphins; the Republic of Iceland for foot-dragging on reintroducing Keiko to their waters, the whale who starred in *Free Willy*; the Irish prime minister for allowing fox-hunting to continue; President Havel of the Czech Republic for their Pardubice steeplechase; Lech Walesa, urging him to stop a "wolf massacre" in Poland; Mobil Corp., for failing to cover smokestacks and thereby protect bats and birds—this in concert with PETA; NASA for sending monkeys wired with electrodes into space; the Belgians for allowing their traditional horse and trap race (as noted, they bowed to the pressure and cancelled); the government of Lebanon, which also banned an annual slaughter of animals, one few believed would make a difference (even during their Civil War, said one conservationist, the Lebanese had only stopped shooting at each other to kill birds); the European Commission for permitting overly long transports of animals before slaughter, and the Australian Prime Minister, John Howard, for allowing sheep to be heaped up in "concentration camp liners" en route to throat slit-tings in the Mideast; the Bulgarian president for failure to adopt an animal protection law in a country newly admitted to the European Union; Russian and Romanian author-ities for planning mass extermination of stray dogs—in Bucharest alone the plan was to get rid of some 200,000 in three years. (Moscow Mayor Yuri Luzhkov took the aging star seriously enough to soften his policies on this issue.)[23]

Bardot's personal vicissitudes of course continued all the while. One was being forced by her sister, Mijanjou, and by Bernard into penning a brief preface for Jeffrey Robinson's biography of her in 1994. Robinson had simply shown up one day at La Madrague, rose in hand. Her arm was twisted, she finally acceded, but when she saw a draft copy, Brigitte had bitter regrets now that this "authorization" had been wangled. Out of bad sometimes comes good, and the good emanating from Robinson's work (despite errors and lacunae, the best on her to that point), was pressure on Bardot to finish her first volume of memoirs, on which she had labored over 20 years. She now put on a full court press, using solitude at Bazoches to near the finish line, which finally was reached in December 1995.

But things grew harder for her per-sonally as the decade wore on. In 1995, while she was giving birth to what became a literary triumph, Bardot lost her dear friend, Yvonne, after fighting so hard to keep her alive. There was also the pass-ing of Paule Drouault, a journalist who had fought for animals in a regular col-umn—an aneurysm snuffing out that exis-tence. Then came news of the passing later that year of Louis Malle, whom Brigitte remembered for his cinematic taste and intellectualism. Vadim too was not so long for this world, but she got closure in the summer of 1995 at a show-ing of *And God...* in Saint-Tropez, where there was heartfelt applause, and she emerged from the hall on the arms of her fourth husband, Bernard, and her first, Vadim. As with Malle, she would now see Roger as a dinosaur in his trade, with a sensitivity and taste not nearly so com-mon in the '90s. Her longest male friend-ship? Ghislain "Jicky" Dussart passed on in May 1996, found dead with a cup of tea in his hand.

Brigitte and her fourth husband, Bernard d'Ormale, demonstrating in the Médoc region of France (spring 1994) against the annual slaughter of wild turtledoves. (SIPA/NewsCom)

And still Bardot soldiered on, meet-ing with the Pope at the middle of the

Pope John Paul II speaks with Bardot at the Vatican, September 27, 1995. She would also meet with other religious authorities, including Islamic leaders, to discuss animal protection and rights. (SIPA/NewsCom)

decade, warmly clasping his hands and speaking Italian to him, trying to get her protectivity toward animals recognized by a pontiff she respected. His response was that St. Francis of Assisi had also cared for animals, which certainly seemed supportive.[24] It was the same year that she paid tribute to the "Joan of Arc of veal," Jill Phipps, a young mother of 31 run over by a truck trundling calves to an airport in England for shipment.[25]

Political connections that would help her cause became tenuous, however, and even her erstwhile friend and supporter, Chirac, drifted away when he became France's president. Bardot's link to Mitterrand (through his sister-in-law Christine Gouze-Rénal) had obviously ended with that politician's death. Christine herself had only come back tearfully to Bardot's side after initially freezing her out due to Ormale (and his friendship with Le Pen). Bardot's old collaborator on a number of films saw one on TV, impulsively called, and both sobbed into the phone. Brigitte apparently asked her hubby at one point if he couldn't become a Gaullist, declaring that she should perhaps have fallen in love with a shoe salesman!

She did not always win with the world's heavy hitters. For example, her letters to Nelson Mandela on the near extinction of the white rhino in South Africa and on elephant poaching there met with disappointing silence. But she kept on fighting and supporting others who put lives on the line, including the great Canadian whaling protestor Paul Watson, a founder of Greenpeace. When Watson was arrested at the Amsterdam

Still a perennial source of heartache: Bardot with a toy baby seal in a demonstration before the Norwegian embassy in Paris, March 20, 1995, beseeching a boycott of countries engaging in the slaughter of seals and baby seals. (AFP/ NewsCom)

airport in 1997 and threatened with extradition to Norway for having tried to sink one of their whaling vessels in 1992, then another in 1994, Bardot intervened with a letter to Holland's Minister of Foreign Affairs. She called Watson an example for all defenders of animals, and was disgusted by Dutch support for a country that still killed thousands of baby seals and several hundred whales each year.[26]

Her most protracted, costly, courageous, and worrisome fight of the '90s was against the practices of France's Muslims during Aïd-el-Kébir or Eïd al-Adha, the four-day spring festival at the end of Ramadan. Known as the Feast of the Sacrifice, it commemorated Abraham's willingness to give his son to God. Bardot had gotten the ball rolling with the 1990 interview in *Présent*, characterizing this sheep slaughter as medieval—particularly given the use of knives to cut throats, rather than the usual French practice of first stunning the animal.[27] She also accused the government of aiding and abetting the spread of Islam in France. From the start the whole matter mixed her concern for animals with larger concerns for France's future. Through the '90s Bardot wouldn't stop speaking her mind, unvarnished. In 1993 she had again condemned the annual ritual as barbaric, arousing the anger of the Marseille mosque's *imam*.[28]

Then in 1996 matters worsened, beginning with an impassioned Bardot column appearing in the newspaper *Le Figaro* on April 26, again showing her fear of an Islamic invasion in her country, and especially focused on the omnipresent slaughter of sheep during the annual festival. She painted a picture of heads of families gruesomely severing sheeps' throats with blades sometimes too dull for the purpose, of children splashing in blood, etc. In the Paris region one of nine places authorized for these killings was her commune of Bazoches, where one farmer wanted to sell off his sheep to Bardot, but was himself fearful of a throat-cutting! The problem was that in her *Figaro* "j'accuse," Bardot again went beyond animals, getting to the raw political nerve of illegal immigration, particularly from the Maghreb. There were varying counts of that North African population in France, with one newspaper estimating it at two million, another at three, another at four.[29]

Bardot's performance of 1996 continued with the imminent appearance of her memoirs (volume one) that September. Interviews associated with the book's coming publication were printed in places like *Figaro* or *Elle*, and again revealed Bardot's concern about the Islamization of France from several points of view. She generally bemoaned the decline of French gentility and civility in the face of rampant immigration. In *Elle* she referred, as elsewhere, to a "Muslim invasion," and on a number of occasions averred that she was only saying what many were thinking. Yet she clung to what she felt was the nub of her anger: omnipresent cutting of sheep's throats in French courtyards, bathrooms, even bedrooms. The April *Figaro* article had already provoked legal action which its proponents now felt had added urgency and weight. Mouloud Aounit's Movement Against Racism group, and also Friendship Between Races pushed for 100,000 francs in a case to be heard December 19 in Paris.[30] Just before the trial Marly-le-Roi (Yvelines) and Quimper (Finistère) got rid of their Marianne busts, modeled on Bardot.[31]

Then came the Paris trial on December 19 at the combined hands of the Movement Against Racism, the League Against Racism and Anti-Semitism, and the Human Rights League. Cheered on by fans and/or those in favor of her animal rights stand, and with d'Ormale in court beside her, Bardot insisted that she had only been pushing for a more humane method of slaughter. She said that people who came to France ought to be subject to French laws—stunning animals before killing them. She feared that the proliferation of mosques meant more such cruelty, for theoretically, every head of a Muslim family must slaughter a sheep.[32]

On January 23 the Paris lower court ruled in her favor, averring that she hadn't broken France's anti-racism laws.[33] But the next year she spoke out again. In April 1997 she issued a statement appearing in newspapers to the effect that Muslim rituals in the festival slated to begin on April 18 would "bathe France's earth in blood." This time—alluding to human beheadings and throat-slittings in Algeria of the era—she went to town, noting heatedly: "They've slit the throats of women and children, of our monks, our officials, our tourists and our sheep, they'll slit our throats one day and we'll deserve it!" Here Bardot had gone well beyond the animal cause; here she was airing private fears of western decadence, barbarians inside the citadel—all of that. "A Muslim France, with a North African Marianne," she sputtered, "why *not*, at the point we are at?" Naturally, she provoked a litigious response for these incautious, some would say discriminatory, some might also say gutsy remarks. Already she was slated for an appearance at the Paris Court of Appeals on September 11, after the original lower court had acquitted her of previous charges.[34] In the fall that appeals court overturned the earlier ruling in her favor, fining her the equivalent of $1,600 for inciting racial hatred in the April 1996

Figaro article, with a symbolic franc payable to each human rights group that had sued. She also had to cover legal costs incurred by these three groups that had gone after her.[35]

Bardot had aroused formidable opponents—and for a lady now in her early sixties, had obviously taken anything but the safe, suburban route in life. At her trial of January 20, 1998, for the remarks made in April 1997, she was again convicted—and this time given a 20,000 franc fine for provocation to hatred and discrimination. Again, she had to pay a symbolic franc to each of three groups, including SOS-Racisme. And her controversial lines kept being re-quoted; for example, Muslims "are born with knives in their hands and they kill everything that falls prey to them." From sheep to humans, she still felt that the divide—especially given sanguinary events in Algeria—was a narrow one. That spring of 1998 Bardot also sided with Christian Serbs against Bosnian Muslims, again citing a Muslim invasion around the world and the issue of animal sacrifices.[36]

The publication of her first volume of memoirs engendered yet another legal battle. At first, like most artists, she didn't quite know the quality of what she had. She had been doing all this privately for a long time, having started on her 40th birthday (September 28, 1974), and had only gotten to the finish line over two decades later.[37] It had been an inordinately long time in the creative rabbit hole; then boxes containing some 1,500 pages of typescript went out to Jean-Claude Fasquelle of Editions Grasset, who was bowled over by what he had. Copyediting ran into 1996 and was a large task; considerately, Brigitte invited her son Nicolas to be involved in the process, and he read some pages, and seemed (in an illusory way) unmoved. Choice of photos occasionally ran into human snags, then Jacques Charrier heard of content, and sent his ex-wife a menacing registered letter, which came back marked "return to sender." Bardot touched the first published copy, a moment of great excitement, at the end of August 1996; *Initiales B.B.* would become hugely popular, with 500,000 copies sold in France within three weeks of publication. It also won her the 11th Paul Léautaud prize of $16,000, fulfilling a requirement that "literature must be physical." Reviews were predictably mixed, and for many notices around the world, writers simply read advance excerpts and didn't bother to labor through the book itself.[38]

Brigitte's telephone then rang off the hook at La Madrague and Bazoches, few caring about her heart problems, sadness from unending animal protection causes, and Charrier's rancor. A suit was indeed mounted by ex-husband Jacques and son Nicolas for unflattering references to Charrier as an alcoholic and abuser, and sometime wimp; and for Bardot's published memories of getting pregnant and fearing the result. A French court fined her the equivalent of $44,000, but she turned the tables when Charrier came out with his own published memoir, winning 50,000 francs for invasion of *her* privacy![39]

Bardot's own present relationship won no prizes, either, for Bernard still went out until all hours some nights, talking politics and doing who knew what. When at home he sometimes ran the TV till 4 a.m. Bardot would pray at her little chapel at La Garrigue, asking the "little Virgin" for aid. Liquor, and for a time Prozac, and just summer heat made her prickly; but she learned, and Bernard also learned as time went by, to carve out a modus vivendi. Finally gone were scenes like his being teargassed by police out of her apartment in Paris! And some exes also came back with acts of generosity, as when Sachs impulsively gave $60,000 to her foundation. And the beautiful woman who had so often spoken her mind and put her existence on the line somehow made it into the next century.[40]

9

Bardot Today

THAT NEW CENTURY STARTED FOR Bardot with the death of her first love to cancer on February 11, 2000, and his funeral in Saint-Tropez. René Descartes had died on the same day as Roger Vadim; however, René's life had been anything but a Cartesian one. His casket proceeded through Tropézien streets and alleys, and behind it, arm in arm, walked Marie-Christine Barrault, Catherine Schneider, Annette Stroyberg, Jane Fonda—and Bardot. (Catherine Deneuve did not appear.) Schneider, Vadim's wife after Fonda, had planned the service for an Episcopal church, with a Scottish minister giving his sermon in accented French. En route out of the church, three Russian violin players then played—this was Bardot's doing, honoring Vadim's heritage on his father's side. It was truly the end of an era.[1]

But it was not the end at all for that survivor par excellence, Brigitte Bardot. During the summer heat wave of 2003, two books were found cheek by jowl on bestseller tables across France—Hillary Clinton's first memoir in translation, and Bardot's *Un Cri dans le silence* (*A Cry in Silence*).[2] The book is an extended diatribe on all the author finds wrong in contemporary France, and at the same time a celebration of the little things that give her comfort at home. She starts with a bang, detailing the sex perversions of our age, then weaves back symphonically to her champestral peace in Provence, then returns to the heritage of a '60s spirit of liberation, ending in what she takes to be contemporary madness. Back to soothing sunsets over the sea, then in chapter 5 (they are short ones) she treats the decline of French patriotism, including the ending of obligatory military service in France. Simultaneously, she tips her cap to President Chirac's stance against the Iraq war, and for peace. But she figures too much has gone by the board: French women in police and military uniforms, turning their backs on other sources of female power; people demanding rights each time they stub toes; the decline of small farmers and shopkeepers; a soulless, assembly-line French health system; the

Bardot visiting her refuge for dogs, Carnoules, October 7, 2001. (Getty/News-Com)

herky-jerky, inane quality of today's remote-control TV; the lack of great actors and actresses (though in the latter category she evinces admiration for France's Isabelle Adjani, Sophie Marceau, Isabelle Huppert, and Arielle Dombasle); music that seems all noise; the obsession today's middle-aged have for eating, while the young turn toward diets of Coke and burgers at "McDo"; a general lack of values—teachers in jeans, priests spat on, young illiterates galore; laws on speed limits, compulsory seat belts, and pooper scoopers (Bardot revealing a libertarian streak here); and not *least*, the horrors that still befall many animals around the world. One part on men blithely knocking down trees in Indonesia, destroying perches of female orangutans trying to protect their young, who then end up as guinea pigs in labs or zoos: like other passages on animals, this one won't top her second volume of memoirs, but reiteration still has its impact. Bardot's continuing guilt for the many suffering creatures she *can't* save again comes through here.[3]

Even in the book's peaceful passages, contemplating, for example, frogs leaping hither and thither, her mind jumps back to frogs' legs she had seen ripped from bodies and heads that keep gibbering in a heap, until death ensues—all so that people may consume this delicacy in tony restaurants. She mentions that when she takes her animals for a daily constitutional, savoring even the breath of her mare, she thinks of recently seeing horses from Eastern Europe brought starving, thirsty, and many dying in 100-degree heat of tight trucks to a transfer point in Italy, before ending up in Western European abattoirs. She recalls their terrible wounds, and how she fought to let some out into the light to eat and drink. Proust-like, her mind then returns to the lucky mare before her.

Does Bardot remain courageous here? No question. She continues to say things few others will about a great increase of illegal immigrants in France, who clamor for rights, and are allowed even to urinate behind the altars in churches; and yes, despite horrid trials she went through in the '90s, and in a pithier, more careful way than before, she remains saddened by the Islamization of France and the omnipresent throat-cuttings of sheep.

Were the old days perfect? No, but near the end of her book she points to an earlier era when French Jews, Protestants, and Muslims worshipped in peace, but didn't inflict values on her country. She also remembers when once-a-week movies at the theater were magical, and when the mailman rode his bike and had plenty of time to stop for a red wine, and things were generally simpler. Occasionally she turns on the TV, seeing herself in an early film, and marvels that this was truly another world.[4]

Again, *Le Cri...* can't touch her memoirs, but Bardot does love to write, and in spots remains quotable here. And she still has so much pain and solitude in her—living that perhaps necessary parallel existence with her husband, Bernard.

And she *has* struck a chord in France, mentioning the continuing pile of fan mail that tells her to keep on going. In a number of interviews, she reiterates that she says out loud what many think inside (and presumably lack courage to say, given job constraints, etc.). She says only fools don't change their minds. For example, she once so opposed the death penalty and the Rosenbergs' execution that she wouldn't have anything to do with the U.S.; but since the 1981 abolition of the death penalty in France, many sadists got prison sentences reduced, returning to plague the population and organizations that work to obtain a bit of justice. All this altered her former opinion, and in some cases, the death penalty now makes sense to her.

Predictably, certain TV interviewers knocked the book and her on shows where Bardot appeared reluctantly. One program that had people talking was "On ne peut pas plaire à tout le monde" (You can't please everyone), airing May 12, 2003, with famed actors like Delon there to welcome Bardot at the studio. However, the show's host, Marc-Olivier Fogiel, a man in his early thirties, criticized Brigitte for cowardice, disdain, and a lack of humanity, making for an evening *Le Monde's* reviewer considered unduly confrontational. The ex-actress then received some 17,000 letters of reassurance, and called this Fogiel "un petit con"—a little imbecile. In response to his lawsuit for her use of that term, the judges eventually decided in her favor, throwing out the case in January 2005. More predictably, Bardot had to shell out cash to other litigants for comments made in her book, approximately $6,000 (in 2004). No wonder she started talking again about decamping—this time to Switzerland. But for any such move, how much life even remained to her? She had been through the mill, and so many of her generation—Vadim, Malle, and in July 2004, Distel—were gone.[5]

For this book I made the decision not to interview eminent people who crossed Bardot's path during that thronged life—it has been done before; nor did I want to hurt her in any way. But I have talked quite a bit to ordinary French humans about Bardot. Concerning her best-selling diatribe, I was surprised to hear from a 40-year-old woman on a bus in Paris that she had already read the book within weeks of its appearance, and that she too felt Bardot was saying what many were thinking. The woman saluted BB's intelligence, and her way of paddling against prevailing currents. She worried also about a crime wave in France, and when I mentioned her nice jewelry, she said it was phony; those who wore real jewelry could have fingers cut off here, losing more than baubles! And finally, this Parisian—before getting off the bus—said she totally supported Bardot's animal crusade.

Michèle, a journalist, said about Bardot that she represents "la grande époque" with Vadim et al. A dear old friend of mine near Paris (old in the sense of being in his mid–90s) surprised me despite his Catholicism by saying that he liked Brigitte's forthright quality.[6] Of course there are people on the negative part of the ledger, too. Some I talked to mentioned her wrinkles and fallen beauty, beauty she now believes means something only when allied to the internal. A nice woman, reading Balzac's *Physiologie du mariage* at a Trocadéro cafe near Bardot Foundation headquarters, says we idealize the past too much when it comes to such figures. But on the same day I met a ditzy, interesting older lady with a dog; she flatly said about Bardot: "I adore her!" She admired her fight for animals vivisected in labs, and noted: "She is so beautiful, so natural!"

In Saint-Tropez during several visits, a typical comment from long-established residents was that Brigitte was a woman of heart ("une femme de coeur"). People also mentioned her arthritic hip, and a cane she uses to help her get around. A lady in an art shop with cats plopped in sofas spoke of Bardot's concern not only for animals but also, and mostly unsung, she said, for needy humans. Yes, she has an apartment in Paris where she lodges old people, but how many know this? An elegant lady running a bed and breakfast with her husband in the hills near Saint-Tropez said Bardot had "sublime" looks in her day, and was a role model to young women, and that she remains a major French figure.[7]

Of course what does "major" mean? At the end of her book Bardot concludes that "to succeed in life means to count only on oneself, to remove oneself forever from dependency, to learn solitude, to no longer endure the disappointments inflicted by others, to no longer disperse one's energies, to only give the gift of one's presence after reflection, to know how to keep quiet, and to listen to what really matters, [and] to look in depth at what really is deserving."[8]

Concluding on an important and wonderful personality, Brigitte Bardot *has* at times spoken out in an extreme, controversial manner; but the issues facing the western world at the dawn of a new millennium are also extreme ones. The oceans are being vacuumed of fish, the ozone layer depleted, the climate altered, and aside from environmental disaster in the offing, a galaxy of other societal problems, including rampant drug use, bad culture, alienation of the young, and general decadence, all amount to something on the possible order of the decline and fall of Rome—especially when one adds a continuing terror threat, reminding anyone with a sense of history of barbarians who eventually toppled Rome's supposedly eternal empire.

Given all this, here is a celebrity who has shown the plain-speaking verve of a Harry Truman, and who has that greatest of virtues: courage, mixed always with heart and soul. Bardot may step on toes and generalize, but at least she takes on big issues, arousing the wrath of some pretty fierce and redoubtable enemies. Perhaps it takes one courageous person to know another: in September 1996 Lech Walesa declared that Bardot

From left to right, French rock star Johnny Hallyday and Secretary of State for Agriculture Nicolas Forissier offer support to Brigitte at her foundation's "Christmas for Animals 2004," held at Levallois Perret, December 18, 2004. (SIPA/ NewsCom)

belongs not just to France "but to the entire post–Communist world."[9] Most graduates of her trade, or those still in it, remain in safer ideological waters.

At this moment—despite all the serious vicissitudes in her life—look up the Fondation Bardot on the Internet, and you will see that it is an organization fighting a very important fight. Bardot's open letters fly out to points around the world. Her petition forms, her pleas for help, her continued calling to conscience of Norwegian and Canadian governments for decimating baby seals (reminding us that for each one captured, a good two or three others are killed), her ongoing fight against elephant and other poaching, complete with lovely elephant pictures on the Internet, her crusade against *foie gras*—it all remains important. And the Fondation Bardot has tried to Americanize and go contemporary in its search for funds, selling Bardot leashes and dog collars in different colors, T-shirts, stickers, key rings, S.O.S. program videos, and so on. On a quarterly basis it also distributes a glossy *Info-journal*, with problems for animals around the world addressed in punchy articles accompanied by color photos. On recent covers Alain Delon and Bardot, both still classy, and then French rock star Johnny Hallyday and Bardot, drew attention to her annual Christmas adoption campaign, finding homes for hundreds of cats and dogs. In the latter issue of 2004 the Foundation's president thanks people for a great outpouring of cards, gifts, etc., honoring her seventieth birthday; but then she gets down to business for what really matters—showing, for example, some of the names gathered for a massive petition against the annual seal hunt (Canada's quota having shot up to well over 300,000 by 2004). On the same page, one sees the searing photo of a blood-ridden, massacred baby seal on reddened ice. The names on this petition include Charles Aznavour, Kim Basinger, and Tippi Hedren, and the total reached over 200,000, all to buttress Bardot's full-court press on the issue with political leaders and the U.N.[10]

In January 2005 Bardot wrote an open letter to the Queen of Denmark, enjoining her to use her influence to end polar bear hunts in Greenland, a Danish dependency. And in her own country she has moved heaven and earth to get the Napoleonic code altered by the French government, and to give domestic animals a protected status.[11] For what she does and, perhaps as important, for what she does *not* do in the gathering twilight of a turbulent, fascinating life, one can easily salute the fragile ex-star who survived to make an extensive difference.

Notes

Preface

1. Having worked on a film (*Vie privée*) with Bardot in the early '60s, the well-known director Louis Malle noted that "no one in our trade doubts her talent...." Malle interview with Yvonne Baby, *Le Monde*, February 1, 1962, 10.

1. A Parisian Childhood

1. Some of the footage still exists; see the documentary made on Brigitte, *Telle quelle*, from the '80s, but now available on video and DVD.

2. Bardot, *Initiales B.B.: Mémoires* (Paris: Grasset, 1996), 26. Much of the rest of the material in this and subsequent chapters rests on these memoirs, and on trustworthy parts of the older biographical studies, and of other memoirs or studies noted in the bibliography.

2. The Vadim Years

1. Dudley Andrew has good pages on the classicism of Allégret, who first came to prominence in the 1930s and was now part of the old guard in the film world. Andrew, *Mists of Regret: Culture and Sensibility in Classic French Film* (Princeton: Princeton University Press, 1995), *passim*. A tribute to his mentor Allégret is in Vadim's first memoir: "He was an intelligent man, sensitive and cultured, curious to learn about other people. He recognized merit in a human being, whether a stripper, a poet, a minister or a future genius. Fascinated by youth, he spotted talent before it had even blossomed. Marc's finest epitaph will be the list of the people he helped at the beginning of their careers and who have become famous in one sphere or another." Vadim, *Memoirs of the Devil* (trans. Peter Beglan; New York: Harcourt Brace Jovanovich, 1975), 62.

2. According to one French actor who came to know Brando well, he later developed into a fluent French speaker. See Daniel Gélin, *A Bâtons rompus: Mémoires* (Paris: Editions du Rocher, 2000), 247.

3. Bourvil (real name André Raimbourg) enjoyed working with the young Bardot, and despite his childish antics on screen, was a stable married man and generous co-worker. But critics in newspapers like *Libération*, *Combat*, *Ce soir*, and the Catholic *La Croix* found him a little too puerile here (in the serious France of *après-guerre*). The film's maker, Jean Boyer, was also damned with faint praise, but a more recent, positive estimate is in Elizabeth Coquart and Philippe Huet, *Bourvil: La tendresse du rire* (Paris: Albin Michel, 1990), 121. To these authors this was a "film charmant, sans prétention" and one where "Brigitte Bardot ... makes a discreet entrance, almost a clandestine one, into her future kingdom." Coquart and Huet, 128, 129 and ch. 5 generally. See also Jean-Jacques Jelot-Blanc and James Huet, *Bourvil* (Paris: Editions Stock, 1990), 109 on critical responses to the film.

4. Only picked up much later by *The New York Times* on October 25, 1958, in the era of her celebrity, the film wasn't highly rated by Richard W. Nason, but seemed to him a "curiosity piece" showing the American public an earlier, more innocent-looking Brigitte. The plot concerning a law student underwater fishing off Corsica involves his discovery of a Phoenician artifact, and intuition that a celebrated

ancient shipwreck is in the vicinity. Bardot plays the daughter of a lighthouse keeper in the area and love blooms, as the booty finally goes the way of many best-laid plans.

5. Gélin and Delorme were then on a topsy-turvy rollercoaster, owing to their celebrity as actor and actress, but also to their lifestyle and his instability, leading to a searing divorce. Gélin's downward spin included an addiction to heroin. See Gélin, *A Bâtons rompus*, 201, 211, and also his *Deux ou trois vies qui sont les miennes* (Paris: Julliard, 1977). Gélin went on to other lives, with evolving film work that included roles in Hitchcock's *The Man Who Knew Too Much* and Louis Malle's *Murmur of the Heart*, published poetry collections, a healthier addiction to gardening, and finally, a stable marriage with a Jewish woman, and trips to Israel.

6. But Louis Chauvet in *Le Figaro* (January 20, 1954) saw real possibilities here for the new *ingénue* on the French cinematic scene.

7. The top female lead was Dany Robin, playing a French woman courted by a G.I. missing home, but trying to stay respectable. Bosley Crowther's review in *The New York Times* (February 12, 1954) found this a good romantic film, though with an unsuitably tragic ending.

8. Vadim notes: "Later, an explanation was found for the enormous attraction she had for the press. It was put down to my genius for publicity [but]... nothing is further from the truth." He believes she just had a certain something that was natural and which drew people. Vadim, *Memoirs of the Devil*, 78.

9. Bosley Crowther reviewed *Helen of Troy* after its Manhattan debut in *The New York Times* (January 27, 1956), finding battle scenes well done, but criticizing Rossana Podesta's Helen.

10. A.H. Weiler would refer to Bardot's physicality when the movie was shown in New York, but with none of the mania that accompanied her full celebrity to come. He also generally praised the film and its cast. See his review in *The New York Times*, March 1, 1956.

11. Roy Armes gives a higher estimate of this film than I would in his *French Cinema* (Oxford: Oxford University Press, 1985), 158. Of the many books on Clair the best is Pierre Billard, *Le Mystère René Clair* (Paris: Plon, 1998). There are also many books on Gérard Philipe (see bibliography). Critical reaction to the movie's mixed modes of frivolity and seriousness, and to its potentially anti-war message, elicited a warm response from intellectuals jumping to Clair's defense, including André Maurois in *Carrefour* and Aragon in *Les Lettres françaises*. For this reaction see Billard, *Mystère René Clair*, ch. 7 (all on *Grandes Manoeuvres*). One critic referred to the movie's schizoid comic-tragic quality in the following manner: "The film itself has its feet in Courteline and its head in Racine." Jacques Audiberti in *Les Cahiers du cinéma*, quoted in Gérard Bonal, *Gérard Philipe: Biographie* (Paris: Editions du Seuil, 1994), 223.

12. A good term for such films is Jean-Pierre Jeancolas' "inexportable," though he uses it more narrowly. See his "The Inexportable: The Case of French Cinema and Radio in the 1950s," in Richard Dyer and Ginette Vincendeau, eds., *Popular European Cinema* (London: Routledge, 1992), ch. 10. When the film finally made it to New York in the era of Bardot's later celebrity, Bosley Crowther gave it a wan review (*New York Times*, July 30, 1957).

13. François Truffaut found the movie verging on pornography! See his review in *Arts*, March 21, 1956.

14. Richard W. Nason's later review in *The New York Times* on April 19, 1958 (of another film that only made it to the U.S. when Bardot was famous) derided the inability of Vadim and Boisrond to decide on *Gamine's* ultimate direction, mixing both light and serious genres. On the French and Jerry Lewis see Rae Beth Gordon, *Why the French Love Jerry Lewis: From Cabaret to Early Cinema* (Stanford: Stanford University Press, 2001), especially 203–215.

15. One of the reasons her hard film work was consistently underestimated was because of a natural quality that endured throughout her career, and the fact that, as Ginette Vincendeau puts it, she seemed to be "blatantly non-actressy." Vincendeau, *Stars and Stardom in French Cinema* (London: Continuum, 2000), 86.

16. The movie once again made it to New York near the end of the next year. See Howard Thompson's unenthusiastic review in *The New York Times*, November 18, 1957.

17. And that of course means physically, as many concur, such as Sarah Leahy: "As the first shots of the film make clear, the narrative details of the film are in fact quite unimportant; the film is really a hymn to Bardot's body." Leahy, "The Matter of Myth: Brigitte Bardot, Stardom and Sex," *Studies in French Cinema* 3 (2003), 73.

18. Truffaut praised the movie and its star actress, provoking a grateful letter in response from Bardot: "Dear Monsieur Truffaut, I was immensely touched by the article you published in *Arts*, it encouraged me and I thank you with all my heart." Quoted in Antoine de Baecque and Serge Toubiana, *Truffaut* (trans. Catherine Temerson; New York: Alfred A. Knopf, 1999), 114. Apparently Jurgens initially demanded top billing, but came to value Bardot's special qualities, and allowed her name to assume a place of prominence in the credits. Bardot would always admire the "class" of this actor. See her interview in the documentary *Telle quelle*.

19. In *Le Monde* (December 5, 1956), Jean de Baroncelli declared that Bardot still needed to mature a good deal as an actress, and that it was easy to be distracted by her beauty on screen. Vadim too needed to develop in his work, but *Et Dieu créa la femme* would make money, the critic predicted. And not because of its dialogue!

20. Crowther found "nothing sublime about the script of this completely single-minded little picture..." and only "sultry fervor" in the performances of Bardot and of the men chasing her in the film. *The New York Times*, October 22, 1957.

21. Quotations 83, article 83–88 with ads and pictures.

22. *Time*, November 11, 1957, quotations 20, 22.

23. *Newsweek*, January 6, 1958, quotes 68. Howard Thompson reviewed *The Bride Is Much Too Beautiful* in *The New York Times* on January 21, 1958, noting how a crowd of people went to the World movie theater simply because of Bardot's name.

24. See for the pre–Bardot era on the Riviera Mary Blume, *Côte d'Azur: Inventing the French Riviera* (New York: Thames and Hudson, 1992), and Michael Nelson, *Queen Victoria and the Discovery of the Riviera* (London: I.B. Tauris, 2001). See also my article, "The Riviera Then and Now," *Contemporary Review* 283 (December 2003), 362–366.

25. A collection of Trintignant's own words on his life and cinematic history, along with estimations by such as Rohmer and Lelouch, is in Jean-Louis Trintignant, *Un Homme à sa fenêtre* (Paris: Jean-Claude Simoën, 1977). Though Trintignant is listed as author, credit should also be given to the editor here, Michel Boujut.

26. Somehow his *Bardot Deneuve Fonda* (trans. Melinda Camber Porter; New York: Simon and Schuster, 1987) would bother her more than *Memoirs of the Devil* from the previous decade.

3. The Era of High Celebrity

1. On Morgan see Claude Bouniq-Mercier, *Michèle Morgan* (Paris: Editions Colona, 1983) and her own memoirs, far less interesting than Bardot's. For Arletty (real name Léonie Bathiat), see Denis Demonpion, *Arletty* (Paris: Flammarion, 1996) and other books in bibliography. For Signoret see also books in bibliography. And for Martine Carol (born Marie-Louise Mourer in Biarritz), Georges Debot, *Martine Carol: ou la vie de Martine chérie* (Paris: Editions France-Empire, 1979); André-Charles Cohen, *Martine chérie* (Paris: Ramsay, 1986), a collection of photos; Arnaud Chapuy, *Martine Carol filmée par Christian-Jaque: un phénomène du cinéma populaire* (Paris: L'Harmattan, 2001); and the chapter on her in Jacques Mazeau, *Les Destins tragiques du cinéma* (Paris: Editions Hors Collection, 1995). Bardot's transformation into an image affecting young peoples' dress, lifestyles, etc., again went well beyond anything of the sort associated with prior French actresses mentioned.

2. See Stanislas Choko's potpourri of posters in *Brigitte Bardot à l'affiche* (Paris: Editions du Collectionneur, 1992) and also Choko, ed., *Affiches du cinéma: Trésors de la Bibliothèque nationale de France 1896-1960* (Paris: Bibliothèque nationale de France/Editions de l'amateur, 1995); Jean-Louis Capitaine, *Les Affiches du cinéma français* (Paris: Editions Segher, 1988); Tony Nourmand and Graham Marsh, eds., *Film Posters of the '50s* (London: Aurum Press, 2000); and for comparisons, René Château, *Les plus belles affiches du cinéma français des années 50: 1950-1960* (Paris: Editions R.C., 1994), a wonder-

ful collection with a whole section devoted to a number of Bardot films (29–50). Advertising posters for her films in Italy or Germany could be as erotic as in France, whereas American ones of that era were less overtly so.

3. Bardot was never a fan of the Cannes festival. In Pierre Billard's book devoted to its history, she appears in only one photograph, but a stunner in fine dress from the back, and facing a stocky François Mitterrand in sober suit. This appearance (spring 1956) was to help Vadim procure money to make *And God...* a color picture. Billard's comment on the photograph: "Even from the back, no one would mistake her for someone else." Billard, *D'Or et de palmes: Le Festival de Cannes* (Paris: Gallimard, 1997), 29 (and photograph 28).

4. Boyer, one of the rare French actors to become famous in English or American movies, was the perfect, prudent opposite number for Bardot here—an authentic representative of *vieille France*, along with an older Hollywood. From Figeac in the French Southwest, he was an only child who became a sober, private adult, deeply devoted to his wife of 44 years. When she passed away on August 24, 1978, he followed, committing suicide two days later. See Larry Swindell, *Charles Boyer: The Reluctant Lover* (New York: Doubleday, 1983), and Guy Chassagnard, *Charles Boyer: Acteur* (Figeac: Editions Segnat, 1999). A.H. Weiler in his *New York Times* review of July 31, 1958, called this film Bardot's best to that point.

5. The film, however, was one where Bosley Crowther considered Bardot "miserably used." But he was perhaps too used to the unclad Bardot of that era. As with other Bardot pictures, this one played in both a subtitled and dubbed version at two different Manhattan movie houses. See Crowther review in *The New York Times*, October 22, 1958. In terms of "screen loving" Bardot spoke interestingly and frankly on that in the documentary *Telle quelle* of the '80s. She found it awful to kiss men she cared nothing for, and even worse to embrace someone publicly who was a significant other!

6. Claude Autant-Lara, the director of *En Cas de malheur* (in English *Love Is My Profession*), was a man born in the Belle Epoque to upper-middle-class parents, but himself a lifelong rebel. See his autobiography *La Rage dans le coeur: chronique cinématographique du 20è siècle* (Paris: Veyrier, 1984). Pierre Billard considers Autant-Lara's virtuosity in subject matter and execution quite unique for his time. See Billard, *L'Age classique du cinéma français: du cinéma parlant à la Nouvelle Vague* (Paris: Flammarion, 1995), 618–621, quotation 618.

7. Jean de Baroncelli headed the list of ambivalents in *Le Monde* (September 24, 1958). Noting that he had seen the film twice within three weeks, he was perplexed by something missing here, despite Autant-Lara's technical mastery, a fine screenplay, the powerful opening scene of Bardot's bungled robbery, Feuillère's wonderful portrayal of the bourgeois wife, and Bardot's palpable progress as an ac-

tress since *And God...* On audience and critical reaction, see also Gerty Colin, *Jean Gabin* (Paris: Presses de la Cité, 1983), 134. Bosley Crowther seemed nonplussed to find Gabin and Bardot on the same screen, making his review in *The New York Times* (April 28, 1959) rather negative. On Gabin see also André Brunelin, *Gabin* (Paris: Editions Robert Laffont, 1987), noting that Bardot and the legend of *Grande illusion* et al. got along on the set, even if he found her "a bit of a dilettante." (452) And on Gabin's reluctance to take the role due to his children, and this being his last love film, see Brunelin, 451.

8. For Bécaud (1927–2002), see Christophe Izard, *Gilbert Bécaud* (Paris: Editions Séghers, 1972); Louis Amade, *Et ce sera ta passion de vivre* (Paris: Hachette, 1982), by probably his greatest lyricist; and Annie and Bernard Réval, *Gilbert Bécaud: Jardins secrets* (Paris: France-Empire, 2001). For a handy, complete compendium of his songs with full lyrics and in chronological order see Gilbert Bécaud, *Alors, raconte...* (Paris: Livre de Poche, 1995).

9. One shouldn't paint Trintignant's subsequent life in entirely bright colors. He had lingering health effects from the difficulties of military service, where he once ate 40 eggs to poison himself (with albumen), and also had several months in prison for his opposition to the war in Algeria. See his interview in Jean-Louis Trintignant, *La Passion tranquille: Entretiens avec André Asséo* (Paris: Plon/France Inter, 2002), ch. 4 ("Brigitte Bardot et le Service Militaire"). A few years back came the tragedy of his daughter, Marie, herself an actress and mother of four children, being beaten about the head after a quarrel with rock singer Bertrand Cantat. Submitting to operations, and in a coma, she died from the blows on August 1, 2003. Many articles appeared in the French press on this tragedy.

10. Vadim, *Bardot Deneuve Fonda*, 126–128; Bardot, *Initiales B.B.*, 166.

11. See my article "French Memories of Algeria," *Contemporary Review* 282 (May 2003), 257–263, on the idealism of a generation of soldiers who in some cases had already been in the Resistance and Nazi camps during World War II, then in Indochina.

12. See Vadim, *Bardot Deneuve Fonda*, 114–115; and more expansively, *Memoirs of the Devil*, 102–107. (Sinatra was in Chicago both for Mike Todd's funeral, which Vadim attended, and a big prizefight.)

13. It also wore thin for Eugene Archer, reviewing the film in *The New York Times* (April 28, 1960), and finding Bardot "briefly hypnotic and ultimately indigestible" here, though directed by Julien Duvivier of *Pépé le Moko* fame. Duvivier was one of the great French directors, but Louis Marcorelles in his review of *La Femme et le pantin* for *Les Cahiers du cinéma* (April 1959) considered the problem partly one of a generational gulf between a director born in 1896 and a star born in 1934. Marcorelles found the "screenplay ridiculous and no figure [in the film] psychologically convincing...." Quoted in Yves Desrichard, *Julien Duvivier: Cinquante ans de noirs destins* (Paris: BiFi/Durante, 2001), 146.

14. On his young life and romance with Bardot, see Sacha Distel, *Les Pendules à l'heure* (Paris: Michel Lafon, 1985), ch. 1–11; and Bardot, *Initiales B.B.*, ch. 12. Distel says they had met in Paris when he decided to cut a record based on Paul Misraki's music for *And God...* Needing to complete his vocal work in studio, they resorted to some spoken dialogue from Brigitte herself. In his version she then asked him to run her home to Paul Doumer, and en route, they had a drink. He dropped her off, and she asked him to stay in touch. See Distel, 101–102.

15. All quotations in a long page cum photos in O'Neill's *Life* article, June 30, 1958, 57.

16. French films also benefited from government aid for nascent projects. In addition, televisions were comparatively rare—only 2,000,000 in 1960, versus 11,000,000 at the outset of the next decade. See Jill Forbes, *Cinema in France after the New Wave* (Houndmills, U.K.: Macmillan, 1962), 6, 8.

17. The full *Match* article (July 26, 1958) is on 54–57, quotes 54; and the first one of August 16 is 25–36, quotes 27, the second (by Hanoteau) is on 37–43, quotes 37, 41.

18. Bardot, *Initiales B.B.*, 207. The media blitz was in part stimulated by Raoul Lévy's love of publicity, which included use of skywriting and sumptuous receptions in palaces. Lévy also managed to become smitten at the time with Jeanne Moreau, which led to his first suicide attempt (apparently to impress her)! See Pierre Billard, *Louis Malle, le rebelle solitaire* (Paris: Plon, 2003), 189.

19. There is less mendacity in Bardot's version than it seems. In earlier interviews that informed secondary source accounts like Joëlle Monserrat's, Bardot had noted her esteem for Charrier's prior theater work. See Monserrat, *Brigitte Bardot* (Paris: Editions PAC, 1983), 37. Memoir writers obviously do not gather up every twig in the river of memory.

20. A good analysis of the use of Bardot as a ravishing Resistance icon is in Leahy, "Matter of Myth: Brigitte Bardot, Stardom and Sex," 75–76. Both Charrier and Bardot would procure relatively high marks from A.H. Weiler in his *New York Times* review of the film, June 8, 1960.

21. The Bardot version of this is in *Initiales B.B.*, 215–16; Charrier's in his interesting but rather bitter and cynical *Ma Réponse à BB: Brigitte Bardot* (Paris: Michel Lafon, 1997), chs. 2–4, including material on his background. Distel noted that Charrier took cover in the bathroom, while he yelled at Brigitte, then slammed the door as he left, breaking mirrors in the process, and shouting that she could bill him! Distel, ch. 13 ("Brigitte, suite et fin").

22. Again, Charrier differs with Bardot's version on the place to which they escaped. He calls it a "romantic five room" apartment that a friend of his on *Le Monde* rented him. He does admit to bohemian ways, and to a bare refrigerator. Charrier, 132–133.

23. Alan Williams, *Republic of Images: A History of French Filmmaking* (Cambridge, Mass.: Harvard University Press, 1992), 286–287. See also Colin Crisp, *The Classic French Cinema, 1930-1960* (Bloomington:

Indiana University Press, 1997), 313 on Clouzot's authoritarian style. And Philippe Pilard's compilation, *Henri-Georges Clouzot* (Paris: Editions Segher, 1969). On Clouzot's choice of Bardot for *Vérité* and his wife's influence in it, see his interview with Yvonne Baby in *Le Monde*, November 3, 1960.

24. The cinematic work of these lawyers played by Paul Meurisse (the abusive husband alumnus of *Diaboliques*) and Charles Vanel, and the courtroom parts generally, are especially lauded by Bosley Crowther in his review (*New York Times*, June 27, 1961). On Vanel, who had a long career and life, see Charles Ford, *Charles Vanel: un comédien exemplaire* (Paris: France-Empire, 1986) and Jacqueline Cartier, *Monsieur Vanel: un siècle de souvenirs, un an d'entretiens* (Paris: Robert Laffont, 1989).

25. She later averred in the documentary *Telle quelle* that she drew from her own travails here, but also felt other fine actors watching on the set, preeminently Vanel and Meurisse. In other words, she felt she had to keep up!

26. Bardot quote in *Initiales B.B.*, 275. Charrier concurs on the fight in his own memoir. Charrier, 239.

27. This scene too seems to have been borrowed for the later Louis Malle film, *Vie privée*, in good part based on Bardot's life.

28. Quoted in, among others, Glenys Roberts, *Bardot: A Personal Biography* (New York: St. Martin's Press, 1984), 163.

29. Reviewing in *Le Monde* (November 5, 1960), Jean de Baroncelli gave high praise to all of the central actors and actresses here—Frey, Vanel, Meurisse, and Bardot, whose transformation into a deep and sincere woman on the stand truly impressed him. He also praised Clouzot for his high, if at times over-conscientious standards.

30. Jean de Baroncelli called all this "léger, léger, léger" in his *Le Monde* review of April 23–24, 1961. There were also repercussions stemming from the initial replacement of the director Aurel by Vadim. An "affair" was spawned when François Truffaut accused Vadim in *France-Observateur* of being an immoralist ready to do anything in the cinematic world. The latter then went to court, accusing Truffaut of defaming his character. Aurel had at the beginning of *Bride*'s production been an inexperienced director, suffering from the fact that the film treatment was originally earmarked for Charrier to star with Bardot. However, Charrier was taken by military service, and the screenplay was altered, and anything but finished in time. Aurel had too much scrambling and plain work to do for Bardot's taste. See Jean-Marc Théolleyre's article in *Le Monde* on January 31, 1962, with a title of "L'envers du cinéma ou Mme Brigitte Bardot témoin." See also Truffaut's letter to Helen Scott dated January 9, 1962, in Truffaut, *Correspondence 1945-1984* (trans. Gilbert Adair; New York: Farrar, Straus and Giroux, 1988): "I'm at war with Vadim who has stolen someone else's film, the one with Bardot that Jean Aurel had been shooting for 3 days; you'll hear talk of it in cer-

tain newspapers, but not in *L'Express* which is shielding Vadim and prefers not to speak about it." (159)

31. Haining, *The Legend of Brigitte Bardot* (London: W.H. Allen, 1983), 115.

32. Bardot, *Initiales B.B.*, 301.

33. Malle feels that Mastroianni was never quite right for this role, and the Italian star and Brigitte did not get along well during the shooting. See Philip French, ed., *Malle on Malle* (London: Faber and Faber, 1993), 32–36. Bosley Crowther also finds Mastroianni "one-dimensional" here (in his *New York Times* review, September 29, 1962), while *Time*'s brief note (October 26, 1962) blamed Brigitte for no longer being the inspiring ball of fire she had been earlier in her career. Brendan Gill in *The New Yorker* (October 13, 1962) praised the director's artful use of the camera in varied locales, while Jean de Baroncelli in *Le Monde* (February 3, 1962) also praised Malle, but felt Bardot didn't translate her emotions into this autobiographical role.

34. See Pierre Billard, *Louis Malle*, 209 on film earnings.

35. See any issue of a newspaper like *Le Monde* in the period when *Vie privée* emerged (January-February 1962). On Malle's trips to Algeria, see Billard, *Louis Malle*, 219–225.

36. Bardot, *Initiales B.B.*, 305.

37. Her announcements of retirement came in interviews, such as with Maurice Chapelan in *Le Figaro littéraire*, February 3, 1962.

38. On how much Bardot was being emulated for her looks, ways, and dancing in certain films, see Sarah Leahy's article, "Bardot and Dance: Representing the Real?," *French Cultural Studies* 13 (February 2002), 49–64. Ginette Vincendeau also notes changes in the clothing industry that resulted from the Bardot "look." Vincendeau, *Stars and Stardom in French Cinema*, 88–89.

39. The O.A.S. was definitely serious, with old members admitting to the kidnap plot on Bardot. See articles (headline "L'OAS Parle") in *France Soir*, June 27, 2003.

40. Jean de Baroncelli was fairly decent to *Repos...* in his *Le Monde* review of September 13, 1962, while A.H. Weiler gave it a more wan estimate in *The New York Times* (December 17, 1963). Vadim confessed to changing his mind about Bardot's character as he put together the movie. See Yvonne Baby's interview of Vadim in *Le Monde*, September 9–10, 1962.

41. Bardot, *Initiales B.B.*, 327.

42. Patrick McGilligan, *Fritz Lang: The Nature of the Beast* (New York: St. Martin's Press, 1997), 449. On the New Wave and Godard's place in it see Michel Marie, *The French New Wave: An Artistic School* (trans. Richard Neupert; Oxford: Blackwell Publishing, 2003); Chris Wiegand, *French New Wave* (Harpenden, U.K.: Pocket Essentials, 2001); and James Monaco, *The New Wave* (New York: Oxford University Press, 1980), among others.

43. See Godard's interview on how the film was made, with Yvonne Baby in *Le Monde*, December 20, 1963. He also said that he made himself Lang's

assistant in the film due to his admiration for that imposing figure, who contributed his own editorial voice as the film was shot. See also Jacques Aumont, "The Fall of the Gods: Jean-Luc Godard's *Le Mépris* (1963)," in Susan Hayward and Ginette Vincendeau, eds., *French Film: Texts and Contexts* (London: Routledge, 2000), ch. 12. Aumont says the entire film is on indecision in filmmaking, and was itself characterized by that indecision! (180)

44. Among many analytical treatments of *Le Mépris* one could start with Wheeler Winston Dixon, *The Films of Jean-Luc Godard* (Albany: SUNY Press, 1997), ch. 2; and Toby Mussman's own pages on the film in Mussman, ed., *Jean-Luc Godard: A Critical Anthology* (New York: E.P. Dutton, 1968), 152–169. In his *Le Monde* review (December 22–23, 1963), Jean de Baroncelli revealed admiration for Godard's classicism and general skill here, but was also put off by flaws like incessant quotations in the script. He noted frustrated sighs and whisperings in the audience when he watched the film. Mainstream New York critics were harder on the movie than more radical ones for the time. Brendan Gill in *The New Yorker* (December 26, 1964) declared: "Jean-Luc Godard has directed [here] with stunning self-indulgence.... The screenplay is credited to Mr. Godard, but I doubt whether an actual script could be found; never have I seen a picture that seemed more surely to have been made up as it went along, and while the backgrounds are beguiling ... what fails to happen in the foreground soon makes one's mind numb with boredom." (73) Bosley Crowther (in *The New York Times*, December 19, 1964) disliked the thin characterizations, and the fact that the husband bringing out Bardot's contempt wore his hat (like Godard) round the clock. Bardot would have a small part a few years later in another well-known Godard film, *Masculin/Féminin*, where Jean-Pierre Léaud (of Truffaut fame) really dominates; though again this picture too seems dated in its intellectual, self-involved rambling.

4. Waning Stardom and the Rise of Sachs

1. With disdain for that era's mainstream, Bosley Crowther gave the film short shrift in his review, appearing in *The New York Times* on January 28, 1965.

2. Malle says that he was thinking of a number of old Hollywood westerns here, particularly *Vera Cruz*. "We thought it would be fun to put Bardot and Moreau in the same situation as Cooper and Lancaster in *Vera Cruz* and to do a pastiche of those buddy films. We started from that." The "we" meant Malle and his co-screenwriter on the project, Jean-Claude Carrière. French, ed., *Malle on Malle*, 51.

3. Those journalists and photographers were often American on this side of the Atlantic, part of

a large publicity machine for the movie. Articles appeared in *Time* on March 5, 1965, with Moreau's portrait on the cover looking like something out of Picasso's "Demoiselles d'Avignon"; in *Life* on April 2, 1965 ("Les Girls in Mexico"); in the *Saturday Evening Post* on April 10, 1965; and in *Look* on May 4, 1965. There was also Marguerite Duras' piece on Moreau in *Vogue* from November 15, 1965 (she had already done a celebrated one on the Bardot phenomenon, "La Reine Bardot," in *France-Observateur* of October 23, 1958).

4. For Malle's problems here, see French, ed., *Malle on Malle*, 49–53. On Moreau see Marianne Gray, *La Moreau: A Biography of Jeanne Moreau* (New York: Donald I. Fine, 1996), and Michel Delmar, *Jeanne Moreau: Portrait d'une femme* (Paris: Editions Norma, 1994).

5. The interview is contained in a variety of the sources on Bardot.

6. For the film's lack of business success in the States Malle partly blamed the quality of American dubbing (French, ed., *Malle on Malle*, 54); today, however, one easily finds the subtitled version on video or DVD, with of course snatches of Spanish in different parts of the picture. The movie did well at European box offices for a variety of reasons. It made an impact both in socialist countries and among the youthful left in non-socialist ones, due to Malle's apparent anticlerical, anticapitalist, antimilitary, and pro-revolutionary stance here. (See Pierre Billard, *Louis Malle*, 255 and ch. 3 generally on the making of *Viva Maria*.) In the U.S. Bosley Crowther essentially called *Viva Maria* hit and miss (*New York Times* review, December 20, 1965), and Brendan Gill in *The New Yorker* (December 25, 1965) thought that Malle had taken on too much as the film's director and co-producer, and as one of its two screenwriters. For Gill the movie didn't come to a proper resolution soon enough. As for Billard, more enthusiastic as a younger reviewer, his judgment today is that despite aiming high, the movie lacked coherence and clarity of purpose. Billard, *Louis Malle*, 256, and see his summary of other French reviews of the movie on that page. Today's Internet is clogged with kudos by a younger generation that in North America and England mostly loves Moreau and Bardot here. They admire a female buddy chemistry outlasting *Charlie's Angels* and the rest, saluting Malle's comic quality, too. In sum, *Viva Maria* has had a resurgent video and DVD life in the 21st century!

7. The erotic "Je t'aime..." only came out in Bardot's version during the mid-'80s. In truth, Gainsbourg-Bardot products (for example, their "Bonnie and Clyde," "Bubble Gum," and "Harley Davidson") seem rather dated in their effort to be '60s cool.

8. On what this turning point era meant for French cinema see Jill Forbes, *The Cinema in France after the New Wave* (Houndmills, U.K.: MacMillan, 1992), especially ch. 1.

5. Playing Out the String

1. See Dmytryk's *Odd Man Out: A Memoir of the Hollywood Ten* (Carbondale, Ill.: Southern Illinois University Press, 1996). Renata Adler in *The New York Times* (November 6, 1968) echoes my estimate, calling *Shalako* a good, old-fashioned western that persuades; while Pauline Kael predictably put it down in *The New Yorker* (November 16, 1968), though praising Connery here.

2. On Tabarly see Benôit Heimermann, *Tabarly* (Paris: Grasset, 2002), Daniel Charles, *Tabarly* (Paris: Arthaud, 2000), Gilles Durieux, *Tabarly: un marin devant l'éternité* (Monaco: Editions du Rocher, 1998), and his own *Mémoires du large* (Paris: Fallois, 1997).

3. See Ellis Amburn, *The Sexiest Man Alive: A Biography of Warren Beatty* (New York: HarperCollins, 2002), 121–122. Fonda does not mention the story in her *My Life So Far* (New York: Random House, 2005).

4. Bardot, *Initiales B.B.*, 518.

5. On Carol and Christian-Jaque, see Arnaud Chapuy, *Martine Carol filmée par Christian-Jaque: un phénomène du cinéma populaire* (Paris: L'Harmattan, 2001).

6. Bardot, *Initiales B.B.*, 532.

7. A blasé review of *Don Juan, ou si Don Juan était une femme* by Martin Even in *Le Monde* (February 23, 1973) found the old tandem of Bardot and Vadim somewhat passé here.

8. *Histoires extraordinaires* (1968) was that trilogy based on tales by Poe, directed respectively by Vadim, Malle, and Fellini. The Malle segment is made in his usual adept way, but the subject matter is Poe-creepy, and sadism (including the cutting up of a woman as a medical experiment) would have repelled any normal viewer. On the making of the film see Billard, *Louis Malle*, 271–274.

6. Goodbye Movies, Hello Animals

1. See, among others, Haining, 201–205.

2. Haining, 201.

3. Brigitte Bardot, *Le Carré de Pluton: Mémoires II* (Paris: Grasset, 1999), 41.

4. For aspects of her fall 1976 state of mind, including extensive reading of classics by Stendhal, de Maupassant etc., see Laurence Masurel's interview of Bardot in *Paris-Match*, November 19, 1976, 24–27, 42.

5. See the secondary sources, especially Jeffrey Robinson's biography, and Bardot's own diary entries in *Paris-Match*, April 1, 1977, 64–69, and in *Carré de Pluton*, 74–90.

6. Bardot, *Carré de Pluton*, 91.

7. On Bardot's attempt to get a ban on the seal hunt with the Conseil de l'Europe, and on her life with Mirko and her dogs on vacation at Méribel, see, among others, an article in *Paris-Match*, February 3, 1978, 16–17. In this period she and Mirko also traveled to Abidjan on the Ivory Coast for an exposition of his sculptures. After beginning the trip in a spirit of enjoyment, Bardot was then moved to tears witnessing baby orangutans miserable behind bars, and pressured the Minister of Culture there to consider freeing the animals. Only on the last night of their trip did she and Mirko get back to celebrating their own lives. See on that trip an article in *Paris-Match*, December 2, 1977, 52–53.

8. Again, mass magazines mainly painted the nice sides of their relationship. The picture of her "relax" time spent with the Bohemian sculptor is rather idyllic in Elizabeth David's article on the couple in *Paris-Match*, June 16, 1978, 54.

9. Brigitte Bardot (with Daniel Dollfuss), *Noonah: Le petit phoque blanc* (Paris: Grasset and Fasquelle, 1978). Eskimo reverence for seals, and therefore, more of an environmental consciousness than in European descendants, is well sketched in a fine book by Allain Bougrain-Dubourg (with Bernard Monier, Bernard Lengelle, and Alika Lindbergh), *L'Agonie des bébés phoques* (Paris: Presses de la Cité, 1978), 52–53. Bardot wrote a preface for the book.

7. Allain and the Animals in the '80s

1. Again, mass magazine articles made things look easier than they were. Readers would see pictures of Bardot mornings at La Madrague inviting a half-dozen dogs and at least twice as many cats to romp on her sumptuous bed, then eat biscuits in a typically communal French breakfast. See article on Bardot of that era in *Paris-Match*, July 18, 1980, 12–14.

2. See Michou Simon's interview of Bardot in *Paris-Match*, March 20, 1981, 80.

3. Rebecca Hall, *Voiceless Victims* (Hounslow, U.K.: Wildwood House, 1984), with Bardot's quote on vii of the preface. See also other such books of the era, such as Jim Mason and Peter Singer, *Animal Fortunes* (New York: Crown, 1980).

4. See, among others, the article on this in the *Washington Post*, August 10, 1982.

5. As an example, see article entitled "Le Coup de cafard de BB" ("BB's Bout of Blues") in *Paris-Match*, October 21, 1983, 24–29.

6. See Denis Taranto's interview of Bardot in *Paris-Match*, July 6, 1984, 22–25, 76.

7. Bardot, *Carré de Pluton*, 274.

8. Bardot, *Carré de Pluton*, 289.

9. On this "world we have lost," the best academic book remains Eugen Weber's *Peasants into Frenchmen: The Modernization of Rural France, 1870–1914* (Stanford: Stanford University Press, 1976).

10. See, among other articles on her displeasure, one in the *Los Angeles Times*, January 15, 1987.

11. Quoted in Bardot, *Carré de Pluton*, 326. On the auction see various secondary sources and her own pages, as well as newspaper articles of the time, such as in the *New York Times*, June 19, 1987.

12. Bardot, *Carré de Pluton*, 339.

13. In her recollections Bardot goes into a dithyramb on this dog's family, and then on others she had, and the character portraits are as deft as any one finds on people. See, for example, *Carré de Pluton*, 343–344.

14. Again, it is easy to quote her on this—"distress without name, inadmissible insalubrity, mud, water everywhere, a humid cold and bowls of frozen water, no food, stiffened cadavers at the back of certain cages...." Bardot, *Carré de Pluton*, 351.

15. Among other articles on Bardot shelling out a good $10,000 for these zoo inhabitants and their eventual transfer to the retreat, see one in *The Daily Telegraph*, December 2, 1988.

16. Roland Gillet, *Dernière croisade* (Brussels: Edipax, 1988) with Bardot's preface. On vivisection see ch. 4.

17. Bardot, *Carré de Pluton*, 386.

18. See her lyrical lament on hunters and hunting, which she despises, in *Carré de Pluton*, 403.

19. Bardot would sometimes say that *La Vérité* was the only film of hers that she cared about—see articles on this in *Los Angeles Times*, December 27, 1990 and *U.S.A. Today*, September 29, 1994; though she would amend that with appreciation for Louis Malle's productions and even *And God Created Woman*, among others.

20. Representative mass-media articles on Bardot and her mentality near the end of the '80s and the dawn of the '90s include Patrick Sabatier, "La vie secrète de Bardot," in *Paris-Match*, June 17, 1988; "Non à Saint-Tropez," an interview with Henry-Jean Servat (whom she respected) in *Match*, August 24, 1989; and his interview with her, primarily about hunting, in *Match*, November 2, 1989.

8. Battles of the '90s

1. Bullfighting generally bothered Bardot both in Spain and in her own France, such as in southern towns like Nîmes. She went after one female bullfighter in the South of France who made big money at it. See on this, articles in *The Times*, September 30, 1990, and *The Daily Telegraph*, October 19, 1990, urging a ban on the "sport." In the next several years Bardot would lead a coalition of associations from thirteen countries, encouraging a boycott of Seville's universal exposition and Spain itself, due to these festivals, some Church-sponsored, where animals were maimed or killed. She also fought for a boycott of bullfighting. (See, among other articles on this, ones in *Agence France Presse*, April 15, 1992, and *The Herald* of Glasgow, April 16, 1992.) She also took on the Italians for their cruel Siena horse race, the "palio," a major tourist attraction going back to the Middle Ages. Frequent horse crashes in mad scrambles over cobblestones occurred there. See articles on this in *Daily Telegraph*, June 28, 1991, and *Sunday Times*, August 4, 1991.

2. Quoted in, among others, Bardot, *Carré de Pluton*, 426.

3. See, among other articles on the impact of these documentaries, one in *Los Angeles Times*, May 19, 1989, and later ones there of April 25 and May 10, 1990.

4. See, among others, the Associated Press article on this (byline by Barry Renfrew) of July 4, 1990; and one in *The Times* (London), July 5, 1990.

5. See on this, articles in *Le Monde* and *The San Diego Union-Tribune* of August 2, 1990.

6. See article on this in, among others, *Los Angeles Times*, August 9, 1990.

7. See an article on the killing of these seal pups off Namibia's coast (by Eddie Koch) for Inter Press Service, October 3, 1990. Opponents still maintained that the killings were really quite humane, and that there were too many of these creatures anyway!

8. Olga Horstig-Primuz (with Ginette Billard), *Moi, j'aime les acteurs* (Paris: Jean-Claude Lattès, 1990).

9. See article on this in, among others, *Le Monde*, March 11, 1991.

10. A full series of articles and numerous photographs grace the pages of *Paris-Match* on March 21, 1991, but Bardot was willingly upstaged there by people such as Jane Birkin, calling Serge her chief mentor.

11. On her support for these commando operations to free baboons, etc., from research centers see an earlier article in *The Times*, June 14, 1990.

12. Members of the foundation would still be reading about this problem in the foundation's *Infojournal* of the third *trimestre*, 2003 (number 45), 12–13. The article appearing there was entitled "Destination vacances" and warned readers: "Don't leave on vacations without your animal." It was accompanied by color pictures of dogs on the two pages, one of them called Péguy after the prolix French intellectual killed at the Battle of the Marne in World War I.

13. Fossey was obviously another idiosyncratic obsessional when it came to besieged animals. An old associate of the legendary Louis Leakey, and herself tortured by an unhappy childhood and by being a six-footer, she then gave her entire life to protect the last of a marvelous species of creatures being decimated by poachers, who often hated her, and by urban sprawl in Zaïre and Rwanda. Fossey's own *Gorillas in the Mist* (Boston: Houghton Mifflin, 1983) is fundamental, but the best book on her passionate life and tragic death is Harold T.P. Hayes' *The Dark Romance of Dian Fossey* (New York: Simon and Schuster, 1990).

14. Looking back, Bardot gives a marvelous summary of where that relationship would evolve, or devolve, in *Carré de Pluton*, 528.

15. See their cover story and photos in the issue of October 29, 1992.

16. The Servat interview of Bardot and the photos of her dancing to guitars are in the *Paris-Match*

issue of August 12, 1993, 17–18. Considerately, she protected Bernard in that interview, saying that he was absent because he liked Saint-Tropez in summer and also had business down there.

17. See Bardot's spirited account in *Carré de Pluton*, 575, and article in, among others, *New York Daily News*, May 15, 1999, summarizing the case.

18. See articles on this in *Agence France Presse*, July 7, 1993; and in *U.S.A. Today*, July 8, 1993, and in *Chicago Sun-Times* on the same date, including reference to gulags.

19. On horse butchers, threats, etc., see articles in *The Herald* of Glasgow, January 29, 1994, *Agence France Presse*, February 22, 1994, and *The Daily Telegraph*, May 10, 1994. And on the Médoc, articles such as one in *Agence France Presse*, May 1, 1994.

20. And again there was a tasteful interview to go with the pictures, conducted by Henry-Jean Servat: *Paris-Match*, June 23, 1994, 37–38. Bardot was thrown her usual quota of questions here on why she had left the cinema, and she answered that movie-making represented another life for her, and that her celebrity only meant something now if it helped animals.

21. See for concerns over pigeons and hunting, articles in *Agence France Presse*, February 23, May 10, and June 2, 1994; *The Daily Telegraph*, June 3, 1994; *The Independent*, January 6, 1995; and *Agence France Presse*, October 9, 1996, on the catfish issue.

22. See on Mitterrand, *New York Times* article of May 11, 1994; on bunting consumption article in the *Cleveland Plain Dealer*, January 20, 1997; on the importation of kangaroo meat (and who needed that?), article in *Agence France Presse*, October 14, 1996. And for the fight against foie gras and frogs' legs, one could simply look up the series of "Principaux Combats" put out by the foundation on the Internet from the late '90s onward.

23. See in order articles in *Agence France Presse*, May 4, 1994, and March 15, 1994; *The Irish Times*, September 24, 1994; *Agence France Presse*, October 14, 1994, and January 10, 1995; *The Houston Chronicle*, October 29, 1994; *The Times-Picayune* (New Orleans), August 30, 1996; *The Herald* (Glasgow), June 15, 1994; *The Times*, September 7, 1995; *Agence France Presse*, February 20, 1995, April 6, 1996, and February 14, 1997; *Agence France Presse*, August 3, 1994; *The Independent* (London), April 22, 1997; *The Guardian*, February 25, 1998; *The Arizona Republic*, July 4, 1998; and *The Independent*, February 7, 1998. Since so much of this was worldwide wire copy, many alternate newspapers could be used here.

24. See Bardot's memoirs, plus an article on this, among many others, in *The Independent* (London), September 28, 1995.

25. See articles on Phipps in *Agence France Presse*, February 14, 1995, and *The Independent*, February 15, 1995.

26. See the article on this support for Watson in *Agence France Presse*, April 10, 1997. Among Watson's absorbing memoirs, one could start with *Ocean Warrior: My Battle to End the Illegal Slaughter on the High Seas* (St. Leonards, Australia: Allen and Unwin, 1994).

27. For the early impact in the press see articles in *Le Monde*, August 2, 1990, and among American papers, one in the *San Diego Union-Tribune* of the same date.

28. See representative article in *The Independent*, June 1, 1993.

29. See articles in *Agence France Presse* and in the *Independent*, April 26, 1996, with Bardot quotations.

30. See summaries in articles appearing in *The Daily Telegraph*, September 24, 1996, and *The Independent*, September 25, 1996.

31. See articles on this in *Sunday Times*, December 1, 1996, and in *Le Monde*, December 7, 1996.

32. See articles on this in *The Herald* (Glasgow), December 20, 1996, and in *Le Monde*, December 21, 1996.

33. See among others, article in *The Daily Telegraph*, January 24, 1997.

34. For quotes, etc., see *The Herald* (Glasgow), April 17, 1997.

35. See articles in *Los Angeles Times* and *The Guardian*, October 10, 1997.

36. See articles in *Le Monde*, January 22, 1998, and *Irish Times*, February 4, 1998, including quotation; and on Serbs, article in *Le Monde*, April 20, 1998. On the Serbs see also Guillaume Apollinaire, Brigitte Bardot, Jean Dutourd et al., *Alliés des Serbes* (Lausanne: Age d'homme, 1998), an anthology. To be fair to Bardot's stand, the Serbs were singled out when their foes had neither perfect pasts nor presents (including the drug-running, terroristic Kosovo Liberation Army). The Americans were perhaps too simplistic in their policies here.

37. The impending finish line of this exhausting enterprise was first announced to the public coincident with her 60th birthday on September 28, 1994. See pictures of her study at Bazoches where she was getting to the end, and Patrick Mahé's interview in *Paris-Match*, October 6, 1994, 80–83.

38. Among relatively positive reviews one could note Claude Imbert's in *Le Point*, October 12, 1996, saluting Bardot's palpability ("in brief, Madame Bardot fascinates, that's how it is!"); and Isabelle de Courtivron in *The New York Times Book Review* (June 22, 1997, 35), averring that "the publication of Brigitte Bardot's memoirs ('Initiales B.B.,' from the title of a song by one of her lovers, Serge Gainsbourg) was met with the same curiosity, opprobrium, fascination and animosity that surrounded the star in her heyday of the 50's and early 60's.... [Bardot] wrote the book over many years; it reflects faithfully, for better and for worse, her qualities and her faults." This review also negates malicious gossip that the book was ghostwritten, as does another mention in an earlier *Le Point* article on BB's birthday, September 28, 1996: "The style proves it superabundantly: Brigitte Bardot wrote her own memoirs." Among other reviewers who actually read the book, Lucy Yeomans is mixed in her assessment given in *The European Magazine*, October 3, 1996, 8,

noting: "The memoirs make simultaneously repulsive and fascinating reading. It is intriguing to discover the thoughts of the sex-kitten turned animal rights campaigner." Katherine Knorr in *The Irish Times*, September 28, 1996, is too clever, but certainly finds Bardot's life an astonishing one. Olivier Schmitt in *Le Monde* (September 25, 1996) is predictably negative. Helen Kennedy in *The Daily News* (New York), September 25, 1996, ferrets out many *People Magazine*–type details, but doesn't offer a real opinion. Among newspapers that simply gave notices or brief summaries, rather than real reviews, one could note *The International Herald Tribune*, September 24, 1996; *The Times* (of London), September 24, 1996; *La Stampa*, September 20, 1996; and the *Boston Herald*, December 1, 1996, though in the latter J.J. Masse mentions the book's extraordinary sales in France (noted above).

39. See representative articles on this in *The Sacramento Bee*, October 25, 1996, and March 6, 1997; *The Independent*, March 7, 1997, and November 6, 1997; and *Le Monde*, November 7, 1997.

40. With of course a second volume of memoirs appearing in the fall of 1999, and not so much reviewed, as summarized. See, among others, representative articles on Bardot's *Le Carré de Pluton* in *La Stampa*, October 8, 1999; *Le Figaro*, October 9, 1999; *The Record* (Bergen, N.J.), October 14, 1999, based on Paul Webster's article in *The Guardian*, noting that Bardot's story outdid any she had played in on screen; and *Le Point*, October 15, 1999, the latter finding this volume sadly full of "combats and mournings." Sales were not as brisk as the earlier, more labored volume on her early life and cinema heyday, but still rose rather rapidly in France to 150,000 copies.

9. Bardot Today

1. The best account of the Vadim funeral is in Fonda, *My Life So Far*, 141–142.

2. Paris: Editions du Rocher, 2003, put out by the estimable Jean-Paul Bertrand of that house in Saint-Germain.

3. As it does in interviews, for example, with Claudette Vaughan in *Vegan Voice* of June 2001. The interviewer asks BB to signal her finest accomplishments for animals, and Bardot answers that there are none, and that in all her battles, it's basically one step forward, several back.

4. In a heartfelt interview with Henry-Jean Servat entitled "Hommage à Romy," in *Paris Match*, June 13, 2002, 94–95, Bardot reiterates her feeling of being lucky that she had gotten off the cinema high-wire just in time (early '70s). By contrast, an actress

of great sensitivity who became her friend, Romy Schneider, died too young, she feels, sacrificing herself, like Monroe, to that career.

5. See on the vituperative talk show hosted by Fogiel, Daniel Schneidermann's article in *Le Monde*, May 17, 2003; and also the *Match* cover article of May 1–7, 2003, discussing preparations for the show. On its impact in Paris, I heard a number of comments; and for its impact on the Riviera, see article in *Var-Matin*, June 29, 2003, noting how Fogiel trapped Bardot, and even invited a shrink to comment! For Fogiel's lawsuit and its resolution in her favor, see articles in *Le Point*, January 13, 2005, and *Sud Ouest*, January 18 of that year.

6. He said it more pungently in French: "Elle en a une paire." Interview June 17, 2003. He then read her book and wrote Bardot a fan letter, describing the five dogs he had had through his life (including one who in advance felt a huge train accident coming in North Africa. He then had to be pried out of the impending, body-strewn wreck!). And would you doubt it? This man of 94 received a gracious reply from the busy Brigitte within weeks, and one from the heart.

7. On Bardot's contemporary Saint-Tropez, see Evgenia Peretz, "Saint-Tropez Babylon," *Vanity Fair* (July 2004), 134–146, beginning with Bardot's own youthful contribution to its frantic popularity via *And God Created Woman*. The article paints Bardot today as a woman decidedly disgusted by a now-decadent jetset capital (especially in summer).

8. Bardot, *Un Cri dans le silence*, 170.

9. Article in *Sunday Telegraph*, September 29, 1996. The ending of wolf hunting in Poland was also in good part due to her foundation's pressure.

10. See the foundation's *L'Info-journal* no. 51 (4th trimestre, 2004) with Johnny Hallyday and Bardot holding a little white dog on the cover; and some of the petition names listed on p. 25, along with the seal photo there. A recent count of petition-signers, mounting to over 200,000 names, is mentioned in an article appearing in *L'Info-journal* no. 52 (first trimestre, 2005), 28. The same issue notes the move of Foundation headquarters to a larger building a few doors down on the Rue Vineuse (15).

11. On Bardot's attempt to ban polar bear hunting in Greenland, see article in *Agence France Presse*, January 23, 2005. And on her letters to the French prime minister and the Minister of Agriculture, asking for alteration of the Napoleonic Code concerning animals, see article in *Agence France Presse*, May 6, 2005; and on their promise (via an announcement by Dominique Perben, Minister of Justice) to reform the code, articles in *Agence France Presse*, May 10, 2005, and *La Nouvelle République du Centre Ouest*, May 12, 2005.

Bibliography

On the French historical background and on Paris see Gordon Wright, *France in Modern Times* (New York: W.W. Norton, 1987); David Pinkney, *Napoleon III and the Rebuilding of Paris* (Princeton: Princeton University Press, 1958); Vincent Cronin, *Paris: City of Light, 1919–1939* (London: Harper-Collins, 1994); Eugen Weber, *The Hollow Years: France in the 1930s* (New York: W.W. Norton, 1994); Oliver Bernier, *Fireworks at Dusk: Paris in the Thirties* (Boston: Little, Brown, 1993); and Brassaï (text and photographs), *Le Paris secret des années '30* (Paris: Gallimard, 1976). For the race to World War II see Alistair Horne, *To Lose a Battle* (Boston: Little, Brown, 1969). On wartime trends and artists, see Robert O. Paxton, *Vichy France: Old Guard and New Order, 1940–1944* (New York: Alfred A. Knopf, 1972); Henri Amoureux, *La Vie des Français sous l'occupation* (Paris: Fayard, 1961); Henri Michel, *Paris allemand* (Paris: Albin Michel, 1980); Gilles and Jean-Robert Ragache, *La Vie quotidienne des écrivains et des artistes sous l'occupation 1940–1944* (Paris: Hachette, 1988); my "Charles Trenet: Troubador of Modern France," *Contemporary Review* 270 (January 1997), 37–44; Maurice Chevalier, *I Remember It Well* (trans. Cornelia Higginson; New York: Macmillan, 1970); and Simone Berteaut, *Piaf* (trans. June Guicharnaud; New York: Harper and Row, 1972). For de Gaulle and the Liberation see, among others, Sir Bernard Ledwidge, *De Gaulle* (London: Weidenfeld and Nicolson, 1982), ch. 22.

On post-war France see Robert Gildea, *France since 1945* (Oxford: Oxford University Press, 1966); Frank Giles, *The Locust Years: The Story of the Fourth French Republic, 1946–1958* (London: Secker and Warburg, 1991); and for continuing influence of the Vichy era, see Henry Rousso, *The Vichy Syndrome in History and Memory in France since 1944* (trans. Arthur Goldhammer; Cambridge, Mass.: Harvard University Press, 1991). See also appropriate chapters of my *Modern France: Mind, Politics, Society* (Seattle: University of Washington Press, 1980).

On Brigitte Bardot see especially Bardot's first volume of memoirs, *Initiales B.B.: Mémoires* (Paris: Grasset, 1996) and the second volume, *Le Carré de Pluton: Mémoires II* (Paris: Grasset, 1999); and her *Un Cri dans le silence: Révolte et nostalgie* (Paris: Editions du Rocher, 2003). She also wrote a children's book (with Daniel Dollfuss), *Noonoah: Le petit phoque blanc* (Paris: Grasset and Fasquelle, 1978); and prefaces for books such as Allain Bougrain-Dubourg (with Bernard Monier, Bernard Lengelle, and Alika Lindbergh), *L'Agonie des bébés phoques* (Paris: Presses de la Cité, 1978) and Bougrain-Dubourg and Marcel Clébant, *Et Dieu créa les animaux* (Paris: Robert Laffont, 1986); Rebecca Hall's *Voiceless Victims* (Hounslow, Middlesex, U.K.: Wildwood House, 1984); Gilbert Picard's *L'Enfer des animaux* (Paris: Le Carrousel-FN, 1986); Roland Gillet's *Dernière croisade* (Brussels: Edipax, 1988); Evelyne Reymond's *Colette et la Côte d'Azur* (La Calade, Aix-en-Provence: Edisud, 1988); and Henry-Jean Servat's *In the Spirit of St. Tropez* (New York: Assouline, 2003).

The earlier books and studies on her include Simone de Beauvoir's essay *Brigitte Bardot and the Lolita Syndrome* (trans. Bernard Fretchman; London: Weidenfeld and Nicolson, 1959); François Nourissier, *Brigitte Bardot* (Paris: Bernard Grasset, 1960), and see also his re-edition *B.B. 60* (Paris: Le Dilettante, 1996) with a new introduction; Souzouki, *Brigitte Bardot* (Paris: Losfeld, 1960); George Carpozi, *The Brigitte Bardot Story* (New York: Belmont Books, 1961); Yves Margueritte, *Brigitte Bardot* (Paris: Pauvert, 1963); Nina Companeez, *Le Livre de Brigitte Bardot* (Paris: Editions Frontières, 1971); Peter Evans, *Bardot: Eternal Sex Goddess* (New York: Drake Publishers, 1973); René Barjavel and Miroslav Brozek, *Brigitte Bardot: amie des animaux* (Paris: F. Nathan, 1976); Tony Crawley, *Bébé: The Films of Brigitte Bardot* (Secaucus, N.J.: Citadel Press, 1977); Willi Frischauer, *Bardot: An Intimate Biography* (London: Michael Joseph, 1978); Peter Haining, *The Legend of Brigitte Bardot* (London: W. H. Allen, 1983); Joëlle Monserrat, *Brigitte Bardot* (Paris: Editions PAC, 1983); Glenys Roberts, *Bardot: A Personal Biography* (New York: St. Martin's Press, 1984); Catherine Rihoit's intellectual *Brigitte Bardot: un mythe français* (Paris: Olivier Orban, 1986); Roger Vadim's popular memoir, *Bardot Fonda Deneuve* (trans. Melinda Camber Porter; New York: Simon and Schuster, 1986), originally *D'une étoile l'autre* (Paris: Edition no. 1, 1986), and also his earlier *Memoirs of the Devil* (trans. Peter Beglan; New York: Harcourt Brace Jovanovich, 1975); Yves Alion, *Brigitte Bardot* (Paris: Editions J'ai lu [Flammarion], 1989); Jeffrey Robinson, *Bardot: An Intimate Portrait* (New York: Donald I. Fine Books, 1994); Sean French, *Bardot* (London: Pavilion, 1994); Dominique Choulant and Jean Dérot, *La Vérité sur Brigitte Bardot* (Paris: Chemins de l'espérance, 1995); Andrew Martin's quirky *Waiting for Bardot* (London: Faber and Faber, 1996); and Gérard Pangon and Pierre Murat, *Brigitte Bardot* (Paris: Editions Mille et une nuits and ARTE Editions, 1997). For pictures and illustrated material see Ghislain Dussart and Françoise Sagan, *Brigitte Bardot: A Close-Up* (trans. Judith Sachs; New York: Delacorte Press, 1976); Sam Lévin and Raymond Boyer, *Brigitte Bardot: And God Created Woman* (New York: Putnam, 1983), featuring the Lévin photographs of Bardot; and for posters of Bardot, Stanislas Choko, *Brigitte Bardot à l'affiche* (Paris: Editions du Collectionneur, 1992), with film synopses and color posters for the films. Two scholarly articles on Bardot are by Sarah Leahy: "Bardot and Dance: Representing the Real?" *French Cultural Studies* 13 (February 2002), 49–64, and "The Matter of Myth: Brigitte Bardot, Stardom and Sex," *Studies in French Cinema* 3 (2003), 71–81. See also my own earlier articles on her, "Brigitte Bardot: Animal Activist," *Contemporary Review* 275 (November 1999), 249–254, and "Bardot: The Making of a Femme Fatale," *Virginia Quarterly* 76 (Fall 2000), 647–660.

On French cinema and its history, and in no particular order, the following have been useful: René Prédal, *Cinquante ans de cinéma français (1945–1995)* (Paris: Editions Nathan, 1996); Susan Hayward, *French National Cinema* (London: Routledge, 1993); Susan Hayward and Ginette Vincendeau, *French Film: Texts and Contexts* (London: Routledge, 2000); Pierre Billard, *L'Age classique du cinéma français: du cinéma parlant à la Nouvelle Vague* (Paris: Flammarion, 1995), and also his earlier published course notes for the Sorbonne's Institut d'Etudes Politiques with Louis Chevalier, *Cinéma et civilisation* (Paris: Les Cours de droit, 1968), 3 vols., and a more recent history of the Cannes film festival, *D'Or et de palmes: Le Festival de Cannes* (Paris: Gallimard, 1997); Ginette Vincendeau and Richard Dyer, eds., *Popular European Cinema* (London: Routledge, 1992), ch. 10; and also Vincendeau's *The Companion to French Cinema* (London: Cassell, 1996), and her *Stars and Stardom in French Cinema* (London: Continuum, 2000), esp. ch. 4 on Bardot; Guy Austin, *Stars in Modern French Film* (New York: Oxford University Press, 2003), esp. ch. 2 on Bardot, and his *Contemporary French Cinema: An Introduction* (Manchester, U.K.: Manchester University Press, 1996); Colin Crisp, *The Classic French Cinema, 1930–1960* (Bloomington: Indiana University Press, 1997); Alan Williams, *Republic of Images: A History of French Filmmaking* (Cambridge, Mass.: Harvard University Press, 1992); Catherine Gaston-Mathé, *La Société française au miroir de son cinéma* (Paris: Editions du Seuil, 1996), from a Sorbonne thesis; Charles Ford, *Histoire du cinéma français contemporain (1945–1977)* (Paris: Editions France-Empire, 1977); Roy Armes, *French Cinema* (New York: Oxford University Press, 1988); Jean-Loup Passek, ed., *D'un cinéma à l'autre: notes sur le cinéma français des années cinquante* (Paris: Editions du Centre Pompidou, 1988) with Bardot on its cover; Jean-Michel Frodon, *L'Age moderne du cinéma français: de la Nouvelle Vague à nos jours* (Paris: Flammarion, 1995); Maurice Bessy et al., *Histoire du cinéma français: Encyclopédie des films 1951–1955* (Paris: Editions Pygmalion, 1995), an excellent source of pictures; Jean-Pierre Jeancolas, *Histoire du cinéma français* (Paris: Editions Nathan, 1995), as well as his *Le Cinéma des français: la Vè République 1958–1978* (Paris: Editions Stock, 1979); Claude Beylie et al., *Une Histoire du cinéma français*

(Paris: Larousse, 2000); Pierre Maillot, *Le Cinéma français: de Renoir à Godard* (Paris: Editions MA, 1988) and also his *Les Français de Marianne: La Société française à travers ses grands acteurs* (Paris: Editions du Cerf, 1996), useful only on Gabin and Delon; Rémi Fournier Lanzoni, *French Cinema: From Its Beginnings to the Present* (New York: Continuum, 2002); Alain Poiré, *Deux cent films au soleil* (Paris: Editions Ramsay, 1988), a personal account; James Reid Paris, *The Great French Films* (Secaucus, N.J.: Citadel Press, 1983), which lists many we all saw in our youth, but only one with Bardot, *And God Created Woman*; and on more specialized subjects, Robert Cravenne, *Le Tour du monde du cinéma français: histoire du cinéma français à l'étranger* (Paris: Editions Dixit, 1995), though too synoptic; Philippe d'Hugues, *L'Envahisseur américain: Hollywood contre Billancourt* (Lausanne: Editions Favre, 1979); Robin Buss, *The French Through Their Films* (London: B.T. Batsford, 1988), a social history; Jacques Kermabon, *Parcours du cinéma en Ile-de-France* (Paris: Editions Textuel, 1995) for studios; Jean-Jacques Meusy, *Cinquante ans d'industrie cinématographique (1906-1956)* (Lyon: Fondation Crédit Lyonnais, 1996), documents from Archives économiques du Crédit Lyonnais. See appropriate parts also of Pierre Sorlin, *European Cinemas, European Societies, 1939-1990* (London: Routledge, 1991), and also his *Sociologie du cinéma* (Paris: Editions Aubier Montaigne, 1977). On the New Wave see Michel Marie, *The French New Wave: An Artistic School* (trans. Richard Neupert; Oxford: Blackwell, 2003); Chris Wiegand, *French New Wave* (Harpenden, U.K.: Pocket Essentials, 2001); Jean Douchet, *French New Wave* (trans. Robert Bonnono; New York: Distributed Art Publishers, 1999); and James Monaco, *The New Wave* (New York: Oxford University Press, 1980). For the period following the New Wave's heyday see Jill Forbes, *Cinema in France After the New Wave* (Houndmills, U.K.: Macmillan, 1992), and see also Forbes (with Sarah Street), *European Cinema: An Introduction* (Houndmills, U.K.: Palgrave, 2000).

For advertising posters relating to Bardot films and others of her period, I have benefited from Tony Nourmand and Graham Marsh, eds., *Film Posters of the '50s* (London: Aurum Press, 2000); Jean-Louis Capitaine, *Les Affiches du cinéma français* (Paris: Editions Seghers, 1988); Stanislas Choko, ed., *Affiches du cinéma: Trésors de la Bibliothèque nationale de France 1896-1960* (Paris: Bibliothèque nationale de France/Editions de l'amateur, 1995); and René Château, *Les plus belles affiches du cinéma français des années 50: 1950-1960* (Paris: Editions R.C., 1994). On the psychology and variety of audience reaction to films, I have used Charles Affron, *Cinema and Sentiment* (Chicago: University of Chicago Press, 1982); Henri Agel, *Métaphysique du cinéma* (Paris: Payot, 1976); Richard Allen, *Projecting Illusion: Film Spectatorship and the Impression of Reality* (Cambridge: Cambridge University Press, 1995); and Jonathan Beller, "The Cinematic Mode of Production: Towards a Political Economy of the Postmodern," *Culture, Theory and Critique* 44 (2003), 91–106, in part on the "labor" of spectators.

For Bardot directors or producers see, among others, Dudley Andrew, *Mists of Regret: Culture and Sensibility in Classic French Film* (Princeton: Princeton University Press, 1995), good on the background of Marc Allégret; Freddy Buache, *Autant-Lara* (Paris: Veyrier, 1981), Claude Autant-Lara, *La Rage dans le coeur: chronique cinématographique du 20è siècle* (Paris: Veyrier, 1984) and his *Le Fourgon du malheur* (Paris: Carrère, 1987); Philippe Pilard's compilation, *Henri-Georges Clouzot* (Paris: Editions Segher, 1969) and Jean-Louis Bocquet, *Henri-Georges Clouzot cinéaste* (Paris: La Sirène, 1993); Raymond Chirat, *Julien Duvivier* (Paris: Premier Plan, 1968), Pierre Billard et al., *Julien Duvivier* (Milan: Il Castoro, 1996), Yves Desrichard, *Julien Duvivier: Cinquante ans de noirs destins* (Paris: BiFi/Durante, 2001), and Eric Bonnefille, *Julien Duvivier, le mal aimant du cinéma français* (Paris: L'Harmattan, 2002), 2 vols.; Pierre Billard, *Le Mystère René Clair* (Paris: Plon, 1998), the best study of Clair, but also see R.C. Dale, *The Films of René Clair* (New York: Scarecrow Press, 1986), 2 vols., Olivier Barrot, *René Clair, ou le temps mesuré* (Paris: Cinque Continents, 1985), Celia McGerr, *René Clair* (Boston: Twayne, 1980), Georges Charensol and Roger Régent, *Cinquante ans de cinéma avec René Clair* (Paris: La Table Ronde, 1979), and Jean Mitry, *René Clair* (Paris: Editions universitaires, 1960); for Godard, among others, see Wheeler Winston Dixon, *The Films of Jean-Luc Godard* (Albany: SUNY Press, 1997), Toby Mussman, ed., *Jean-Luc Godard: A Critical Anthology* (New York: E.P. Dutton, 1968), Richard Roud, *Jean-Luc Godard* (London: Secker and Warburg, 1967), and Royal S. Brown, *Focus on Godard* (Englewood Cliffs, N.J.: Prentice-Hall, 1972); Philip French, ed., *Malle on Malle* (London: Faber and Faber, 1993) and the definitive biography by Pierre Billard, *Louis Malle, le rebelle solitaire* (Paris: Plon, 2003); and for insights into Bardot, Antoine de Baecque and Serge Toubiana, *Truffaut* (trans. Catherine Temerson; New York: Alfred A. Knopf, 1999). Also interesting Edward Dmytryk, *Odd Man Out: A Memoir of the Hollywood Ten* (Carbondale, Ill.: Southern Illinois University Press, 1996), by the director of *Shalako*; and François Guérif,

Claude Chabrol: un jardin bien à moi (Paris: Denoël, 1999).

For male French actors Bardot worked with see, among others, Jacques Lorcey, *Bourvil* (Editions PAC, 1981), Jean-Jacques Jelot-Blanc and James Huet, *Bourvil* (Paris: Editions Stock, 1990), and Elizabeth Coquart and Philippe Huet, *Bourvil: La tendresse du rire* (Paris: Albin Michel, 1990); Larry Swindell, *Charles Boyer: The Reluctant Lover* (New York: Doubleday, 1983) and Guy Chassagnard, *Charles Boyer: Acteur* (Figeac: Editions Segnat, 1999); Gerty Colin, *Jean Gabin* (Paris: Presses de la Cité, 1983), Claude Gauteur and André Bernard, eds., *Gabin ou les avatars d'un mythe* (Paris: Editions PAC, 1976), Jean-Claude Missiaen and Jacques Siclier, *Jean Gabin* (Paris: Henri Veyrier, 1977); André Brunelin, *Gabin* (Paris: Robert Laffont, 1987), and Claude Gauteur and Ginette Vincendeau, *Jean Gabin: Anatomie d'un mythe* (Paris: Editions Nathan, 1993); Gérard Bonal, *Gérard Philipe: Biographie* (Paris: Editions du Seuil, 1994), the best work on that actor, and also Philippe Durant, *Gérard Philipe* (Paris: Editions PAC, 1983), Georges Sadoul, *Gérard Philipe* (Paris: Lherminier, 1979), Maurice Périsset, *Gérard Philipe* (Paris: J.P. Ollivier, 1975), Monique Chapelle, *Gérard Philipe, notre éternelle jeunesse* (Paris: Robert Laffont, 1966), and Anne Philipe and Claude Roy, *Gérard Philipe* (Paris: Gallimard, 1960); Charles Ford, *Charles Vanel: un comédien exemplaire* (Paris: France-Empire, 1986) and Jacqueline Cartier, *Monsieur Vanel: un siècle de souvenirs, un an d'entretiens* (Paris: Robert Laffont, 1989); Philippe Barbier, *Alain Delon* (Paris: Editions PAC, 1982), Olivier Dazat, *Alain Delon* (Paris: Editions Seghers, 1988), Emmanuel Haymann, *Alain Delon: Splendeurs et mystères d'une superstar* (Lausanne: Favre, 1998), and Henry-Jean Servat, *Alain Delon: L'Insoumis, 1957–1970* (Paris: Michel, 2000). See also Robert Hossein, *Nomade sans tribu* (Paris: Fayard, 1981).

For female French actresses whose celebrity preceded Bardot's, see Claude Bouniq-Mercier, *Michèle Morgan* (Paris: Editions Colona, 1983), and Michèle Morgan (with Marcelle Routier), *With Those Eyes* (trans. Oliver Coburn; London: W.H. Allen, 1978); Michel Perrin, *Arletty* (Paris: Perrin and Perrin, 1952), Philippe Ariotti and Philippe de Comès, *Arletty* (Paris: Editions Henri Veyrier, 1978), Pierre Monnier, *Arletty* (Paris: Editions Stock, 1984), Christian Gilles, *Arletty ou la liberté d'être* (Paris: Seghier, 1988), Denis Demonpion, *Arletty* (Paris: Flammarion, 1996), and Arletty (with Michel Souvais), *Je suis comme je suis ...* (Paris: Carrère, 1987); Georges Debot, *Martine Carol: ou la vie de Martine chérie* (Paris: Editions

France-Empire, 1979), Arnaud Chapuy, *Martine Carol filmée par Christian-Jaque: un phénomène du cinéma populaire* (Paris: L'Harmattan, 2001), and the chapter on her in Jacques Mazeau, *Les Destins tragiques du cinéma* (Paris: Editions Hors Collection, 1995); Joëlle Monserrat, *Simone Signoret* (Paris: Editions PAC, 1983), Philippe Durant, *Simone Signoret, une vie* (Lausanne: Favre, 1988), Catherine David, *Simone Signoret* (trans. Sally Sampson; Woodstock, NY: Overlook Press, 1993), Jean-François Josselin, *Simone: deux ou trois choses que je sais d'elle* (Paris: Grasset, 1995), and Simone Signoret, *Nostalgia Isn't What It Used to Be* (New York: Harper and Row, 1978). For the actress who most rivaled Bardot's popularity in her era see Michel Laclos, *Jeanne Moreau* (Paris: J.J. Pauvert, 1964), Jean-Claude Moireau, *Jeanne Moreau* (Paris: Editions Ramsay, 1994), Michaël Delmar, *Jeanne Moreau: Portrait d'une femme* (Paris: Editions Norma, 1994), and Marianne Gray, *La Moreau: A Biography of Jeanne Moreau* (New York: Donald I. Fine Books, 1996). See also memoirs by female stars Bardot appeared with near the end of her career: Annie Girardot, *Ma vie contre la tienne* (Paris: Robert Laffont, 1993), and Claudia Cardinale, *Io, Claudia, tu Claudia* (with Anna Maria Mori) (Milan: Frassinelli, 1995).

Aside from Vadim's, mentioned above, memoirs or published interviews on the era and/or on Bardot include Dirk Bogarde, *Snakes and Ladders* (New York: Penguin Books, 1988); Charles Aznavour, *Yesterday When I Was Young* (London: Crescent, 1979); Daniel Gélin, *Deux ou trois vies qui sont les miennes* (Paris: Julliard, 1977) and *A Bâtons rompus: Mémoires* (Paris: Editions du Rocher, 2000); Jacques Charrier, *Ma Réponse à Brigitte Bardot* (Paris: Michel Lafon, 1997); Olga Horstig-Primuz (with Ginette Billard), *Moi, j'aime les acteurs* (Paris: Jean-Claude Lattès, 1990); Jean-Louis Trintignant, *Un Homme à sa fenêtre* (Paris: J.C. Simoën, 1977), a collection of his own words on his life and career and those of others, put together by Michel Boujut; and more recently, Trintignant, *La Passion tranquille: Entretiens avec André Asséo* (Paris: Plon/France Inter, 2002); Sacha Distel, *Les Pendules à l'heure* (Paris: Michel Lafon, 1985); Giangiacomo Schiavi, *Ho ammazzato Gigi Rizzi: io, BB, et le altre: diario segreto di un seduttore* (Milan: Rizzoli, 1996), among others. For Gilbert Bécaud see Christophe Izard, *Gilbert Bécaud* (Paris: Editions Séghers, 1972), Louis Amade (one of his lyricists), *Et ce sera ta passion de vivre* (Paris: Hachette, 1982), and Annie and Bernard Réval, *Gilbert Bécaud: Jardins secrets* (Paris: France-Empire, 2001). For Warren Beatty, see Ellis Amburn, *The Sexiest Man Alive: A Biography of Warren Beatty* (New

York: HarperCollins, 2002). And for Jane Fonda, her best-seller, *My Life So Far* (New York: Random House, 2005).

On other animal protectors Bardot has admired there is of course a flood of literature, memoirs, etc. See, for example, Paul Watson's *Sea Shepherd: My Fight for Whales and Seals* (New York: Norton, 1992), his *Ocean Warrior: My Battle to End the Illegal Slaughter on the High Seas* (St. Leonards, Australia: Allen and Unwin, 1994), and also his *Seal Wars: Twenty-Five Years on the Front Lines with the Harp Seals* (Buffalo: Firefly Books, 2003). For Dian Fossey see her *Gorillas in the Mist* (Boston: Houghton Mifflin, 1983), as well as Harold T.P. Hayes' passionate book on this tragic figure, *The Dark Romance of Dian Fossey* (New York: Simon and Schuster, 1990). Bardot has also admired Jane Goodall, author of, among others, *My Life with the Chimpanzees* (New York: Pocket Books, 1996). Monographs germane to Bardot's fight for animals

include Chantal Nadeau, *Fur Nation: From Beaver to Brigitte Bardot* (New York: Routledge, 2001).

On the making of the Riviera see Mary Blume, *Côte d'Azur: Inventing the French Riviera* (New York: Thames and Hudson, 1992); Michael Nelson, *Queen Victoria and the Discovery of the Riviera* (London: I.B. Tauris, 2001); and my article, "The Riviera Then and Now," *Contemporary Review* 283 (December 2003), 362–366; also for Saint-Tropez, see Evgenia Peretz, "Saint-Tropez Babylon," *Vanity Fair* (July 2004), 134–146.

I have also used many articles in the press, both in France and in English-speaking countries, and a few from other countries, such as Italy; not to mention the Bardot movies, television programs now available on video or DVD, including Allain Bougrain-Dubourg's marvelous documentary on her, *Telle quelle*; and record collections (such as "Best of BB," put out by Philips in 1996).

Index